Aspects of Educational and Training Technology XXIX

Aspects of Educational and Training Technology XXIX

Implementing Flexible Learning

Edited for the Association for Educational and Training Technology by

Chris Bell, Mandy Bowden and Andrew Trott

KOGAN
PAGE

First published in 1997

Apart from any fair dealing for the purposes of research or private study, or criticism or review, as permitted under the Copyright, Designs and Patents Act 1988, this publication may only be reproduced, stored or transmitted, in any form or by any means, with the prior permission in writing of the publishers, or in the case of reprographic reproduction in accordance with the terms of licences issued by the Copyright Licensing Agency. Enquiries concerning reproduction outside those terms should be sent to the publishers at the undermentioned address:

Kogan Page Limited
120 Pentonville Road
London N1 9JN

© The Association for Educational and Training Technology, 1997

British Library Cataloguing in Publication Data

A CIP record for this book is available from the British Library.

ISBN 0 7494 1874 5
ISSN 1350-1933

Typeset by N C Murray
Printed and bound in Great Britain by Biddles Ltd, Guildford and King's Lynn

Contents

Editorial: Hail, Farewell and Thanks!

All good things must come to an end. The Association for Educational and Training Technology (AETT) has been running highly successful conferences for 29 years now, but the 1995 Plymouth event was the last. All who were fortunate enough to attend will agree that it was one of the best ever, and will provide us with happy memories for a long time to come.

The reason why the Plymouth Conference was the last of the series is that AETT ceased to exist as an independent organisation on 31 December 1995. On 1 January 1996, it was transmogrified into the Learning Technologies Group of the Staff and Educational Development Association (SEDA). Why did this happen? To understand the reasons, it is necessary to take a brief look at the history of AETT, and at the changing educational environment in which it has had to operate in recent years.

AETT began life in 1962, as the UK-based Association for Programmed Learning (APL). The next few years were the true 'golden age' of the Association, which had a clear focus, was at the cutting edge of progressive educational thinking, and had a large, highly active membership – over 1200 at its peak. Indeed, it regularly attracted over 1000 people to its annual conference – a figure that can only be dreamed of by today's conference organisers!

During the late 1960s, the focus of the Association began to change. The programmed learning movement was now past its peak, and 'educational technology' (the application of the systems approach to all aspects of curriculum development and instructional design) was beginning to replace it as the dominant paradigm of educational development. This was reflected by the Association's first change of name in 1969 to the Association for Programmed Learning and Educational Technology (APLET).

The Association continued to thrive during the 1970s, continued to have a large and active membership, and continued to attract large numbers of people to its annual conference – albeit not so many as in the 1960s. It also attempted to move with the times by undergoing a second change of name in 1979 to the Association for Educational and Training Technology (AETT). This reflected the fact that 'programmed learning' had by then become a somewhat unfashionable term, and belatedly recognised that a large proportion of the Association's members worked in the training sector – although this had always been the case.

I think it is fair to say that the 1980s were a period of decline for AETT – a decline that continued throughout the 1990s, despite the strenuous efforts of the Association's Officers and Council to reverse it. Two main factors contributed to this decline. First, the Association gradually lost its original constituency (the programmed learning activists of the 1960s and the educational and training technologists of the 1970s) through retirement and, increasingly, death. Second, Britain went through two major recessions, and these had a drastic effect on the funding of educational and training technology. As a result, both membership of the Association and attendance at its conference fell steadily from year to year.

In the light of the above developments, AETT's Council eventually came to the reluctant conclusion that the only way of guaranteeing the Association's continued existence was to merge with a larger organisation. A number of possible partners for such a merger were considered, but it was unanimously agreed that the Staff and Educational Development Association (SEDA) was by far the most appropriate. The merger was overwhelmingly approved by the memberships of the two bodies at their 1995 Annual General Meetings, thus enabling AETT to become the SEDA Learning Technologies Group at the start of 1996.

I am delighted to report that the new SEDA LTG has made an excellent start. It has an active and highly enthusiastic membership, and has already made plans to hold its first conference. I wish it all success, and am confident that it will continue to fly the flag for educational and training technology.

It remains for me to say but three things:

- Hail SEDA Learning Technologies Group – may you live long and prosper!
- Farewell AETT – I and my fellow 'old fogies' will miss you!
- And finally, many, many thanks to Chris Bell, Mandy Bowden, Debbie McCarthy, Shirley McLean, Nick Rose, Serena Vellacott and all the other members of the Plymouth Conference Team; you certainly gave AETT a memorable 'wake'!

Professor Henry Ellington,
Chairman of AETT

1. Flexible Learning – Your Flexible Friend! Keynote Address

Professor Henry Ellington, *The Robert Gordon University, Aberdeen*

SUMMARY

Back in 1988, Chris Bell did me the singular honour of asking me to give the opening keynote address. He has invited me back to give a further keynote address. This time, he has asked me to follow the 'interactive keynote' that opened the conference by presenting a broad overview of what flexible learning is all about. I will do this by attempting to answer the following three questions:

- what is flexible learning?
- what different forms can it take?
- what are the benefits?

I will begin by showing how the term 'flexible learning' has evolved over the years, and how it is now gaining widespread acceptance as a generic term covering virtually all situations where the learner has some control over the way in which learning occurs. I will then try to give you an idea of the wide diversity of forms that flexible learning can take. I will do this by looking at some of the ways in which my colleagues and I at The Robert Gordon University have adopted a more flexible approach to teaching. As you will see, this is helping us to make our teaching more user-friendly and more effective in preparing our students to cope with the challenges that they will face in the outside world.

What we mean by 'flexible learning'?

From a search through the material in the ERIC database, it appears that the term 'flexible learning' originated in the United States during the 1970s, when the Flexible Learning System (FLS) was developed for use in schools. This was a multi-unit package that provided guidance for teachers on how to help children develop problem-solving skills and attitudes, with particular emphasis on shifting the responsibility for solving classroom problems from teacher to pupils (Yinger and Eckland, 1975).

As far as I can tell, the term started to be used in Britain during the early 1980s. By 1986, there was sufficient activity in the area for AETT to make Flexible Learning Systems the theme of its Edinburgh conference (Percival *et al.*, 1987). At this conference, Gaye Manwaring defined such systems as 'student-centred approaches involved in removing barriers', and regarded them as a subset of open learning (Manwaring, 1987). At the same conference, Martyn Roebuck defined 'flexible learning' as an approach 'characterised by flexible approaches to the provision and design of ways of meeting learners' needs' (Roebuck, 1987). Indeed, he anticipated the modern usage of the term by regarding it as 'embracing open-learning, self-study, individualisation and the like'. At the following year's AETT conference in Southampton, Phil Race gave a similar interpretation of the term, regarding 'flexible learning' as a 'wider term than *open* or *distance* learning', and 'including many things that can be done in college environments' (Race, 1988).

During the intervening years, 'flexible learning' has come to be interpreted very loosely indeed, and now is widely taken to mean the same as 'open learning', in its broadest sense. This is certainly the interpretation that has been adopted by the recently formed Flexible Learning in Higher Education Network (FLHEN). Indeed, when I asked Rachel Hudson, one of FLHEN's joint coordinators, how they defined 'flexible learning', she told me that FLHEN had deliberately *not* attempted to define the term. They preferred to leave it to practitioners to interpret it in any way they liked! Just how widely practitioners *have* interpreted the term can be seen from the great diversity of the papers and workshops that are included in the programme of this conference. Therefore, I would suggest that we all try to promote the general adoption of this wider interpretation, and start using 'flexible learning' as a generic term that covers all those situations where learners have some say in *how*, *where* or *when* learning takes place – whether within the context of traditional institution-centred courses or in non-traditional contexts such as open learning, distance learning, CAT schemes, wider-access courses or continuing professional development.

Different forms of flexible learning

Let me now turn to my various case studies – all examples of ways in which I and my colleagues have made use of flexible learning in one form or another. These case studies will give you some idea of the great diversity of flexible learning, and will also show you some of the very real benefits that can result from such an approach.

Case Study 1: Using open-learning, self-study methods to train lecturers
My first case study shows how the problem of providing in-service training in basic teaching skills for lecturing staff was tackled by the Scottish Central Institutions (CIs – the Scottish equivalent of the polytechnics) during the late 1980s. At the time (as now) there was increasing pressure to improve the overall quality of teaching and introduce a wider range of teaching methods within the CIs. Since the traditional method of undergoing training in these areas – ie undertaking an appropriate course at a college of education or university – was seldom practicable for lecturers who were already in post, the CIs, through the Central Institutions Committee for Educational Development (CICED), decided to provide such training in-house. They also decided to make it available on an open-learning, self-study basis so that staff could fit it into their normal work. It was felt that a conventional taught course would not work.

The resulting course, leading to a Postgraduate Certificate in Tertiary-level Teaching Methods, was developed by myself and a group of colleagues from six other CIs during 1987–88, and was piloted in my own institution (then The Robert Gordon Institute of Technology, RGIT) in 1989 (Ellington, 1990). It consisted of eight largely self-contained modules, each of which involved working through a series of structured activities with tutor support and then carrying out a negotiated assignment based on the material covered. The summative assessment for the module was based on this assignment. The eight modules were:

Module 1: Educational Objectives
Module 2: Selection of Instructional Methods
Module 3: Production of Instructional Materials
Module 4: Student Assessment
Module 5: Use of Mass Instruction Techniques
Module 6: Use of Student-Centred Learning Methods
Module 7: Use of Group-Learning Methods
Module 8: Evaluation.

The RGIT pilot proved extremely successful, and the course was subsequently taken up by several other Scottish CIs. Indeed, it is now being run in all four Central Institutions which gained university status in 1992. Feedback from course teams and from staff undertaking the course suggests that it is now having a very real impact on the overall quality of teaching wherever it has been adopted (Ellington and Land, 1995). In the case of my own university, for example, 23 people have now obtained the PG certificate, and all 23 have reported significant improvements in their performance as teachers as a result of undertaking the course. Thus the decision to adopt a flexible approach to staff training has been completely vindicated.

Case Study 2: Converting traditional taught courses into distance learning

My second case study shows how it is possible to widen the access to a conventional taught course by making it available in distance-learning format, and, as a result, greatly increase the uptake. The course in question is RGIT's Diploma in Occupational Health Nursing, a one-year, post-experience, professional course that was originally developed during the late 1980s. The original version of the course was itself highly innovative, since it made it possible for students to spread their studies over a period of up to three years. This was done by dividing the course into six self-contained modules, teaching these consecutively over a period of one academic year, and allowing the students to take them in any order.

A market survey carried out in 1989 showed that the course was still not fully meeting the needs of the Occupational Health Nursing Community. Of the UK's 10,000 OH nurses, over 50% had no formal qualification in the field, but few of these could afford the 27 weeks off work needed to undertake the RGIT course even when spread over three years. The logical solution was to convert the course into distance-learning format. The conversion work was carried out during 1990–91, with the new version of the course being run in parallel with the traditional 'taught' version starting in September 1990 (Ellington and Lewis, 1992).

Some of the details of the conversion work may be of interest. First, attendance at RGIT was reduced from 27 weeks to 6 weeks, with the 'taught' element of each module being reduced to a single week. This effectively made the course available to *all* the UK's unqualified OH nurses, since these six weeks of attendance could still be spread over a time span of up to three years. As a result, applications for the course increased several times. Second, the conversion work was carried out *as the course was actually being delivered*, and was completed in just over one year. This was only possible by separating the writing of the 'textbook' sections of the self-study packs from the writing of the 'study guide/workbook' sections, thus enabling the packs to be produced much more quickly than traditional self-study materials. This approach had been used successfully in the development of the PG certificate in Tertiary-level Teaching Methods (Ellington, 1990), and proved just as successful with the Diploma in OH Nursing.

Comparison of the performance of students undertaking the distance-learning version of the course with that of students undertaking the traditional, taught version of the course revealed 'no significant difference' between the two groups (Lowis and Ellington, 1992). Once the distance-learning course became available, however, enrolments for the taught course fell off rapidly. Indeed many 'traditional' students asked to be transferred to the distance-learning course! As a result, the 'traditional' course was phased out and the course converted entirely to distance-learning format.

Because of the great success of its distance-learning course in OH Nursing, The Robert Gordon University's Department of Nursing subsequently developed full distance-learning BA degrees in Community Health Nursing and in Nursing (Lawton, 1993). Indeed, the original OH Nursing Diploma course has now itself been phased out, since an Occupational Health Nursing qualification is now available via one of the routes of the former.

Case Study 3: Resource-based learning opportunities for part-time students
Aberdeen has been the operational centre of Britain's offshore oil industry since the early 1970s. This has presented Aberdeen's colleges and universities with both great opportunities and with new challenges, not the least of which has been the problem of meeting the learning needs of the people who work in the industry. Many of these want to enrol on our various degrees and other courses, but this is made difficult by the fact that a high proportion work offshore – typically on two-week tours interspersed with two- or three-week periods at home. The irregular pattern of these tours makes it practically impossible for workers to undertake conventional courses, even on a day-release or block-release basis.

One of the courses that large numbers of offshore oil workers wanted to undertake was the linked HND/BSc in Mechanical Engineering run by The Robert Gordon University's School of Mechanical and Offshore Engineering. In order to enable them to do so, the course team has developed a part-time version of the course, supported by a comprehensive bank of self-study and support materials available on an open-access basis (Edward, 1994). Students on this course attend formal day or evening classes whenever they are onshore, catching up on any classes that they missed while they were offshore by making use of self-study materials in the School's steadily expanding Resource Centre.

Although the initial intention was to develop new materials for use in the course, this was not found to be practicable. Instead, at the present time, the resource materials are being built around materials already available within the school, which are being edited and combined into integrated 'resource packs'. The materials in such a pack include a list of references, a directed reading list, video lectures and textual notes, student worksheets with model solutions, and a 'substitute laboratory' kit. Typically, this comprises a workbook, a video illustrating laboratory equipment and its use, a computer-based simulation of the actual experiment(s) with specimen results for the student to analyse, and a tape/slide pack.

At the moment, a total of roughly 40 students a year are enrolling for the part-time mechanical engineering course, with half attending on a daytime basis and half during the evening. All are mature individuals with a high level of commitment and motivation. Student reaction to the self-study materials has been very favourable, and there is a demand for more materials of this type in a wider range of subject areas. Development of such materials has been given high priority by the host school, which has formed a Teaching and Learning Support Group comprising four lecturing staff and a technician. It is planned to extend the approach to other courses.

Case Study 4: Self-study methods as lecture substitutes/supplements
One of the most common, and most effective, manifestations of flexible learning is the use of self-study methods of various types as a substitute for, or supplement to, conventional lectures. The various weaknesses of the lecture as a didactic method have long been recognised (Bligh, 1972; Percival and Ellington, 1984). Indeed, recent work by Phil Race suggests that the lecture is an extremely inefficient vehicle for bringing about effective learning, with students retaining as little as 5% of the material covered in some cases (Race, 1992). Lectures will no doubt continue to play an important role in most courses (eg to provide introductory overviews and cover key topics) but I expect many 'run of the mill' lectures to be replaced by more active, student-centred methods over the coming years. This is certainly beginning to happen in my own university, where more and more course teams are recognising the benefits that such an approach can bring (more effective student learning, greater student involvement, reduced class contact time, and so on).

Let us look at four specific ways in which RGU staff are now using self-study methods to replace or support their lecture programmes.

The first is an integrated lecture/tutorial/self-study course in basic economics that was developed by Jim Duncan of RGU's Business School in 1991–92, as part of the school's Enterprise in Higher Education programme. The course was piloted in the school's BA in European Business Administration with Languages, and is now used in five separate degrees (Duncan, 1994). Introduction of the course has enabled formal lectures in Basic Economics to be reduced to one a week (previously two a week), and tutorials to be reduced to one a fortnight (previously one a week). Much of the content previously covered by lectures is now delivered via directed study of material in a standard textbook, which is an essential purchase for students. In Term 1, students are provided with study guides incorporating lecture summaries, but the latter are replaced by lecture guides in Terms 2 and 3 in order to encourage the students to take progressively greater responsibility for their own learning.

Feedback from students indicates that a few do not like the new approach because it puts too much onus on them and involves 'too much reading', but that the great majority are perfectly happy with it, if not wildly enthusiastic. Certainly, their overall performance in examinations does not appear to have been adversely affected, and the approach seams to be succeeding in making the students more self-reliant. Another benefit is that timetabling has been made much easier. Because of its success, the approach is now being extended to other courses.

My second example is the use of a commercial American package on Basic Economics by Alistair Wood, of RGU's School of Public Administration and Law. Unlike Jim Duncan, Alistair uses the package as a *supplement to* rather than a *substitute for* lectures, thus providing his students with the opportunity to complement the passive learning that they experience with more active, student-centred learning. The package is made available via networked PCs in one of the school's computer laboratories, and Alistair estimates that it is used regularly by roughly 20% of the 160 enrolled students. Feedback from these indicates that they have found the package extremely useful.

My third example is the experimental use of multimedia packages on bibliographic classification and indexing by Douglas Anderson and Robert Newton of RGU's School of Librarianship and Information Studies, both as a replacement for and as a supplement to formal classes. Feedback from students indicates that they are very happy with the use of such packages in the latter role, and find them extremely helpful. The great majority of students do not want to see formal classes in the subject completely *replaced* by self-study, since they greatly value the social interaction and help from tutors that such classes provide. Let all those who advocate replacing live teachers by computers please note!

My fourth example is an integrated 25-week course in Environmental Politics, Policy and Management that Alistair McCulloch of RGU's School of Public Administration and Law runs in Year 4 of their BA in Public Policy and Management. This is designed to make *the students themselves* responsible for delivering the bulk of the content (and also to ensure their participation in learning activities that they often do their best to avoid!) Following an intensive five-week introduction to the subject area via lectures, videos and visiting speakers, the students spend the remainder of the session first preparing in-depth seminar papers and then presenting these in class. Each student is also provided with a full set of the seminar papers, so that the students also effectively write their own course 'textbook'! The students are assessed on the quality of their papers and presentations, the defence of their papers and their overall contribution to the seminar programme. This method of course delivery has proved extremely popular with students, and is highly recommended as a way of introducing flexible learning into the later years of a degree.

Case Study 5: Simulations/games to develop process skills

It is generally acknowledged that the various forms of *group learning* (class discussions, group tutorials, seminars, simulation/games, interactive case studies, etc) are extremely powerful vehicles for developing transferable process skills of virtually all types (Elton, 1978; Percival and Ellington, 1984; Jaques, 1991). Such methods constitute what Lewis Elton describes as the 'interdependent' mode of learning – the mode in which students *learn from one another* rather than from the teacher or from pre-packaged resource materials. Group learning should therefore be regarded as an important subset of flexible learning.

For the last 22 years, I have been heavily involved in the design, promotion and use of simulation/games, one of the most versatile and useful types of group learning activity (Ellington, 1994a). One of the first was the Bruce Oil Management Game, a computer-based team exercise that simulated the process of bringing a newly discovered offshore oilfield into production (Ellington *et al.*, 1975). This was developed by a multidisciplinary team of RGU staff in collaboration with Aberdeen's local newspaper, *The Press and Journal*, during the early 1970s, and was used as the basis of a national, and later an international, competition for six successive years.

The management game was also run as an exercise for our own business and offshore engineering students. It is still so used. It is designed to give the participants a feel for what goes on in the offshore oil industry by giving them the chance to make the type of decisions that real-life managers have to take – and to see the consequences of these decisions in terms of profit or loss for their company.

Another exercise developed in The Robert Gordon University during the 1970s was The Power Station Game, a manual simulation/game based on the choice of type and siting of a large new power station (Ellington *et al.*, 1978). Here, the participants take the role of three competitive design teams, developing detailed plans for building a coal-fired station, an oil-fired station and a nuclear station and trying to persuade the Generating Board to adopt their particular scheme. It is designed to develop a wide range of skills, including problem-solving, decision-making, planning, interpersonal and presentation skills. The exercise has been in regular use with our engineering students since 1975, and has undergone three major rewrites in order to keep it up to date. The last (and most radical) involved changing it to an East European scenario, since Britain no longer builds the three types of station on which the game is based (Ellington, 1994b).

The game that has probably been most widely used in The Robert Gordon University, however, is Power for Elaskay. This is a simulated planning exercise in which the participants have to exploit the natural energy resources of an offshore island in order to meet its future electricity needs (Ellington and Addinall, 1978). Although originally designed as a case study on alternative energy, this exercise has proved to be an ideal vehicle for helping students to develop interpersonal, communication and presentation skills. It has been in regular use by our Communication Studies staff for the last 17 years. Two versions of the game are now available – the original Scottish version and a Far Eastern version that I wrote in 1989 for use with Singaporean students (Ellington *et al.*, 1991).

Case Study 6: A problem-based approach to course design
My sixth case study shows how it is possible to build problem-based learning into an otherwise conventional degree course. In this case, the course is the BSc in Mathematical Sciences with Computing that is run by RGU's School of Computer and Mathematical Sciences. It differs from many conventional mathematics courses in that it is specifically designed to produce mathematical consultants capable of working in industry and commerce. Such consultants must possess both mathematical modelling skills (the ability to apply mathematical techniques to the solution of real-life problems) and interpersonal and communication skills (the ability to work

as an effective member of a professional team and to relate to, and communicate with, non-mathematicians).

Staff of the school collaborated both with personnel from Industry and Commerce and with the university's Communication Studies and Educational Technology staff during the mid-1980s in developing a highly innovative Mathematical Models and Methods course within their degree (Usher and Earl, 1987; Usher *et al.*, 1991). This combines basic instruction in mathematical modelling and communication studies with a systematic programme of group modelling exercises in which the students have to put what they have learned into practice when solving their client's problems, the client usually being a person from industry or commerce.

In each group modelling exercise, the students (working in small cooperative groups of three to five) take the role of 'consultants' who have been brought in to help their 'clients' solve real-life problems by applying the principles of mathematical modelling. These problems vary enormously in nature: 'helping a dental practice to optimise its appointment system'; 'predicting the overall reliability of the inspection schedule for a paper production line'; and 'determining the optimum shape of the battens used in racing skiffs', being three of the many that have been used so far. The team have to establish the nature of the problem, decide how to tackle it, allocate tasks, agree on a recommended solution, and present this to their client both orally and in writing (including posters).

The approach has now been in use for over 10 years, and has proved extremely successful – particularly in terms of preparing students to cope more effectively with working in the outside world and making them attractive to prospective employers. Feedback from the various firms that have employed our students has also been extremely positive, and testifies to the effectiveness of the approach.

Case Study 7: Incorporating work-based learning into courses

It has long been recognised that learning, often of an extremely high level, takes place at the workplace as well as in formal educational contexts. It is only comparatively recently, however, that serious attempts have been made to analyse this learning and accredit it as satisfying some or all of the outcomes of a recognised academic award. During the early 1990s, the UK Government's Training, Education and Enterprise Department (TEED) funded a number of collaborative projects involving higher education institutions and industrial organisations in order to address this issue. One of these was a partnership between RGU's School of Mechanical and Offshore Engineering and Shell Expro UK. This has now led to the establishment of a scheme whereby Shell staff who are enrolled on the school's HND/BSc in Mechanical Engineering as part-time students can gain accreditation for work-based learning (Edward, 1993).

As we saw earlier, the above course has a part-time route that caters for offshore oil workers whose shift patterns make it difficult or impossible for them to undertake conventional study. Shell had several technicians enrolled on this course, and it was recognised that their work was highly technical and involved considerable responsibility. It was also recognised that Shell have a formal scheme for assessment of employees' competence, a scheme whose criteria overlapped considerably with the learning outcomes of the course. Areas of commonality were identified in four specific subjects, and it was agreed that students who had met Shell's competence criteria in respect of these should receive appropriate accreditation once they had produced supplementary evidence of underpinning understanding.

Following a successful pilot with seven students, the scheme has now been extended. Similar schemes have also been introduced in respect of a number of other RGU courses, and the practice of formally accrediting work-based learning seems likely to be widely adopted throughout the university.

Case Study 8: Computer links to provide remote learning/assessment facilities

One of the most exciting areas in which flexible learning is now manifesting itself is the use of the so-called 'new media technologies' to provide opportunities for interactive remote learning (Ray, 1992). A number of RGU staff are currently working in this area, including Ian Pirie of Gray's School of Art. He is the Course Leader of the university's new BSc in 'Design for Industry', and is anxious that the teaching methods used should reflect the highly innovative nature of the course. For this reason, he is exploring some of the possibilities that the marriage of new media technologies and digital communication are now making practical. Specifically, he is looking at possible ways of linking design students on work placement and their industrial supervisors with staff and students working at the university. These include:

- *remote tutorials*, whereby students on work placement can demonstrate their work to and discuss their work with university-based tutors on a one-to-one basis;
- *group crits,* whereby students can have a 'joint crit' of their work carried out simultaneously by their industrial and academic support teams;
- *remote seminars*, whereby placement students and their industrial support teams can deliver interactive seminars to a student group at the university;
- *external industry crits,* whereby industry-based groups can conduct interactive crits with students based at the university;
- *joint assessment,* whereby industry support teams can participate in the assessment of university-based students' project work;
- *virtual visits,* whereby industry-based groups can take students based at the university on 'mediated tours' of a production or other facility.

Ian hopes to turn all of these ideas into practical schemes by the time the new course builds up to full operation in two years' time, so that the first cohort of students can benefit from them in their final year.

Conclusion

I would like to think that I have now achieved my objectives for this keynote address by answering all three of my initial questions.

Firstly, I have tried to show you what we now mean by the term 'flexible learning', and hope that you agree with my suggestion that we should start using it as a generic term covering all the areas that were previously included under 'open learning' in its broadest sense. I am trying to persuade my colleagues in my own university to adopt this usage, and I hope that you will do the same.

Secondly, I have tried to show you some of the many ways in which flexible learning can manifest itself, including traditional open learning, distance learning, resource-based learning, self-study methods of various types, simulation/games, problem-based learning, work-based learning and interactive remote learning. There are further examples of wider-access courses and CAT systems of the type that are operated so successfully at Napier and Paisley Universities which I have not explored.

Thirdly, I have tried to show you, through my various case studies, some of the very real benefits that a more flexible approach to learning can bring. These include greater student ownership of the learning process, more participative (and hence more effective) learning, and greater variety of experience for students.

I am convinced that flexible learning will be one of the dominant paradigms of progressive education during the remainder of the 1990s. We at this conference can help make it so, and thus help ensure its success. I end with a modified version of the advice given to Jacob in the Book of Genesis – 'go forth and flexify'.

References

Bligh, D (1972) *What's the Use of Lectures*? Penguin Books, Harmondsworth.

Duncan, J (1994) 'Student-centred learning in economics', in D Eastcott, B Farmer, and G Gibbs (eds) *Course Design for Resource Based Learning: Business*, Oxford Centre for Staff Development.

Edward, N S (1993) 'Work-based learning in an offshore environment', *European Journal of Engineering Education,* **18**, 2, 207–12.

Edward, N S (1994) 'Meeting the needs of shift workers studying on a part-time mechanical engineering course', in F Percival and G Gibbs *Course Design for Resource Based Learning: Technology,* Oxford Centre for Staff Development, 52–4.

Ellington, H I (1989) 'Problem-based learning in education and training', in C Bell, J Davies and R Winders (eds) *Aspects of Educational Technology XXII*, Kogan Page, London, 99–105.

Ellington, H I (1990) 'Training in-post college lecturers by open-learning methods', in B Farmer, D Eastcott and B Lentz (eds) *Aspects of Educational and Training Technology XXIII*; Kogan Page, London, 99–102.

Ellington, H I (1994a) 'Twenty years of simulation/gaming: reminiscences and thoughts of a Scottish practitioner', *Simulation & Gaming*, **25**, 2, 197–206.

Ellington, H I (1994b) 'How The Power Station Game was rescued from obsolescence: a case study', in R Armstrong, F Percival and D Saunders (eds) *The Simulation and Gaming Yearbook Volume 2,* Kogan Page, London, 175–86.

Ellington, H I and Addinall, E (1978) 'Power for Elaskay', *School Science Review*, **59**, 298, 747–50.

Ellington, H I and Land, R (1995) 'Providing initial training for university teachers through open learning', in F Percival, R Land and D Edgar-Nevill *Aspects of Educational and Training Technology XXVIII*, Kogan Page, London.

Ellington, H I and Lowis, A (1992) 'Converting a taught course into distance-learning form', in D Saunders and P Race (eds) *Aspects of Educational and Training Technology XXV*, Kogan Page, London, 8–13.

Ellington, H I, Addinall, E and Langton, N H (1975) 'The Bruce Oil Game', *Petroleum Review*, April 1975, 263–5.

Ellington, H I, Allinson, M and Chen, J (1991) 'Introducing simulation/games into the curriculum of a Singapore college', in R Winterburn (ed.) *Aspects of Educational and Training Technology XXIV*, Kogan Page, London, 98–102.

Ellington, H I, Langton, N H and Smythe, M E (1978) 'The use of simulation games in schools: a case study', in P Hills and J Gilbert (eds) *Aspects of Educational Technology XI*, Kogan Page, London, 399–406.

Elton, L R B (1978) 'Educational technology – today and tomorrow', in P Hills and J Gilbert (eds) *Aspects of Educational Technology XI*, Kogan Page, London, 236–41.

Jaques, D (1991) *Learning in Groups*, 2nd edn, Kogan Page, London.

Lawton, S (1993) 'The development of a BA in Community Health Nursing/BA in Nursing', *Nurse Education Today*, **13**, 310–14.

Lowis A and Ellington, H I (1992) 'Teaching nursing by distance learning', in *Open and Distance Learning*, National Board for Nursing, Midwifery and Health Visiting for Scotland, Edinburgh, 15–29.

Manwaring, G (1987) '"Flexibilities" – a simulation on the resource implications of flexible learning systems', in F Percival, D Craig and D Buglass (eds) *Aspects of Educational Technology XX*, Kogan Page, London, 9–12.

Percival, F and Ellington, H I (1984) *A Handbook of Educational Technology*, Kogan Page, London.

Percival F, Craig, D and Buglass, D (1987) 'Editorial', *ibid*.

Race, P (1988). 'Approaches to flexible learning', in H Mathias, N Rushby and R Budgett (eds) *Aspects of Educational Technology XXI*, Kogan Page, London, 225–32.

Race, P (1992) 'Developing Competence', Professorial Inaugural Lecture, The Polytechnic of Wales, Pontypridd.

Ray, B (1992) 'Overview of remote learning. Part 2: The potential role of the "new technologies", in D Pemberton (ed.) *Proceedings of Conference on Education and Training for Remote Areas*, Highlands and Islands Enterprise, Inverness, 12–19.

Roebuck, M (1987) 'Flexible learning – developments and implications in education', in F Percival, D Craig and D Buglass (eds) *Aspects of Educational Technology XX*, Kogan Page, London, 326–32.

Usher, J R and Earl, S E (1987) 'Group modelling and communication', in J S Berry *et al.* (eds) *Mathematical Modelling Courses*, Ellis Horwood, Chichester, 133–44.

Usher, J R, Simmonds, D G and Earl, S E (1991) 'Industrial enhancement through problem-based learning', in D Boud and G Feletti (eds) *The Challenge of Problem Based Learning*, Kogan Page, London, 225–33.

Yinger, J and Eckland, R (1975) *Problem Solving with Children*, Far West Laboratory for Educational Research and Development, San Francisco, California.

Professor Henry Ellington is Director of the Educational Development Unit at The Robert Gordon University, Aberdeen. He is currently Chairman of the Association for Educational and Training Technology.

2. Flexible Learning or Learning to be Flexible?

Brian Chalkley, *University of Plymouth*

SUMMARY

This chapter highlights the distinction between flexibility as a mode of teaching and learning and flexibility as a quality to be developed in our students. It challenges the assumption that flexible learning automatically produces flexible graduates. This is an important issue because increasingly the world of work is demanding that employees be flexible not only on a day-to-day basis but also throughout their careers. The era of a single job for life may well be over. The chapter therefore considers how best to strengthen our students' capacity for flexibility and how far this objective can be achieved through the kinds of activities commonly undertaken in the name of flexible learning.

Introduction

The growth of interest in flexible learning can be ascribed to a variety of circumstances, including new technologies, resource constraints, a growing dissatisfaction with traditional modes of curriculum delivery and the stimulus for change and improvement provided by the new systems for monitoring the quality of educational provision. Clearly, however, it is also a response to government demands that students should be better prepared for the world of work. There are increasing expectations that education should provide students with a range of learning experiences and a variety of transferable skills which will enable them to prosper in the rapidly changing world of employment (Wright, 1990).

Against this background, it is not surprising that in 1988 in the schools sector, flexible learning was incorporated as a key element in the government's Technical and Vocational Educational Initiative or TVEI (Temple, 1991; Tomlinson and Kilner, 1991). Similarly, within universities one of the main vehicles for the advancement of flexible learning has been the Department of Employment's Enterprise in Higher Education programme, which has also had strongly vocational aims (Guirdham and Tyler, 1992; Sneddon and Kremer, 1994; Prickett, 1994).

There is therefore a not unreasonable expectation, often implicit but sometimes explicit (Department of Employment, 1991), that flexible learning will make students more adaptable and versatile and thereby help them to succeed in a business environment where the pace of technical and economic change is continuing to accelerate. The purpose of this chapter is both to question how far flexible learning is likely in practice to produce flexible graduates and to highlight the hitherto neglected distinction between flexibility as a mode of teaching and learning and flexibility as a desirable capability to be developed in our students. University teachers may adopt flexible learning methods without articulating any clear view of the type of person they are hoping to develop. Similarly, students may experience flexible learning techniques without themselves internalising the value of flexibility or learning the art of thinking and acting in a flexible manner.

In pursuing this argument, this chapter's aim is emphatically not to discredit flexible learning or the battery of new technologies which are used to enrich it. It is recognised at the outset that whatever the limitations of flexible learning, it is more likely to promote versatility than traditional chalk-and-talk teaching methods. It is appreciated also that flexible learning can be highly beneficial as a means of strengthening student motivation, understanding and knowledge, even if its role in promoting graduate flexibility is open to question. Indeed, much of the literature on flexible learning focuses strongly on new teaching and learning methods and says surprisingly little, directly or in detail, about how, if at all, these may encourage flexibility as a desirable personal and intellectual quality (Wade *et al.*, 1994; Rowntree, 1994; Birch and Latcham, 1984). For these reasons, a capacity to produce flexible graduates is by no means the only criterion by which flexible learning should be judged.

The distinctions and issues outlined and introduced above are not merely of semantic or academic interest. The next part of this chapter underlines how recent technological and economic developments have significantly intensified the need for a workforce which is flexible, which can respond effectively to the demands for rapid change and frequent innovation, and which can adjust successfully to the business dislocations associated with ever-shortening product lifecycles. Later sections go on to explore how far flexible learning can engender the newly required levels of professional adaptability and versatility and to consider what further steps educationists can take to provide learning experiences that will nurture in our students the flexibility which many of them are going to need.

Technology, post-Fordism and flexible production

During the last two decades in Britain and in other advanced economies there has been a major restructuring of economic activity. Principally in response to technological change, there has been a shift from Fordist to post-Fordist modes of business organisation (Lipietz, 1987; Scott, 1988).

Up till the 1970s the major industries of capitalist economies, such as car manufacture, engineering and consumer durables, adopted Fordist production techniques, as epitomised in the assembly lines introduced in Henry Ford's car plants. Fordism involved mass production, standardised goods and closely regulated and routinised factory operation. Among the labour force there were high levels of trade unionisation, and job roles even at middle-management level were tightly demarcated and characterised by specialisation and routine. The skills required of many graduate employees were those associated with operating in a large, centralised organisation: the emphasis was on working within a closely defined job description, transmitting information from the layer above to the layer below, monitoring production and ensuring conformity with existing procedures.

In recent years, however, Fordism has increasingly been replaced by new more diverse and differentiated modes of business activity. The pace of technical change, the IT and communications revolution, the rise of new product markets and the shift to a service economy have all exposed the rigidities of the Fordist paradigm. In its place we are seeing less standardised, more customised forms of operation, which can respond quickly to technical or consumer change and which can adjust designs, products and services to meet the tastes and requirements of particular market segments. Large organisations are now operating with less centralised forms of management and are encouraging more local autonomy. They are also subcontracting nonessential activities to smaller companies: for this and other reasons, there has been a substantial increase in the number of small businesses, whose shorter production runs and greater ability to customise add greatly to the economy's flexibility. The growth in part-time and temporary employment is another facet of the new post-Fordist world (Watson, 1994). This new economic paradigm, often referred to as 'flexible production' obviously has different labour requirements and expectations. Increasingly, businesses are looking for graduates who are multi-skilled, adaptable, responsive to change, able to take on new tasks, willing to keep abreast of technical innovation and prepared to be lifelong learners. Even in what used to be relatively secure occupations such as banking, insurance and the civil service, the notion of a job for life is probably over. There are, of course, limits to flexibility: it is not envisaged that bankers will become biotechnologists or that derivative traders will turn their hands to radiography. Nonetheless, within broad professional areas, and sometimes beyond, there will need to be an increased capacity for career change.

If Britain's economy is to flourish in this new highly competitive, post-Fordist world, our education systems will have to respond accordingly and themselves become more flexible. Although not explored here, clearly there are, for example, implications for areas such as credit-transfer, accredited prior learning, distance learning and the promotion of access and flexibility in the timing and mode of course delivery (Edwards, 1991). There are also potentially important implications for the process of teaching and learning if higher education is to ensure a supply of graduates with the necessary intellectual and personal qualities to succeed in an era of flexible production. Graduates will have to possess an increased range of skills, to accept and welcome technical innovations, to be prepared for career changes, to cope with uncertainty, to work to tight deadlines, to be able to exploit a wide range of information types and sources, to meet the challenge of the unforeseen and to operate effectively in different working and cultural environments.

The question now arises, therefore, of how far flexible learning activities can successfully contribute to producing graduates who possess these capabilities. Does flexible learning at university provide the basis for flexible operation in the workplace?

Does flexible learning produce flexible graduates?

One immediate difficulty in addressing this question is the ambiguity surrounding the definition of flexible learning. Indeed, the whole arena of innovative teaching and learning is a confusing swamp of overlapping concepts and poorly defined terms. Among the labels in use are: open learning, autonomous learning, self-directed learning, active learning, student-centred learning, individualised learning, self-managed learning and independent learning. The confusion is compounded by the fact that different authors have used these terms in different ways. In the absence of a clearly circumscribed and agreed definition of flexible learning, for the purposes of this present discussion I have simply itemised below five key features which are commonly included in the flexible learning literature. For each of these key features in turn the issue considered is how far this particular aspect of flexible learning is likely to promote real flexibility in the students involved.

1. Student choice of learning methods

Flexible learning is often defined as the provision of a variety of learning methods so that the student can select the form of study that they personally find most effective. This approach relates closely to the concept of autonomous learning (Boud, 1988) and recognises that individual students learn in different ways. In practice, of course, although students commonly do have some freedom to select the precise balance of their learning modes, it is extremely rare for individual degree modules to be offered in a choice of formats (lecture-based, workshop-based, project-based, etc). That in these terms completely flexible learning is therefore largely mythological is probably beneficial rather than detrimental to the cause of promoting real flexibility in our students. If undergraduates were allowed a completely free choice of learning mode, there is a clear danger that across modules they would too often opt for the same approach and thereby narrow their educational experience. Graduate flexibility demands that students experience a variety of different learning modes and not merely the one or two with which they feel most comfortable. Flexibility requires a level of challenge and change that is not entirely compatible with the high levels of autonomy sometimes encouraged by flexible learning.

2. Student choice of curriculum

Flexible learning is associated with giving students a wide measure of choice over what they learn as well as how they learn. Students are encouraged to take responsibility for their own programme of study. In this respect modular structures are often thought to be advantageous because they provide flexibility in the sense that students can select a pattern of modules tailored to their individual needs and interests (Jenkins and Walker, 1994).

In terms of producing adaptable graduates, the flexibility associated with modularity has certain clear benefits in that it can lead students to encounter a wider range of teachers and methods of learning. It can also allow students to experience a number of academic disciplines, each with its own distinctive culture, perspectives and expectations. Exposing students to these different ways of thinking and working is obviously likely to encourage graduate flexibility. Students schooled in more than one discipline may also find it easier to switch career directions and to adapt more readily to changing circumstances in the labour market.

The downside of student choice and the curriculum flexibility permitted by modularisation is that in a unitised framework it can be difficult to provide for each student a coherent, balanced and progressive programme of transferable skills. With respect to graduate flexibility, this is obviously a key concern. There is also a danger that students will choose to avoid skills or subjects which they find difficult or stretching. Technophobes, for example, may deliberately minimise their contact with IT, computer-assisted learning (CAL) and multimedia. In this way flexible learning and choice may once again limit the educational experience and disempower the student, leaving them less equipped to face the challenge of working in an environment of flexible production that demands a diversity of skills and a capacity to cope with the difficult and the unfamiliar.

3. Information technology

The literature on flexible learning regularly includes chapters and case studies on the use of IT and CAL (see for example, Wild, 1994; Birch and Latcham, 1984). IT represents not only an alternative medium for curriculum delivery but one that supports flexible learning because it allows for student independence. In the words of Saunders (1986) 'information technology is revolutionary in that it puts learning into the hands and control of the learner'. Students are free to determine when they will learn and at what pace they will learn. They also have increasing flexibility as to where they will learn.

It can also be argued that learning through IT can promote adaptability in the workplace. Indeed, IT has revolutionised so many areas of work, from financial services to the daily press, that computer literacy is absolutely essential for the modern graduate. So many innovations in working practices are prompted by or delivered through developments in information systems that adaptability and IT are often closely interwoven in the fabric of job change.

The use of IT and CAL as study vehicles or learning aids does not by itself guarantee a high level of computer literacy, but it does assist familiarisation and enable students to feel increasingly comfortable with different forms of computer applications. Moreover, some computer-based simulations pose challenges and require a speed of problem-solving which may, in a modest way, help to nurture flexibility of thought and response. However, among the well-known downsides to CAL is that some educational software requires little by way of active learning and gives the student only a limited degree of initiative and freedom. There is also, of course, the much discussed anxiety that too much time spent in front of a computer might result in student isolation and produce a passivity which would certainly not promote the cause of flexibility, versatility and the spirit of enterprise.

4. Resource-based learning

It is sometimes suggested that flexible learning has its roots in resource-based learning (Erant et al., 1991) and certainly the literature on flexible learning contains numerous examples of study activities based heavily on materials such as course handbooks, study guides, textbooks, worksheets, tapes and videos.

The implications of resource-based learning for graduate flexibility depend very much on the quality and variety of the materials employed and whether they are kept up to date. At its best, student adaptability can be enhanced through experience of different kinds of source materials. This training in study and information skills can have lasting benefits and be put to use later in a variety of business and professional settings. At its worst, however, resource-based learning can simply be a device for reducing staff-contact hours; producing for the student a rigid and impersonal form of instruction in which the worksheets or reading give little scope for individual initiative and demand little by way of flexibility, creativity or imagination. Where it is introduced as a mechanism for coping with growth in a mass higher education system, resource-based learning can represent in effect a Fordist mode of curriculum delivery. Mass-produced, prepacked information kits may result in spoonfed students who are denied the challenge of researching their own information. Resource-based learning is therefore an example of a flexible learning approach which, if not carefully designed, can induce dependency and inflexibility. It raises the question of whether Fordist styles of teaching and learning can effectively prepare students for a post-Fordist world.

5. Self-pacing

Flexible learning involves a preference for allowing each student to determine the pace at which they work (Boud, 1988). This is another facet of the autonomous learner concept. Students progress through a planned sequence of units or tasks at a speed that suits their background, aptitude and inclinations.

Although self-pacing certainly gives the student flexibility in their studies, it does not promote the flexibility increasingly required in the workplace. In the post-Fordist world of just-in-time delivery systems, customised services, intense competition and perpetual change, employees are rarely allowed the luxury of proceeding at a pace of their own choosing. There is instead a premium on speed of response and meeting deadlines. In these terms, self-paced flexible learning is perhaps the very antithesis of post-Fordist flexible production.

Education for flexibility: some concluding remarks

Having established that certain aspects of flexible learning are not entirely helpful in creating flexible graduates, this final section of the chapter considers what kinds of higher education might be most effective in creating the versatile and adaptable graduates society needs, while recognising, of course, that there are institutions and degree programmes that already give at least some attention to the importance of flexibility. The question explored here is: 'What would the educational experience and curriculum look like if flexibility really were prioritised?' In addressing this question and outlining some preliminary suggestions, I am only too well aware of merely scratching superficially at the edge of a subject of massive proportions and one that remains as yet largely unexplored.

A first priority must clearly be breadth in the curriculum and in the skills acquired. British higher education programmes are at present, by international standards, excessively specialised, and there is still a strong emphasis on the traditional single honours degree and the narrow subdisciplines taught within it. We academics like to indulge ourselves in teaching our own special research interests, but although there is certainly a place for research-led teaching, it must not be at the expense of a wide and diverse curriculum for the students. In the new modular frameworks we need to ensure that breadth is achieved not just by a small minority of students who choose to be adventurous but that many more undergraduates receive the stimulus of exposure to a variety of areas of knowledge, each with its own different style of thinking and working. Similarly, we need deliberately to design in and embed the acquisition, practice and assessment of a wide range of transferable skills, among the most important of which is an approach to study skills that enables and encourages students to become lifelong learners. The pace of technical change and the speed at which information dates make it essential that students are equipped for keeping abreast of innovation and for developing new areas of expertise.

The increasingly global economy will also demand more graduates who have language skills and who can adjust successfully to living in different cultures and environments. Employers will be looking for students who can transfer their transferable skills from one country to another. More language training and requiring or encouraging more students to take a study period abroad would obviously play a part in achieving this cultural and linguistic versatility.

In terms of teaching and learning methods, the keynote must be diversity – a message no doubt close to the heart of many who have advocated and promoted flexible learning. It is essential, however, that diversity becomes compulsory rather than merely optional. Degree programmes need to be structured to ensure student exposure to the full range of learning modes: cognitive, behavioural and experiential. Debates, brainstorming, work experience, individual projects, groupwork, guest lectures, industrial visits, problem-solving exercises, fieldwork, role plays and many more learning experiences need to be part of the student agenda.

In preparing for diverse teaching, staff will need to make good use of the flexible learning literature and of texts such as Habeshaw *et al.*'s (1988) *53 Interesting Things to do in Your Seminars and Tutorials*. Diversity will also be important in assessment, with students being challenged to adapt to different ways of demonstrating their skills and knowledge. In modular frameworks the key will be to find ways of planning and coordinating this variety so as to ensure that individual students cannot opt for the quiet life by choosing exclusively the familiar and the relatively undemanding.

The philosophy needed to underpin and inform the curriculum is therefore one of providing a range of challenges. The role of the teacher is no longer to facilitate 'comfortable learning' but rather to design learning experiences that stretch students both intellectually and personally in ways which lead them towards new and alternative forms of thinking and working. If accepted, this cultural shift would make fresh demands on staff and challenge some of the traditional assumptions about what is good practice.

For example, beautifully prepared course guides warning in advance of every aspect of the curriculum and detailing every hour of the programme may be seen as a recipe for a disabling predictability that can pacify and disempower the student. Learning will have to include coping with the unforeseen and responding to the unexpected. The good practice of giving long lead-times for assignments, on every occasion, may come to be regarded as failing to prepare students properly for the real world of unexpected and sometimes extremely short deadlines. Similarly, always circulating specimen examination papers may be criticised for eliminating the challenge of coping with new and unforeseen demands.

I am not at all advocating here a chaotic or ill-prepared curriculum, nor that adaptability should become the only skill to be developed. I recognise also that if universities are to be successful in promoting flexibility, ideally it should be nurtured much earlier in life in primary and secondary education. I appreciate too that students may not welcome some of the new challenges envisaged here. Similarly, some staff would prefer to carry on with a curriculum that all too often remains subject based and lecture delivered. But can we really demand flexibility from our students, if we are not prepared to be flexible ourselves?

In setting the future agenda, the starting point must be to adopt and champion flexibility as a key educational aim and then to consider how best to achieve that aim within the context of our own institutions and courses. There is a need to review both modular and traditional single-honours frameworks in order to ensure that students experience a broad curriculum and acquire a diverse portfolio of IT and other transferable skills. There is a need for staff development to assist teachers to design learning experiences that promote adaptability and versatility. There is similarly a need for 'student development' so that they too participate in these curriculum debates and are fully aware of how and why course objectives like flexibility are chosen and pursued. It is also important, in responding to the need for flexible graduates, that further research is undertaken so that we understand more precisely both the changing needs of employers and also the long-term outcomes of different kinds of educational experiences. Do combined graduates prove to be more versatile than their single-honours counterparts? Do students who have experienced the full range of flexible learning methods actually fare better in the workplace than those from more traditional courses?

Pursuing the theme of flexibility therefore opens up interesting agendas for both teaching and research, the latter in time perhaps helping to refashion the former. It may well also stimulate more exciting and imaginative approaches to the design of learning, as well as equipping our students more effectively for a world where technical and economic change are endemic and accelerating. In summary, therefore, the essence of this chapter's argument is that the flexible learning movement needs to become more sensitive to the goal of producing flexible graduates. The call is for approaches to teaching and learning that are in tune with the new world of flexible production and will foster in our graduates the flexibility they will need to succeed.

Acknowledgements

I am grateful to Dr Mark Brayshay (Department of Geographical Sciences, University of Plymouth), for his helpful comments on a first draft of this chapter.

References

Birch, D W and Latcham, J (1984) *Flexible Learning in Action: Three Case Studies of Flexibility*, Department of Education and Science, London.

Boud, D (ed.) (1988) *Developing Student Autonomy in Learning*, 2nd edn, Kogan Page, London.

Department of Employment (1991) *Flexible Learning: A Framework for Education and Training in the Skills Decade*, London.

Edwards, R (1991) 'The inevitable future? Post-Fordism and open learning', *Open Learning*, **6**, 2, 36–42.

Erant, M *et al.* (1991) *Flexible Learning in Schools*, Department of Employment, London.

Guirdham, M and Tyler, K (1992) *Enterprise Skills for Students*, Butterworth-Heinemann, Oxford.

Habeshaw, S, Habeshaw, T and Gibbs, G (1988) *53 Interesting Things to Do in Your Seminars and Tutorials*, 3rd edn, Technical and Educational Services Ltd, Bristol.

Jenkins, A and Walker, L (eds) (1994) *Developing Student Capability Through Modular Courses*, Kogan Page, London.

Lipietz, A (1987) *Mirages and Miracles: The Crisis of Global Fordism*, Verso, London.

Prickett, S (1994) 'Enterprise in higher education: Nice work or ivory tower versus exchange and mart?', *Higher Education Quarterly*, **48**, 3, 169–81.

Rowntree, D (1994) *Preparing Materials for Open, Distance and Flexible Learning*, Kogan Page, London.

Saunders, M (1986) *Trends, Influences and Future Curriculum Provision*, Future Curriculum Trends Working Party, Southern Examining Group, Guildford.

Scott, A J (1988) *Metropolis*, University of California Press, Los Angeles.

Sneddon, I and Kremer, J (eds) (1994) *An Enterprising Curriculum: Teaching Innovations in Higher Education*, HMSO, Belfast.

Temple, H (1991) 'Starting them young: Flexible learning in the TVEI Programme', *Open Learning*, **6**, 2, 28–35.

Tomlinson, P and Kilner, S (1991) *The Flexible Learning Framework and Current Educational Theory*, Department of Employment, London.

Wade, W, Hodgkinson, K, Smith, A and Arfield, J (eds) (1994) *Flexible Learning in Higher Education*, Kogan Page, London.

Watson, G (1994) 'The flexible workforce and patterns of working hours in the UK', *Employment Gazette*, **10**, 2, 7, 239–47.

Wild, P (1994) 'Flexible learning and information technology in higher education', in W Wade *et al.* (eds), *Flexible Learning in Higher Education*, Kogan Page, London.

Wright, P W G (1990) *Industry and Higher Education: Collaboration to Improve Student's Learning and Training*, Open University Press, Buckingham.

Address for correspondence: **Brian Chalkley**, Associate Head, Geographical Sciences, University of Plymouth PL4 8AA.

3. Virtually There: Flexible Learning in the New Millennium

Ray Land, *Napier University, Edinburgh*

SUMMARY

The potential of new learning and networking technologies, allied to distributed multimedia systems, will transform flexible learning in the next decade. This raises disconcerting questions for educators.

As educators we find ourselves in a unique period of transition. How will the current generation of educators, products of a print-based generation, cope when required to teach in ways in which they themselves have not been taught? What will be the effects on current models of learning and on the educator's role, of a shift from the book (a constant, stabilised medium, which is ordered, linear, hierarchical and standardised) to the computer interface (a dynamic medium, which is exploratory, multidimensional, anarchic and comparatively unregulated)? What happens when a curriculum based on enduring truths and academic authority moves to one in which the most trustworthy data is the most recent? This chapter considers the likely effects of learning technologies that are currently being adopted in higher education. From a postmodernist perspective of education it argues that a new paradigm of learning is likely to be ushered in through the advent of advanced learning technologies and that this paradigm will have its most noticeable impact in flexible learning. The chapter seeks to encourage debate of an educational theory and practice for a new generation of online learners in an information society.

Introduction

> 'My consumers are they not my producers?'
> (James Joyce, *Finnegan's Wake*)

The last two decades have, of course, witnessed many grand claims for the application of information technology in higher education and we are all aware that there have been many false dawns. Just as television was not widely adopted as a teaching and learning technology through its lack of interactivity, many computer-assisted and computer-based learning (CAL and CBL) packages disappointed educators through their degree of closure and lack of transferability to other environments. The availability in recent years, however, of computer-mediated communications (CMC) technologies, coupled with distributed hypermedia systems such as the World Wide Web, is already offering teachers and learners in higher education rich opportunities to construct genuinely interactive and collaborative learning environments. These new learning technologies are now well beyond their development stage and though it would be rash to predict exactly how they might eventually come to be used it is reasonable to argue that they are already having considerable impact in US higher education and increasingly so within the UK.

The attraction and the value of new online learning technologies are explicable mainly in the ways they seem to be addressing the current needs of higher education and the perceived needs of learners in the next century. Most UK universities are now struggling to maintain quality against increased student numbers but in a climate of declining resource. Quality assessment exercises are often critical of learning environments for not fostering a deep approach to learning, yet the individual tutorial contact and the smaller group-based activity that are more likely to promote the deeper processing of information are often the first casualties of resource constraints. Online learning would seem to offer at least one valuable way of redressing this loss of personal student interaction. In an increasingly diverse student population this approach can also provide a means of minimising the barriers faced in conventional HE by non-traditional students. The flexibility of access to such a virtual learning community and the control over one's participation in it offered by CMC will be of particular benefit to mature students, women returning to work, disabled and economically disadvantaged students, those engaged in continuing professional development and any other social groups who are faced with complex arrangements for managing their time, work and domestic commitments.

A 'distinct and unique domain'

Harasim (1989) has drawn attention to the 'distinct and unique' properties of online learning in terms of its being:

- asynchronous
- place independent
- a many-to-many interactive communication medium.

She points out that the capacity of online learning to offer a new domain for learning has not been fully appreciated:

> 'Until now educational computer conferencing has been approached from one of two traditional perspectives: as a variant of distance education or as an extension of classroom activities. However, neither perspective is entirely adequate or appropriate; in fact, holding on to traditional perspectives may limit our understanding and realisation of the full potential of this new medium.'

She demonstrates in diagrammatic form how the most useful properties of both classroom-based learning and paper-based modes of distance education come together in a unique synthesis in online education (see Figure 1).

Other commentators have pointed out that the capacity of online learning to bring group-based work into the domain of flexible learning may in the long term be seen to be its most powerful feature.

> 'Collaborative knowledge construction environments enable all members of a class or learning group the opportunity to contribute their interpretation.' (Jonassen et al., 1993)

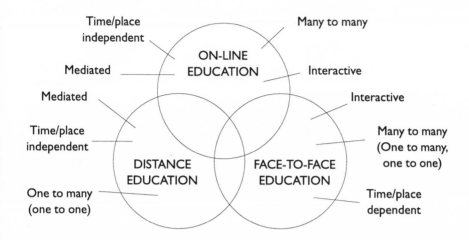

Figure 1 *Online learning as a distinct domain (after Harasim, 1989)*

Important considerations concerning equality arise from a learning environment that offers guaranteed turn-taking and freedom from the constraining behaviour of dominant peers such as one may encounter in conventional group settings. Moreover, the opportunity for reflection and considered response is also emphasised as a means of encouraging the deeper processing of information. The online learner is not pressured, as the face-to-face learner often is, into a hasty or ill-considered reply but has space for the application of judgement and the marshalling of an argument. It is, however, not only the collaborative nature of online learning but its multi-dimensionality, its multiplicity of perspectives and its complex environment of many voices and interpretations that is the key to understanding this new learning technology, not just as a more powerful tool for flexible learning – flexible learning, as it were, with added functionality – but as offering a new paradigm for learning in higher education.

> 'It is important for advanced knowledge acquisition that learners realise that there exist multiple interpretations for every event or object. Those inter-pretations may be dissonant or consonant, but they reflect the natural complexity that defines most advanced knowledge domains. Collaborative environments enable learners to identify and reconcile those multiple per-spectives in order to solve problems.' (*ibid.*)

These notions of multidimensionality, multiple perspective and competing interpre-tation lead us into a consideration of online flexible learning as the potential site for the development of a postmodern approach to learning.

A postmodern education?

'When technology extends our senses a new translation of culture occurs as swiftly as the new technology is interiorised.' (McLuhan, 1967)

When Marshall McLuhan offered this insight over 30 years ago, the cultural translation with which he was primarily concerned was the shift from an oral to a typographical culture, as well as with the social effects of television in his own time. His observation, however, provides a valid key to understanding the powerful translation of culture that is taking place within our own generation from typographical to electronic modes of communication, or, as others would argue, from a culture of modernity to one of postmodernity. As Jencks (1992) has argued:

'The uncontested dominance of the modern world view has definitely ended. Like it or not, the West has become a plurality of competing subcultures where no one ideology and *episteme* dominates for long. There is no cultural consensus, even if the actual dissensus and fragmentation into many sub-cultures has been exaggerated.'

This is not the place to become embroiled in the protracted, impassioned exchanges and manifestos which seek to explain the nature of the postmodern. Suffice it to say that it may be viewed as a condition that we face, a view to be held or an agenda to be adopted. However, the much-touted pluralism and ambiguity that most analyses would attribute to postmodernism would seem to be a key defining characteristic of the experience of online education. The ambiguities of online learning take many forms. As Mason (1993) has pointed out, the technology creates a culture in which there are new possibilities for playing with identities online. Communication can be degendered and existing hierarchies in relationships and organisations can be destabilised and reconstructed along quite different lines of interaction. Indeed, the fact that both the author and the subject of communication are dislocated both temporally and spatially often renders such hierarchies and espoused assumptions regarding, say, disability, ethnicity or social origin, either redundant or of lesser intrinsic interest than the immediate task or issue under consideration. Furthermore, the complex ambiguities that surround the ethical and legal issues of online learning environments that can straddle the globe merit a study of their own.

The emphasis we have already noted within this medium on the collaborative, the participatory and the exploratory would also seem to locate the medium within a postmodern perspective, as would its tendency to operate within parallel environments (eg multiple conferencing) and within markedly dialogic settings. Pickering's (1995) characterisation of the translation of culture might be depicted as follows:

Postmodern		*Modern*
pluralism	vs	positivism
emergence	vs	determinism
systems thinking	vs	reductive approaches
multidimensionality	vs	linearity

While Harvey (1992), in a similar list of binary oppositions (which seem to be ubiquitous within this debate) includes the following 'schematic differences':

play	vs	purpose
chance	vs	design
anarchy	vs	hierarchy
art object/finished work	vs	process/performance/happening
participation	vs	distance
text/intertext	vs	genre/boundary
combination	vs	selection
anti-narrative	vs	narrative
anti-form	vs	form
(disjunctive, open)	vs	(conjunctive, closed)

Hassan offers as *The Eleven 'Definiens' of the Term Postmodern* (1992) these characteristics:

1. Indeterminacy
2. Fragmentation
3. Decanonisation
4. Self-less-ness, depth-less-ness
5. The unpresentable, unrepresentable
6. Irony
7. Hybridisation
8. Carnivalisation
9. Performance, participation
10. Constructionism
11. Immanence.

Now this might seem a disconcertingly tall order for the poor lecturer struggling simply to offer a more flexible and supportive programme! Nonetheless, for those familiar with the experience of online learning environments, the remarkable degree of correspondence between many of these attributes and the radically different patterns of ownership and knowledge construction within computer-mediated communication, are evidence that such environments may well be seen as offering a new paradigm of learning. Readers might also have noted the correspondence between these postmodern characteristics and the attributes of such networks, distributed systems and technologies as the Internet, the World Wide Web and Hypermedia. Pickering points out that in such learning environments 'The textual base of a course is no longer the exclusive property of teachers'. He goes on:

> 'The postmodern tradition is away from authoritative monologue and towards pluralist dialogue. Instead of linear texts owned and imposed by teachers on passive recipients, future pedagogy will deal in parallel hypertexts obtained and explored by participatory, autonomous, lifelong learners.' (*op. cit.*)

Or, as the earlier quotation from Joyce reminded us, our course consumers are as likely to be our course producers in a collaborative online learning environment.

The 'text' that is continually 'emerging' in postmodern fashion from the process of the course in turn becomes a retrievable and reusable resource for the benefit of all. It forms what is in effect a collective 'course history' which, almost as soon as it is produced, can be consumed – revisited, reworked, reinterpreted.

Through the electronic wardrobe, or the new Narnia

Such a shift in the culture of learning is both exhilarating but also dislocating. Spender (1994) has pointed out the sense of threat experienced by a print-based generation of teachers who are now required to teach in ways in which they themselves were not taught. Giving up the familiar for the unfamiliar is always threatening and for those of us brought up in a literary tradition the recognition that print is no longer the primary medium of information will bring an inevitable and painful sense of loss. It will require of teachers, suggests Spender, a willingness to learn from the next generation of learners and a readiness to embrace a new educational theory and practice. This will involve moving from the comparatively stable medium of print to the dynamic media of electronic communication.

For many the thought of this transition might open up dystopian perspectives in which traditional bodies of knowledge will be undermined and standards fall. Indeed it will most probably involve a shift from an existing academic culture which places emphasis on enduring truths, canonical texts, and the use of precise reference to one concerned with swift change, obsolescence, recycling and updating, in which ''the most trustworthy data is the most recent' (ibid.). But as Spender reminds us, the transition from a monastic manuscript culture to a typographic culture in the fifteenth and sixteenth centuries was equally traumatising for academics.

Some 20 million books were printed in Europe between 1530 and 1580. But the effects of the information revolution sparked by the Renaissance printers were to go far beyond typographical design. As Postman has demonstrated, technologies always bring with them unseen social and cultural implications:

> 'In every tool we create, an idea is embedded that goes beyond the function of the thing itself.' (Postman, 1987)

In this way the advent of the printing press led to an enlargement of the reading population beyond the monopoly of the select few. The democratisation of reading begun in this manner led away from passive transcription and memorising associated with manuscript culture to an academic practice based upon books and enquiry. Reading was to provide a road to radicalism in the form of Protestantism and the rise of scientific thought. Similarly with the advent of electronic media in our own time we find ourselves moving from a print medium, based on stability, order and linearity to an extraordinarily different medium of communication. The computer screen now available to us has become an electronic window through which we enter a new realm, partly strange, partly familiar, where we will be presented with new tasks and challenges, and where we will have to grow up and come to know ourselves in a new way, in a new community. Whereas in the culture of print it remains quite reasonable to ask what a particular book contains, the question 'What does that computer contain?' becomes highly problematic. The most helpful response might simply be 'New communities'.

Conclusion – towards a new learning paradigm

If we begin to recognise the potential of computers not just as systems for course delivery, through closed courseware, but (with such learning technologies as CMC, Hypermedia, desktop video-conferencing and the World Wide Web at our disposal) rather as interpersonal communication systems, then we can see the emergence of a new paradigm of learning. This will be characterised by an emphasis on collaborative activity, on enquiry and questioning rather than on answers. As the print culture led to the democratisation of reading the new learning technologies seem to be leading to the democratisation of authorship.

Periods of transition are always problematic. The virtual realm will not be all sweetness. The traditional role as source and deliverer of information which many teachers feel comfortable with and in which they have developed and invested a high degree of expertise will probably be less in demand than roles which involve needs analysis, marketing, course design and evaluation. Requiring our students to put undue emphasis on memorisation will come to be seen as an obstacle to flows of information, to problem formulation and definition. The new learners will be more interested in doing things with the information they have located and put together rather than passively receiving and storing it.

This is not to take lightly the pressing issues that will face online learners in the new millennium. There will remain serious problems of access and equity in the use of the new learning technologies. The democratisation of authorship will add to the problem of information glut. Students will need to develop a new repertoire of online learning skills, a repertoire that will necessarily involve skills of navigation, information management, discrimination and selective negligence.

> 'The successor to print literacy will be the set of skills needed to locate and usefully organise information for ourselves and others in cyberspace.' (Lemke, 1993)

Coping with the complexity and multidimensionality of online environments may very well favour students with particular preferred learning styles. For tutors there will be difficult issues to resolve in the course design of online learning environments and particularly in the area of assessment. Establishing the authenticity of work produced in collaborative learning environments is fraught with difficulty. The way forward will inevitably entail a reduction of our dependence on content and a readiness to emphasise evidence of learning outcome achievement and to test students through questions of principle rather than through prescribed reading. To add to the complexity, the disposition and compartmentalisation of knowledge with which we are currently familiar in universities will most probably undergo reorganisation at an accelerating rate.

Yet as a generation of teachers working through this historic transition we are in a unique position. Although we are not originally educated ourselves with these technologies, we have an opportunity to demonstrate our openness to development and our capacity to critique our own assumptions and values in relation to educational theory and practice.

It behoves us as educators to be willing to take this step. And the first and most fitting demonstration of such critique should and most probably will be in the domain of flexible learning.

References

Harasim, L (1989) 'Online education: a new domain', in R Mason and A Kaye (eds), *Mindweave: Communication, Computers and Distance Education*, Pergamon Press, Oxford.

Harvey, D (1992) 'The condition of postmodernity', in C Jencks, *The Postmodern Reader*, Academy Editions, London.

Hassan, I (1992) 'Pluralism in postmodern perspective', in C Jencks, *The Postmodern Reader*, Academy Editions, London.

Jencks, C (1992) *The Postmodern Reader*, Academy Editions, London.

Jonassen, D, Mayes, T and McAleese, R (1993) 'A manifesto for a constructivist approach to uses of technology in higher education', in T M Duffy, J Lowyck and D Jonassen (eds), *Designing Environments for Constructive Learning*, NATO ASI series, F105, Springer-Verlag, Heidelberg.

Joyce, J (1992) *Finnegan's Wake*, Minerva, London.

Lemke, J (1993) 'Education, Cyberspace and Change', *The Arachnet Electronic Journal on Virtual Culture*, **1**, 1 (retrievable from: jllbc@cunyvm.cuny.edu).

Lewis, C S (1988) *The Lion, the Witch and the Wardrobe,* Lions, London.

McLuhan, M (1967) *The Medium is the Message: An Inventory of Effects*, Penguin, Harmondsworth.

Mason, R (1993) 'Introduction: written interactions', in R Mason, *Computer Conferencing: The Last Word*, Beach Holme Publishers Ltd, Victoria, BC.

Pickering, J (1995) 'Hypermedia and Postmodern Education', paper delivered to the conference, Hypermedia at Work, University of Kent at Canterbury, 11 January.

Postman, N (1987) *Amusing Ourselves to Death: Public Discourse in the Age of Show Business*, Methuen, London.

Spender, D (1994) 'From Learner to User: The Role of the Computer in Changing Learning, and Theories', address delivered to the International Experiential Learning Conference, Washington DC, 11 November.

Address for correspondence: **Ray Land**, Senior Lecturer, Educational Department, Educational Development Unit, Napier University, 219 Colinton Road, Edinburgh EH10 6EY.

4.   A Metacognitive Approach to Self-Directed Learning

Elaine Cox, *Westminster College*

SUMMARY

Research into the education of adults often focuses on the concept of self-direction. This frequently results in the design of learning programmes which presuppose, either directly or indirectly, that the learning endeavours of adults are not only planned by the individual, but that the whole process can be self-controlled. Since the capacity to be self-directing is not innate, any ability in this respect has to be encouraged and developed and, consequently, the learning processes of adults, although frequently seen as planned and controlled by the student, require input at some stage from educators. It is suggested that learning behaviour is a creative and dynamic process involving knowledge of the self just as much as knowledge of a subject or discipline, but that the development of this self-knowledge often needs help. With this in mind, metacognition is identified as a tool for educators which can foster awareness of cognitive processes, increase the student's psychological control and contribute to understanding of what helps or hinders their own capacity for learning.

Following an initial theoretical discussion of the role of metacognition in the promotion of self-direction, these ideas are related to an example of a strategic programme designed to enhance metacognitive ability in adults. The Programme for Essential Learning in Communications and/or Numeracy (PELICAN), which has been developed by the Oxfordshire Adult Basic Skills (ABS) Unit, is discussed and evaluated in the light of metacognitive theory. Since the programme is validated by the Open College Network (OCN) a brief overview of the aims and operation of OCN accreditation is included, together with a description of the assessment criteria for the PELICAN programme.

The concept of metacognition

Metacognition entails being conscious of the processes involved in a learning endeavour. It has been described as:

> 'our ability to plan a strategy for producing what information is needed, to be conscious of our own steps and strategies during the act of problem solving, and to reflect on and evaluate the productivity of our own thinking.'
> (Costa, 1987, p.106)

Whereas cognitive activity entails the active engagement of the mind relative to the subject under consideration, metacognition can be defined as 'cognition about cognition', where the mind has as its subject the processes surrounding the acquisition of knowledge. The development of self-consciousness therefore, forms an integral part of the operation.

There appear to be at least two activities involved in the metacognitive process and Flavell (1976) has differentiated between 'metacognitive knowledge', which is knowledge about one's own consciousness, and 'metacognitive experience', which incorporates the development of techniques and strategies to remedy or improve learning. The development of self-direction in the learning situation depends upon both of these activities in as much as it requires not only an awareness of cognition but also the regulation of the cognitive processes in the planning, control and evaluation of the learning situation. Metacognitive techniques to improve self-direction in learning will therefore involve devising a cognitive schema, which can be either intrinsically or extrinsically formulated, and which is then used as a guide both for strategic action and for mental reflection.

Self-direction is seen as an important and valuable skill which gives insight into individual strengths and weaknesses, personal preferences and methods for learning. Furthermore, it would appear to be an ability only acquired through the management of cognitive processes. However, although metacognitive aptitude is seen as a peculiarly human activity, research suggests that its development is not automatic (Costa, 1987). Few people analyse or try to understand their daily tasks. Thinking is an automatic process and more often than not we are unaware of how we think and are only concerned with the outcome or the idea that it produces. Consequently, few people can be genuinely self-directing and Costa (1987) has suggested that those who do practice self-direction are the ones who tend to possess well-developed metacognitive skills already.

Part of the rationale behind encouraging metacognitive skills is that they can compensate for any lack of previous knowledge by making the acquisition of that knowledge easier and more probable. Thus, metacognitive ability becomes an important precondition for the independent acquisition of knowledge and skills. Laursen (1993) illustrates the value of metacognition as a learning tool:

> 'apprehension of ourselves as thinking and learning individuals is the most
> important aspect of the ego as a self-regulating and self-producing subject
> in relation to the learning processes inherent in the learning-to-learn idea.'

This definition indicates that the practice of metacognition is instrumental in the development of self-direction. Long (1990) also confirms that self-directed learning only occurs when the student is in control of cognitive processes and goes as far as to state that 'psychological control is the necessary and sufficient cause for self-directed learning'. The development of control or responsibility, therefore, is of prime importance in the metacognitive process. Similarly Brockett and Hiemstra (1991) maintain that one of the cornerstones of self-direction in learning is personal responsibility and in their Personal Responsibility Orientation (PRO) model individuals are seen to assume ownership for their own thoughts and actions so that, even if they have little control over life circumstances or environment, they can still control how to respond to a situation. The use of metacognition in the learning/teaching situation could have an important part to play in the development of such responsibility.

The particular skills involved in the metacognitive process have been identified by several researchers. For example, Brown (cited in Laursen, 1993) identifies metacognitive ability as:

- knowing when you know;
- knowing what you know;
- knowing what you do not know;
- knowing what you need to know;
- knowing the advantage of actively changing your own level of knowledge.

Brown confirms that as long as the strategies used in learning remain unconscious it is merely a cognitive process: only giving thought to the actual processes of learning is metacognition. Smith (1983) also gives a list of features which, he maintains, the adult who has learned how to learn knows:

- how to take control of his or her own learning;
- how to develop a personal learning plan;
- how to diagnose strengths and weaknesses as a learner;
- how to chart a learning style;
- how to overcome personal blocks to learning;
- the criteria for sound learning objectives;
- the conditions under which adults learn best;
- how to learn from life and everyday experience;
- how to negotiate the educational bureaucracy;
- how to learn from television, radio and computers;
- how to lead and participate in discussion and problem-solving groups;
- how to get the most from a conference or workshop;
- how to learn from a mentor;
- how to use intuition and dreams for learning;
- how to help others learn more effectively.

Although this ambitious and somewhat idealistic catalogue tends to reinforce the view that the majority of adults can never be self-directing in all circumstances, nevertheless it prompts us to consider whether the process of metacognition is self-perpetuating, and whether once a student has learned the method of process awareness in one context he or she is able to put it into practice in different contexts. It seems probable that metacognitive experience, to use Flavell's distinction, brings about metacognitive knowledge Smith has suggested that:

> 'Learning intersects learning how to learn, because as we learn things happen that affect our motivation for further learning and our potential for learning more efficiently, effectively and meaningfully.' (Smith, 1983, p.58)

Students of any age and ability would need assistance to achieve the levels of skill identification suggested in the list given by Smith, but once they have been encouraged to use metacognitive techniques it is hoped that they would be able to transfer the skill to other situations. Since previously learned knowledge and skills influence subsequent learning, if a student has internalised the process of metacognition (ie the ability to plan strategically and to reflect on the process) he or she should be able to transfer the skills to other situations with the result that the ability becomes habitual.

At the basic skill level at which PELICAN is aimed, the primary intention is to kindle the habit of reflective thought and evaluation. Any psycho-cultural assumptions that may be implicit in the material used in the PELICAN programme are not emphasised, although it is possible that, as the student gains in confidence and self-critical ability, these forms of analysis may occur. It is suggested that a combination of subject teaching and separate skills might consolidate the learning more readily, by providing both real and hypothetical opportunities to practice metacognitive skills.

Gestalt psychologists claim that the understanding of a situation in all its aspects forms the basis of transfer in learning and, as the metacognitive strategies advocated here involve complete understanding of the processes required in learning, the transfer would appear to be optimised.

One essential part of the meta-learning process, which should not be underestimated, is evaluation. In order to be effective this should be conducted with respect to specific learning objectives. If the objectives are clear a meaningful appraisal can be carried out. Time should be set aside at the end of each learning session to examine progress and this kind of feedback is closely connected to motivation, since it can be used to inspire new goals and create new strategies. Reflection on the experience and the matching of what was expected with what actually happened leads to the development of metacognitive skills.

It has been suggested that 'the adult education programme which gives top priority to the individual, actively involves him in the educational experience and provides him with useful feedback will be helping him learn how to learn' (Jensen, cited in Smith, 1982). This is because the inclusion of detailed and positive feedback and evaluation in the learning programme can greatly increase motivation. Internal incentives to certain kinds of activity can often be induced by external motivational factors with the result that motivation can often be achieved by the positive analysis of needs. Thus a major part of the process, if metacognitive skills are to be encouraged, is the development of a plan of action, incorporating needs analysis and evaluation, and the maintenance of that plan over a period of time.

PELICAN

Frequently in the design of learning programmes the idea of self-direction in adults is assumed. But more often than not, as Long (1990) recognises:

> 'independence is provided for students who are not sufficiently proficient,
> either psychologically or in terms of content, to address the learning goals.'

This is particularly noticeable at the basic skill level, where any attempt to thrust such independence on students can result in participation problems. Consequently, because of the implicit heavy student reliance upon the tutor, any programme of work for basic-skills students is normally prescriptive in nature. Furthermore, the previous learning experiences of adults conditions them to believe that the development of the learning programme is part of the teacher's domain. Accordingly, since autonomy and self-direction are viewed as desirable attributes in adults, students in these circumstances appear to be in a paradoxical situation. On the one hand they need to develop self-direction, but on the other they have no inner resources on which to call. They have not learnt how to learn.

PELICAN has been designed specifically for adult basic-skills students in an endeavour to assist with the development of student autonomy in learning how to learn. Learning how to learn involves the learner's ability to create strategies, define goals and analyse ways of achieving them. The PELICAN programme encourages the ability to make the appropriate plans and ensures that decision making and control are promoted. Indeed, the element of control is made concrete by the development of a visible action plan which forms the foundation of the programme. The fundamental aim of the programme is to encourage the student to achieve his or her own learning goals and to obtain recognition for doing so.

The PELICAN programme incorporates the majority of the components of metacognition identified earlier, including identification of student needs. The main procedures involved are as follows.

- Negotiation (or renegotiation) to help the student to explore their present situation and establish long- and short-term goals.
- Student goal-setting with specific focus on aspects they want to change.
- The planning of learning with emphasis on the time required to complete.
- The creation of a personal action plan that also identifies resources which can be utilised in the learning process.
- Continuous student and tutor evaluation and regular progress reviews and negotiations.
- The building of a portfolio.

The process is designed to involve the student at every stage of the development of the learning programme, thus helping to develop metacognitive abilities.

In the notional 30 hours of learning (required to attain one Open College Network credit) students are encouraged to develop skills that enable them to analyse their present position and to focus on aspects they want to change; to discuss and establish long- and short-term goals and to create a personal action plan. The programme aims to build confidence and autonomy by recognising and addressing the student's own needs and aspirations and providing Open College Accreditation for this achievement.

Prior to the first learning session the student and tutor complete an indepth analysis of the goals and ambitions of the student, together with recognition of the skills already available and those that need to be learnt or improved. Specific learning goals are identified and prioritised and a time constraint suggested. In this way realistic objectives can be ascertained. Strategies for achieving the goals are then outlined and appropriate materials and resources chosen. An account of the interview is made on the first page of the Record of Work (see Figure 1). During this interview the tutor helps to construct a learning programme, but in order to confer ownership, and thereby increase motivation, it is necessary that the learner also be instrumental in its construction.

30-Hour Action Plan

Date:

What do I want to be able to do by the end of the programme?

What do I need to do to get there?

What materials will I need?

How will I know I have got there?

Review date:

Figure 1 *PELICAN 30-hour action plan*

Careful identification of a learner's goals and aspirations at this stage will help to overcome the barriers to learning which many adult learners have. Similarly each learning session has to relate to the original aims of the student and be structured in such a manner that the student is aware of the relevance and purpose of the activities. The learning should therefore have recognisable outcomes and progress should be easily identifiable. Breaking down the tasks into competencies has some value at this level and, if there is involvement by the student in the breakdown, the metacognitive approach will be further enhanced. Evaluation criteria are also set down at this early stage in order to focus on the desired result.

Space is set aside at the end of each subsequent session for the work to be recorded, together with the amount of time spent on each activity, in order to show a developing skill in organising time and planning work. This, together with an evaluation ('How did it go?') provides ongoing self-monitoring which is very important since it gives insights into progress being made and difficulties encountered. The formal recording system ensures that the student comes to the learning situation aware of the successes and failures of the previous sessions, although the tutor does have a responsibility to ensure that minor as well as major successes are recorded and that disappointments are analysed to find a positive solution. The evaluation, effected in this way, is valuable in increasing self-esteem and/or realism. Work for next time is also recorded as part of the process and completed pieces of work are dated and timed before being added to the portfolio of work. Although the portfolio is secondary in the development of metacognitive skills, nevertheless it provides a focus for the achievement of the learning goals outlined in the initial action plan. At the end of the programme, normally 30 hours, both the portfolio and the Record of Work booklet will be assessed for OCN accreditation.

Open College Network

The OCN is a partnership of education providers who are committed to increasing access to higher education. Its aims are primarily to improve the quality of learning opportunities available for adults and to promote a national system which will give access to education and training, particularly for those groups of individuals who, in the past, have been unable to benefit from existing provision. Many courses and learning programmes for adults do not offer their learners any record or certificate for learning achieved; through the OCN recognition can be given for such learning in the form of credits which are then accumulated by the student in a Credit Record. As well as helping learners to progress to further learning activities the credits can be used to help in job and training applications. Credits are available at four levels, ranging from foundation to preparation for higher education. Assessment is usually through the formation of a portfolio.

Accreditation of PELICAN by the OCN acknowledges the development of student autonomy in learning how to learn and is based on the negotiated learning programme. It is set at two levels, both of which require the essential parts of the programme to be taken into account with the evidence provided by the student's portfolio of work. The criterion for assessment at level 1 states that the tutor is responsible for recording information in the Record of Work booklet and for suggesting materials for the learning sessions. At level 2 the student takes respon-sibility for entering most of the information, as well at taking the initiative for researching and identifying further learning opportunities. The ability to renegotiate the individual programme is an important part of the process and its assessment.

The OCN moderator checks that the items in the Record of Work accord with the work in the portfolio and that the pieces of work meet the original aims of the negotiated programme. The comments under 'How did it go?' will provide evidence that the learner has increased in confidence in the desired skills. In particular the moderator is checking adequate production of the following.

At level 1:
- negotiated learning programme;
- recorded goals in Record of Work;
- recorded work done in class (with time spent);

- how well the work went weekly;
- planning of work to be done next;
- recording of attained goals;
- regular review of work and discussion of feelings and achievements;
- evidence of renegotiation;
- file of work to show skills worked on and achievements.

In addition, at level 2, evidence of the following skills will be expected:
- recording of own Record of Work;
- finding of own materials and resources;
- independent organisation of work;
- independent time management;
- setting long-term goals with realistic time constraints;
- finding out about activities that will build on skills once original goals have been met.

Conclusion

The PELICAN Record of Work booklet was used successfully at the beginning of 1994 to record the literacy and numeracy work done by a group of unemployed adults attending a compulsory six-week intensive Learning for Work course at North Oxfordshire College. The use of metacognitive strategies in the learning sessions proved worthwhile. Testimonials from the eight students on the course suggest that being made aware of the learning process, often several times each day, increased their awareness of themselves as learners and highlighted to them the importance of their own input. The improvement in the motivation of the students was discernible to both learners and tutors, particularly towards the end of the course when almost every student was motivated to arrange some kind of further study. Bearing in mind that these adults all had negative educational experiences that they needed to exorcise, it was evident that the strategic metacognitive approach used on the course had paid dividends.

In 1983 Carl Rogers suggested that the goal of education in the future should be the 'facilitation of change and learning'. He stated that the only man who is educated is the man who has learned how to learn, and that a reliance on process rather than static knowledge is the only thing that makes any sense as a goal for education in the modern world. The metacognitive strategies discussed here have an important role to play in the process and development of self-direction in the learning situation, and especially for those requiring basic-skills help who have not yet learnt how to learn. The use of metacognitive approaches increases confidence and the likelihood of self-direction in learning and stresses the value of regular reflection and evaluation of progress. In particular the PELICAN programme is aimed at encouraging the learner to question his or her own learning behaviour, it gives support and encouragement for basic-skills learning and thereby increases levels of motivation and self-esteem. Any programme using the concept of metacognition or meta-learning as its guiding philosophy enhances the learning ability of its students and equips them for success in many areas of life. It provides less proficient students with a means of developing responsibility for their own learning, and subsequently fosters psychological independence, both of which, despite careful planning, are absent from many programmes of independent learning.

References

Brockett, R G and Hiemstra, R (1991) *Self-direction in Adult Learning*, Routledge, London.

Costa, A (1987) 'Mediating the metacognitive', in H F Clarizio *et al.* (eds), *Contemporary Issues in Educational Psychology*, McGraw-Hill, Singapore.

Flavell, J H (1976) *Cognitive Development*, Prentice Hall, Hemel Hempstead.

Garrison, D R (1991) 'Critical thinking and adult education: A conceptual model for developing critical thinking in adult learners', *International Journal of Lifelong Education*, **10**, 4, October–December, 287–303.

Kidd, J R (1973) *How Adults Learn*, Association Press, Chicago.

Laursen, E (1993) 'Problem-controlled learning processes and metacognition in adult learning', in P Gam *et al.* (eds), *Social Change and Adult Education Research,* Copenhagen.

Long, H (1990) 'Psychological control in self-directed learning', *International Journal of Lifelong Education*, **9**, 4.

McGuinness, C (1993), 'Teaching thinking: New signs for theories of cognition', *Educational Psychology*, **13**, 3 & 4.

Mezirow, J (1981) 'A critical theory of adult learning and education', in M Tight (ed.), *Adult Learning and Education*, Croom Helm, Beckenham.

Rogers, C (1983) *Freedom to Learn from the '80s*, Merril, Columbus, Ohio.

Smith, R M (1982) *Learning How to Learn*, Open University Press, Buckingham.

Address for correspondence: **Elaine Cox**, Lecturer and Career Development Programme Coordinator at Westminster College, Oxford, OX2 9AT.

5.   Using Flexible Resources for Learning

Sally Brown, *University of Northumbria at Newcastle*

SUMMARY

Any university that chooses to ignore the current developments in flexible learning resources does so at its peril, risking the loss of important opportunities for enabling autonomous student learning and the potential to provide exciting, adaptable and cost-effective curriculum delivery methods.

This chapter aims to examine some of the key questions and issues associated with flexible learning resources in higher education in the 1990s. It also suggests strategies for those who wish to extend their repertoire of teaching and learning techniques by developing a greater variety of improved resources for learning.

The importance of flexible learning resources in HE

Higher education is changing rapidly, and it is apparent to many of us that we need to review the techniques we use for curriculum delivery, not only to cope with the new environment in which we are working, but also to harness the new technologies now available to us. On the one hand, the use of learning resources is seen as a way of coping with a whole range of issues including:

- larger numbers of students;
- diverse kinds of students who don't share common assumptions and knowledge bases;
- problems with students who lack motivation or who are content with very low standards of achievement;
- decreasing units of resource in real terms;
- increasing pressure on academic staff;
- restrictions on conventional resources such as accommodation;
- pressures towards more autonomous student learning;
- requirements to provide more support for non-standard, part-time and access students;
- the changing role of personal tutors, who often have little time to cope with individual or personal support and more responsibility for tracking and monitoring student progress;
- modularisation and unitisation prompting changes in curriculum design;
- changes such as modularisation leading to the need to make better use of contact time;
- student expectations of better presented, more interesting materials.

At the same time, opportunities are being provided to allow university teachers to make use of a range of resources that have not previously been available to them including:

- CD-ROM facilities for computer mediated teaching and learning;
- interactive video disks;
- opportunities for computer conferencing for tutorials and student-led group activities
- e-mail for communications and interactivity;
- off-air recordings of television programmes;
- Internet and the World Wide Web for information retrieval, communication, mind-bending, surfing and fun!

For all these reasons, staff in universities are looking at ways of doing things differently, and making learning resources more readily available.

The benefits of learning from resource materials

Learning resources can provide for students:

- a sense of ownership and control over the material being studied;
- a chance to pace work at a rate to suit individual circumstances (so long as university regulations permit this!);
- the opportunity to go back and have another try when things go wrong;
- the comfort of privacy to make mistakes in, and then to remedy them without looking foolish;
- the ability to skim rapidly through things that are already understood, saving time for the elements of learning that are new and challenging;
- built-in feedback on their work, when feedback from tutors is increasingly under pressure.

Staff can benefit from:

- opportunities for advanced planning and production of course materials, which may save time overall (although energy and finance inputs may be heavily front-loaded!);
- the possibility of long-term savings of resources, or at least a change in the resource mix of materials available to students;
- a change to the role of tutors who become 'expert witnesses' and process supporters rather than information transmitters;
- chances to exchange or sell materials produced with other academics in the same field (with due consideration given to copyright issues);
- an assurance that students have been provided with good learning support, even when absenteeism is common.

Resources for flexible learning are not a quick fix!

Some universities have moved with such speed to implement the wider use of learning resources that inevitably problems have occurred. It now has become apparent that resources for learning cannot:

- replace teaching contact in its entirety, since students still often want and need personal contact for inspiration, motivation, role models and human interaction;
- be produced without substantial investment of time, effort and money (although there are notable examples of a great deal being achieved by the creative use of relatively small investments, for example in the Department of Continuing Education at Lancaster University);
- be devised to standard templates without modification for different circumstances and contexts;
- be developed without staff development for the academics who are writing the materials and administrative and technical staff who are producing them;
- be implemented within existing courses overnight;
- be used for long periods without regular updating;
- be introduced without providing induction for students in the study methods necessary for resource-based learning and for staff in how to support student learning when flexible resources are used;
- solve all the potential problems brought about by modularisation, such as loss of course coherence and difficulties in tracking students' performance;
- remedy all the perceived difficulties that arise from semesterisation, such as compression of teaching programmes or awkward blocking of study periods within the academic calendar.

Flexible learning resources often work best if there is:

- support for their development from the highest level within a university;
- shared responsibility for their production and implementation;
- a strategic approach to their development and usage;
- a rewards system for the pioneers and the practitioners;
- a clear focus of responsibility for development and use;
- sensible planning providing sufficient lead times for production;
- substantial support provided for academics by librarians, computer specialists, technicians and administrators;
- good teamwork and morale among the producers and users of resources for learning;
- a commitment to the development of cohesion of materials;
- an understanding of the need for learner interaction;
- a consistent house-style for all materials produced within a learning environment (although not everyone believes this to be essential);
- standardisation of equipment used, to ensure compatibility;
- a variety of approaches to prevent student malaise and boredom;
- opportunities for piloting and revision;
- effective evaluation by all users, with built-in provision for continuous improvement.

What kinds of resources for learning exist?
The range of resources available to support and enable learning include:

Paper-based learning resources including course guides, booklets, manuals, self-help diagnostic tests, study units, textbooks with textbook guides, reading guides, systematically organised lecture notes, logs and learning diaries, profiling systems.

Computer-based materials including: Keller plan programmes, computer-based tutorials, online objective testing, CD-ROM learning programmes, multimedia.

Networked learning resources such as online tutorials, networked study programmes and computer conferences.

Media-based materials including audio tapes, video tapes, slide transparencies, interactive video disks which make use of barcode technology (see the Exeter TLTP project, 1995).

The kinds of areas for which resources for learning may be used encompass:

Study skills guides: ranging from basic hints and tips sheets to full-blown multimedia packages.

Teaching packages: where staff produce or repackage new or existing material into accessible form, where students can work independently, particularly in the information transfer domain.

Materials used to promote student activity including seminar guides, tutorless group-work briefings, fieldwork guides, project work, laboratory work guides, visit guides for galleries and museums.

Simulations: which provide opportunities for students to try out dangerous or problematic activities without risk.

What factors make learning resources work well?
There has been a great deal of effective development in this area in recent years, sometimes based on learning by doing things wrong! The features that make learning resources really effective tend to be as follows.

Materials that are interesting and attractive
We are working with a generation raised on sophisticated computer games and inventive media techniques on television and video, and magazines read for pleasure come in full colour and have user-friendly text. Learners in the mid-1990s are accustomed to being presented with well-produced materials, so the resources they use for study need to be seen as modern, stimulating and accessible in style. However, this doesn't mean that everything has to be produced to glossy, expensive standards, as long as it is appealing and has high standards of production.

Packages that provide a sense of ownership
Learners need to feel that the resources are theirs and not merely things belonging to a resource room or library. When, for example, learners use packages in learning

resource centres, it makes a big difference to the effectiveness of such media if they can be issued with their own interactive workbooks or manuals, in which they can log their personal use of the materials, and which they can take away with them afterwards. With computer-based packages, a learner identification system can be valuable, enabling students to be recognised and have their results recorded.

Opportunities for learning by doing
From print-based open learning packages to facilities such as the World Wide Web, the driving force for learning is that students don't just read information, but make decisions. Accessing the WWW is a complex sequence of decisions, where learners can be in control of searching for what they need, and of the depth to which their searches will go.

In-built feedback
When learners have made choices (for example, picked options in multiple-choice questions) they need to know whether their decisions were correct or not. When they give the 'wrong' responses, they need feedback explaining exactly what was wrong with their thinking. An advantage of many forms of resource-based learning is that feedback information can be built in, and can be instantly available to learners. Indeed, a disadvantage may be that the feedback can be available to learners rather too readily, and they can 'cheat' by exploring the feedback they would have received on decisions they have not yet made. However, this sort of exploration may well be an equally legitimate way of going about using learning resource materials as any planned sequence the authors of the packages may have intended!

Provision of 'time out' for reflection
Students need to be given opportunities to make sense of the learning they have been doing. Well-designed learning resource materials don't just say 'stop now and think about what you have learned'. Good learning resources build in exercises or tasks that necessarily involve learners in consolidating the learning they have just undertaken.

A sense of control and power for the learners
Good learning materials empower students. Learners can control the speed at which they work through the materials, and they can be empowered regarding the routes they take through the materials. For example, the best computer-based learning packages have menu facilities enabling learners to go rapidly backwards as well as forwards through the package, and to choose exactly which parts of the package they wish to simply scan, and which parts they will engage in actively.

Getting started with resources for learning

Having said that a strategic approach is the best way to implement resource-based and flexible learning, there are some stages that can be fairly readily initiated. Individual lecturers on their own might:

• systematically collect existing handout material and edit it into a course guide;
• create a reader for a unit or module, comprising copyright-cleared extracts from

books, journals and other key texts;
- collect resource materials, especially non-book resources into special topic boxes or packages and make these available to students, for example, for project work;
- negotiate a location where learning resources can be safely stored and readily accessed;
- replace selected lectures within a unit with resources for learning including text self-assessment questions and guidance for wider reading;
- investigate what learning resources already exist in their subject area in other universities and look at ways to use it, adopt it or emulate it. (The Oxford Centre for Staff Development project materials derived from the HEFCE-funded Course Design for Resource Based Learning projects are a useful source of contacts, Gibbs *et al.*, 1994.)

Course route teams and larger departmental groups can:

- set up learning resources groups to work collaboratively on the production of materials;
- establish a standard format or house-style for learning resources produced by the group;
- agree on compatible equipment for using computer-based learning materials;
- bid for funding to support the development and production of learning resources.

Institutions as a whole might consider:

- learning from the experiences of universities who have already gone a long way along this route;
- investing in a strategic approach to the development of resources for learning designed to fulfil the needs of the institution;
- providing staff with release-time/funding to enable them to work on materials (expecting staff to develop resources for learning in their own time with no reward rarely works!);
- exploring the capital requirements for the provision of learning resources including computers and other equipment, learning resource centres, academic, technical, administrative and librarian staffing requirements;
- investigating the best balance of investment between people and technology. It is all too easy to buy lots of computers and other equipment without investing in appropriate infrastructure to support it.

There is also a need for individuals, departments and institutions to find ways of working together as member-led consortia to produce and utilise materials that can be held in common and customised locally. This will save waste in terms of energy and resources, as well as contributing to a genuine community of knowledge.

Who is currently using learning resources in higher education?
Everyone! Most of the learning that takes place in higher education is done from learning resource materials of one kind or another, ranging from textbooks and handouts to interactive learning packages. The idea that learning can only take place

when there is a teacher around is obsolete. The roles of teachers are changing from being information providers, towards being guides, inspirers, and trouble-shooters. In addition, the roles of libraries and librarians are changing, becoming more central in the learning process as a whole. (Developments in nine key subjects are described in Gibbs and others in the Resource Based Learning Projects, 1994.)

How can we evaluate the uses of flexible learning resources?
One of the pitfalls for developers of resources for learning has been in failing to evaluate properly the learning resources that have been developed. The kind of questions that should be asked include the following:

- Are the learning resources accurate and appropriate in terms of content?
- Is the material pitched at the right level for the target group of students?
- Are they relatively easy to update and to customise for different audiences?
- Are they produced to a standard of which we can be proud?
- Are they easy to use by students and sufficiently attractive to draw students to use them?
- Do they achieve the purposes for which they were designed?
- Are they cost-effective?

This last question is a very significant one. The HEFCE-funded Course Design for Resource Based Learning project proposed that resource-based learning is not automatically cheaper than conventional curriculum delivery. Indeed, in the developmental stages, there can be considerable initial start up costs, and benefits may not be reaped for five years or so if the investment is substantial. However, there is often a significant gain in overall effectiveness of student learning and economies of scale, together with potential reduction of class contact time can make this option very attractive. (Detailed guidance on establishing the true costs of developing learning resources is given in the Resource Based Learning Projects, Gibbs *et al.*, 1994.)

How can we know what students think about learning resources?
Learning resources are of little value if students can't use them or don't find them effective. There are a range of ways in which we can discover what students think.

Make videos of students using resource materials
A lot can be learned just by watching facial expressions as they work with learning resource materials.

Track their usage
Even more can be learned by watching exactly how learners route themselves backwards and forwards through the packages. Many computer-based learning packages can indeed be programmed to track the exact sequences that individual users take, and even the time spent on each stage.

Ask learners
Whether using questionnaires or face-to-face interviews, valuable information can be gathered by asking basic questions such as:

- What do you like most about this package?
- What do you like least about this package?
- What changes would you suggest to make the package better?
- What is the most important thing you have learned from the package?

Measure learners' achievements
Any good resource-based learning package should have well-defined outcomes. Probably the best way to evaluate the effectiveness of the package is to design assignments that test the extent to which the intended learning outcomes are achieved. With computer-based learning packages, such tests can be built into the packages directly.

Working through the materials ourselves
It may seem obvious, but we don't always find the time to work through the packages that we give to our learners. In particular, it is valuable to identify the points at which learners could find themselves stuck and needing extra information and guidance.

Get groups of learners to evaluate packages
One danger of resource-based learning materials is that they can be too isolating. When materials are used by two or three learners working together, the benefits of peer discussion and peer feedback are maximised.

Horror stories

In the production of learning resources, things can sometimes go horribly wrong. Some of the worst (perhaps apocryphal) stories are listed here, not in the spirit of *schadenfreude* but in the hope that we may learn from them. These include:

- The university where the computer that had on its hard disk all the materials for a whole course to be delivered through learning packages was stolen, together with all the back-up disks which had been stored alongside.
- The learning package that had gone all the way up to final (expensive) production before the course team realised that it used the old polytechnic title throughout, rather than the new university one.
- The materials that had been widely advertised for sale, linked to a large launch event, and were not ready on time.
- The booklets that were dispatched for use by a consultant on a training course, which were found to be incorrectly assembled, so the page numbers were wrong.
- The member of staff who wrote and piloted a unit, only to find that the head of department would not fund the essential design and print costs.

References

Exeter TLTP project (1995) *Critical Encounters in the Classroom*, Exeter TLTP project (contact Penni Tearle, School of Education, Exeter University).
Gibbs, G (1994) *Institutional Support for Resource Based Learning*, Oxford Centre for Staff Development, Oxford.

Gibbs, G and Brown, S (1994) *Course Design for Resource Based Learning: Built Environment*, Oxford Centre for Staff Development, Oxford.

Gibbs, G and Cox, S (1994) *Course Design for Resource Based Learning: Social Sciences*, Oxford Centre for Staff Development, Oxford.

Gibbs, G and Parsons, C (1994) *Course Design for Resource Based Learning: Education*, Oxford Centre for Staff Development, Oxford.

Gibbs, G and Percival, F (1994) *Course Design for Resource Based Learning: Technology*, Oxford Centre for Staff Development, Oxford.

Gibbs, G and Wilks, M (1994) *Course Design for Resource Based Learning: Art and Design*, Oxford Centre for Staff Development, Oxford.

Gibbs, G and Wisdom, J (1994) *Course Design for Resource Based Learning: Humanities*, Oxford Centre for Staff Development, Oxford.

Gibbs, G, Attrill, P and McLane, E (1994) *Course Design for Resource Based Learning: Accountancy*, Oxford Centre for Staff Development, Oxford.

Gibbs, G, Eastcott, G and Farmer, B (1994) *Course Design for Resource Based Learning: Business*, Oxford Centre for Staff Development, Oxford.

Race, P (1988) *The Secrets of Study* (interactive learning package), Mast Learning Systems, London.

Race, P (1995) *Effective Learning Skills*, Napier University prototype materials due to be available in CD and networkable form (contact Fred Percival, Educational Development, Napier University, Edinburgh).

Address for correspondence: **Sally Brown**, Educational Development Adviser, Educational Development Services, University of Northumbria at Newcastle, Newcastle-upon-Tyne NE1 8ST.

6. Cost-Effective Autonomy Learning

Lewis Elton, *University College London*

SUMMARY

Autonomy learning, with its aim of leading to lifelong learning, is not only pedagogically desirable, but could actually be made more readily cost-effective than more traditional approaches to learning. However, the introduction of autonomy learning constitutes a major change in any educational system and it will fail, unless it is handled at the system level. This chapter illustrates these points in terms of past attempts at educational innovation and concludes with an analysis of the problems – educational, managerial and financial – that stand in the way of a successful introduction of cost-effective autonomy learning.

Introduction

Autonomy learning is learning that develops a student's capacity of learning how to learn. Some seven years ago I wrote a paper in which I demonstrated that it was possible to develop autonomy learning at a distance (Elton, 1988). At that time we in higher education were not quite as cost conscious as we are now, and the problem that I tackled then, was that of how to facilitate learner autonomy when teacher and learner do not meet face to face. This had been a problem at the Open University and arose from a paradoxical feature of the learning materials for which the OU was rightly famous: by and large they were so good that students did not have to fill in for the deficiencies of their lecturers, as they regrettably often had to in live lectures. Unfortunately, this meant that students often grew to be extremely dependent on their learning materials; the very opposite of independent and autonomy learning.

Towards autonomy learning at a distance

The way that I approached the problem, as in a similar manner did Liz Beaty (Taylor and Kaye, 1986) in what I believe is still the only OU course to tackle the problem of learner autonomy, was to argue that if students were to learn how to learn, they had to start from their own life and/or work experience and build their learning on this. This meant that the learning situation was different for each student, which was the very opposite of the normal OU learning situation, which starts from where the OU decrees it to be in terms of its 'oh so excellent' course materials. I do not wish to suggest that this is necessarily wrong, because autonomy learning is a rather sophisticated form of learning and may quite legitimately not be one of the aims for a particular course. If it is not, then the OU way of learning is very good indeed. On the other hand, it ought to be an aim of any degree course as a whole that the students who take it have been led towards autonomy learning by the time that they get their degrees. How else can we achieve a 'learning society'?

Autonomy learning in traditional universities

There is in fact no sharp dividing line between learning that leaves students dependent on their teachers and learning that leads to their autonomy. Any form of learning that allows students some say in how their learning is governed and managed is a step towards full autonomy learning. In traditional university teaching this includes reading in the library, writing essays, solving problems (as opposed to finding the answers to practice examples), conducting project work. The touchstone is that the learning process leaves at least some initiative to students, but not so much that (at the stage that their learning development has reached) they are left to flounder. Thus to give an example, even in a first year course, reading lists should be structured but not prescriptive, while final year students may well be left to their own devices in searching the literature in a given topic.

There is therefore nothing new about autonomy learning as such, although traditional university teachers, with their over-emphasis on content over method in their approach to student learning, have often left the development of learner autonomy to the ineffable aspects of a university education, with the result that many students never achieve it.

Autonomy learning in mass higher education

The move from elite to mass higher education has had two very serious effects on the development of autonomy learning. Firstly, the majority of students no longer arrive at university from small sixth forms, where dedicated teachers working at very favourable staff–student ratios had often prepared students so well for university that they had effectively covered what I call the 'ineffable' aspects of first year university education. This was far more important than the fact that these students also had learned a great deal of material that in other countries (including Scotland) they would only learn at university, but it is typical of the perverse concern of university staff with 'content knowledge' rather than 'learning maturity' that present complaints are generally expressed in content terms. Secondly, most of the traditional means of developing learner autonomy are labour intensive; they require personal contact between teachers and very small groups of their students, with the extreme case of the one-to-one Oxbridge tutorial. With constantly worsening staff–student ratios, teachers are fighting a losing battle with traditional methods of autonomy learning and yet do not know what other and more cost-effective methods there might be.

Where and how can educational technology help?

It is here that traditional universities can learn from the OU. The most obvious first step towards autonomy learning is to allow students to govern the pace at which they study, something that is of course the norm at the OU, but almost unknown in the timetable-driven and lecture-dominated courses at all other universities. Another discovery in the OU is that the solution to the problems of mass higher education may not lie in a technological fix, but rather in a deep analysis: applying the technology of education rather than technology in education. At a very early stage the OU discovered that its first idea of replacing live lectures by television was unsound and they turned to printed materials to replace lectures. The dominant technology which the OU used was therefore that of Gutenberg, not that of Baird, although the latter too found its uses. This lesson, that the choice of a particular technological development or device can only be made in terms of a particular learning situation, is fundamental and one which technological enthusiasts ignore at their and the tax-payer's peril.

The way that the OU made this discovery was through the understanding of the technology of education in its Institute of Educational Technology, which has continued its good work to the present day, as is apparent from the recent book by Laurillard (1993) with its subtitle 'A framework for the effective use of educational technology', the lessons of which she has presented pithily in a recent article (Laurillard, 1994), in which she writes:

'Ironically, if the use of new technology were to begin with an analysis of what students need, instead of what the technology can offer, we should make far better use of it.'

Papert (1994), one of the great innovators in the technology of education, puts it in a similar vein:

'Printing press and book, pencil and paper, chalk and blackboard are technologies as much as a computer, and their properties play a capital role in shaping what schools teach and how they teach it.'

Mayes (1994), the Director of Research at the Heriot-Watt University Computer-based Learning Institute, has this to say in the same excellent *Times Higher Education Supplement* 'Synthesis':

'The main problem to address with innovative methods is not the students' access to subject matter or even their primary exposure to it through a lecturer's personal interpretation, but rather how to deal with the individual misconceptions, questions and discussion necessary as each learner struggles to come to an acceptable level of understanding.'

The same sentiments have been echoed by Reinhardt (1995):

'In study after study, a vital conclusion emerges: technology alone is not the solution. Reaping the benefits of computers first requires extensive teacher training, new curricular materials, and, most important, changes to educational models.'

Thus, to use technology effectively in a learning situation involves an interactive analysis of both the learning situation and the potential of the technology. Out of this comes the realisation that what is important in introducing technological change into learning, and before into teaching, is to link such change to learning objectives rather than match it to teaching methods. In retrospect this may be a rather obvious conclusion, but set against the historical development of replacing live lectures by televised ones, live tutorials by computer programmes which simulated tutor–student interaction and live laboratory experiments (and I mean experiments) by computer simulations – all of which related to methods rather than objectives – it still needs stressing.

Changes to traditional teaching: doing better

In trying to improve teaching which facilitates autonomy learning before we turn to more radical change, we must not ignore the possibility that much could be gained by doing better what is at present not done as well as it might be. In view of the enormous prevalence of lecturing in higher education, it is likely that an improvement of 1% in the learning effectiveness resulting from an improvement in lecturing will do more for the improvement of learning than an improvement of 100% through computer-assisted learning. Any lecturers who have read, marked, learned and inwardly digested the just over 100 pages of *Lecturing and Explaining* (Brown, 1978) will almost certainly have improved by more than 1%, even if they have now to lecture to 100 or even 300 students, where previously they lectured to, say, 30. A little book by Abercrombie (1979) can have the same effect on tutorial work and I dare say that my chapter on 'Some problems in teaching and learning' (Elton, 1987) could also be read with profit. Not all of the help and advice contained in these references is directly concerned with autonomy learning, but much of it is, and all of it makes learning more effective, thus freeing more time and resources to foster autonomy learning.

Changes to traditional teaching: doing it differently

However, doing better is not enough, not only because of the radical changes in the circumstance under which teaching now takes place, but because traditional teaching was never in fact geared deliberately towards autonomy learning. So we have to do it differently. And here I must issue a very serious warning. The first result of doing differently is almost certainly to do worse, for the simple reason that any innovation, however well thought out and prepared, will need to be improved in the light of evaluation and feedback at the pilot stage. This developmental stage of any innovation ought to be but hardly ever is within the thinking of Funding Councils, whether they are concerned with funding or with quality assessment.

Let me illustrate the above in terms of three very different innovations that have now been with us for over 20 years:

- *Project work in science laboratories*. This was introduced into higher education in the 1960s as a result of efforts by the National Council for Technological Awards and spread rapidly. It is in fact the only innovation that I can think of as having spread rapidly and the reason for this is undoubtedly that academic staff saw it as something very close to what they liked best and knew most of, ie research. Unfortunately this has also meant that the huge differences between undergraduates and postgraduates – in maturity, ability and motivation – have not been given adequate attention, and this has been particularly serious in connection with the development of learner autonomy, for which project work in principle is well designed.

- *Self-instructional learning*. This started with programmed learning in the 1960s, moved to Keller Plan in the 1970s, and to the use of OU and other materials in traditional universities in the 1980s. In attempting to replace lecturing, it has had a particularly hard task, since lecturers quite understandably did not wish to be replaced. There is, however, a more subtle reason for this failure, which is that it is very difficult to move on from small-scale pilot developments to anything on a larger scale, since that would require changes at departmental and institutional level, which affect timetabling, space provision, the production of materials and the management of learning.
- *Computer-assisted learning*. This has been the panacea round the corner at least since the National Development Programme in Computer Assisted Learning in the 1970s and, with the Teaching Learning Technology Programme, is still in that position in the 1990s. For success it will require not only all the changes at departmental and institutional levels needed for self-instructional learning, but in addition similar changes at national level.

Although all three of the above developments were in principle capable of contributing to autonomy learning, they were driven by changes in method rather than objectives; all have suffered from a lack of appreciation of the need for substantial staff development if they were to succeed. A development that in many ways is in striking contrast to the previous three is the Enterprise in Higher Education Initiative (EHE) of the Employment Department (Macnair, 1990). This initiative aimed at a change in the objectives of higher education (ie added explicitly a new objective: the development of life and work skills) but was happy to accept any learning method that promised to further this new objective. It also put the need for staff development high on its agenda and followed the principles of well-established change theory (Elton and Cryer, 1994). The evident success of the initiative (Elton, 1995a) may indicate that this time we have got the process of educational innovation more nearly right than before.

Autonomy learning in mass higher education: some obstacles

In principle, autonomy learning (ie students being responsible for their own learning) ought to be more cost-effective than learning for which the students' teachers are responsible, since it implies the active involvement of students in both teaching and learning. Such learning is more effective – it is more likely to be deep than surface (Marton and Säljö, 1976) and more likely to match students' motivation (Elton, 1995b) – and it makes good use of the financially cheapest learning resource, namely students' time. However, some caveats are appropriate.

- The learning objectives appropriate for autonomy learning are not the same as those for more traditional teaching and learning. They put a greater emphasis on the development of learning skills ('learning to learn') and a correspondingly lesser emphasis on the acquisition of knowledge. These changes in objectives must be reflected in corresponding changes in student assessment, and this will not be easy. Not only are most academics at present heavily content-oriented, but very different forms of assessment would have to be introduced to match these skill objectives.

- Traditional teaching methods associated with autonomy learning are likely to prove too expensive in the future, but new methods being developed require changes not only in the methods themselves, but in the whole teaching and learning system at institutional and national level. This is beginning to be appreciated (MacFarlane, 1992; Elton, 1994).

- Nothing significant will happen without a major effort in staff development, eg such as is implied by the existence of the compendium on *Effective Teaching and Learning in Higher Education* (Cryer, 1992). Students also need help and training with study skills and practices for which previous experience may not have equipped them. Some of the more spectacular failures of self-instructional learning are due to students not having been adequately prepared for it.

- There are two major financial matters, without which the new developments cannot succeed. The first is for the Funding Councils to realise that all innovatory work needs pump-priming and to develop funding mechanisms for this. The EHE Initiative has set a good example. The second is that the direct financial support for students must actually be increased if they are to have the time to be in part their own teachers. The present continuing cut-back in student support is difficult to accommodate even in traditional teaching and learning situations; it becomes impossible for autonomy learning. Part of what is being saved on teachers' salaries must be used to increase student support; to attempt to save on both simultaneously is a sure prescription for loss of quality.

Autonomy learning in mass higher education: towards solutions?

I said earlier that to use technology effectively in a learning situation involves an interactive analysis of both the learning situation and the potential of the technology. Out of this comes the realisation that what is important in introducing technological change into learning, and before that into teaching, is to link such change to learning objectives rather than match it to teaching methods. This prescription will take us to an appropriate use of low and high technology or no technology at all in the light of our understanding of relevant pedagogy and of the need for staff development at all levels, from probationary lecturer to vice-chancellor. The latter is actually more important than the former, for the changes required at institutional and national levels demand efforts of leadership and management that are completely new to most of those who have to carry them out (Middlehurst and Elton, 1992). A daunting agenda but a hopeful one.

To all this must be added the overriding need to use all the resources at our disposal in the best manner. Now, as I have argued, the most under-used resource is student time and effort in supporting their own learning, and that is why I see autonomy learning as the most cost-effective way forward in higher education. It can take many forms – individual and team project work, self- and peer-assessment, negotiated curricula and many others. What all have in common is that they put a much greater stress on each student's life and work experience and thereby create strong student motivation, which is a prime contributor to cost-effectiveness. Incidentally, because of the greater individualisation of each student's learning programme, modern technology will be more valuable as a provider of learning resources than as a means of delivering courses.

Finally, there is the effect of autonomy learning on the resulting graduates who will have developed the skills and attitudes needed for lifelong learning. Since they will be the leaders in any learning society of the future, and since the development of a learning society is essential for national prosperity, and indeed survival, the increased prosperity will in due course make it possible to increase the contribution of society to higher education. However, before that can happen, there is an imperative need for a pump-priming operation in both educational and industrial investment on a massive scale – an operation which has been carried out in an exemplary manner by the Tigers of the Pacific Rim, but which Britain has not yet begun. It is time that government stopped blaming higher education for ills largely due to its own negligence.

References

Abercrombie, M L J (1979) *Aims and Techniques of Group Teaching*, 4th edn, Society for Research into Higher Education, Guildford.

Brown, G (1978) *Lecturing and Explaining*, Methuen, London.

Cryer, P (ed.) (1992) *Effective Teaching and Learning in Higher Education*, Universities Staff Development and Training Unit, Sheffield.

Elton, L (1987) *Teaching in Higher Education: Appraisal and Training*, Kogan Page, London.

Elton, L (1988) 'Conditions for learner autonomy at a distance', *Programmed Learning and Educational Technology*, **25**, 3, 216–24.

Elton, L (1994) *Management of Teaching and Learning: Towards Change in Universities*, Committee of Vice Chancellors and Principals and Society for Research into Higher Education, London.

Elton, L (1995a) 'Enterprise in higher education: issues of evaluation', *Higher Education Quarterly*, **49**, 2, 146–61.

Elton, L (1995b) 'Student motivation: A conceptual analysis', *Studies in Higher Education*, 20.

Elton, L and Cryer, P (1994) 'Quality and change in higher education', *Innovative Higher Education*, **18**, 3, 205–20.

Laurillard, D (1993) *Rethinking University Teaching: A Framework for the Effective Use of Educational Technology*, Routledge, London.

Laurillard, D (1994) 'Reinvent the steering wheel', *Times Higher Education Supplement: Synthesis*, 13 May, p.iii.

MacFarlane, A G J (1992) *Teaching and Learning in an Expanding Higher Education System*, Committee of Scottish University Principals, Edinburgh.

Macnair, G (1990) 'The British Enterprise in Higher Education Initiative', *Higher Education Management*, **2**, 1, 60–71.

Marton, F and Säljö, R (1976) 'On qualitative differences in learning', I & II, *British Journal of Educational Psychology*, **46**, 4–11 and 115–27.

Mayes, T (1994) 'Intensely personal relations', *Times Higher Education Supplement: Synthesis*, 13 May, p.viii.

Middlehurst, R and Elton, L (1992) 'Leadership and management in higher education', *Studies in Higher Education*, **17**, 3, 251–64.

Papert, S (1994) 'Grasping a dragon tail', *Times Higher Education Supplement: Synthesis*, 13 May, p.ii.

Reinhardt, A (1995) 'New ways to learn', *Byte*, March, 50–62.

Taylor, E and Kaye, T (1986) 'Andragogy by design? Control and self-direction in the design of an Open University course', *Programmed Learning and Educational Technology*, **23**, 62–9.

Lewis Elton is Professor of Higher Education, University College London and a Consultant in Higher Education to the Department for Education and Employment. He is a Fellow of the American Institute of Physics and of the Society for Research into Higher Education, and an Honorary Life Member of the Staff and Educational Development Association.

Address for correspondence: 3 Great Quarry, Guildford, Surrey GU1 3XN.

7. Inspiring Learning with Adult Distance Learners in Higher Education

Sally Lawton, *The Robert Gordon University, Aberdeen*

SUMMARY

This chapter describes how a supportive model of learning being developed by the author may help to inspire distance learning students during their educational experience. The model recognises the difficulties distance learners may face at the beginning, during and at the end of a course, and places great emphasis on the relationship that develops between the student and tutor during a course. This relationship is concerned with the mutual trust that is needed between the tutor and the student and which could provide the student with the confidence they need to develop and, in so doing, inspire their learning.

Introduction and background

This chapter explains the reasons why a supportive model of learning has been developed in a department of nursing located in a Scottish university and its links with the inspiration of learning. The model is described and suggestions made about ways to evaluate both the model and the notion of inspiration.

In this context the definition of the inspiration of learning through tutor support is the process of identifying factors that may promote or hinder the educational experience of a student; the provision of support and guidance during the educational experience to enhance the experience; and the evaluation of that experience at the end of the student's programme of studies.

Having worked with adult distance learners undertaking a top-up degree in nursing, it is evident that the part-time educational process is similar to being on a roller-coaster, with very positive experiences being followed by very negative ones. Students may react to these highs and lows by a loss of motivation and self-confidence. As Elwood (1987) noted, motivation cannot be maintained at a high level throughout a course. However, the tutor can provide the support to show how a student is progressing if there is personal contact and continuity.

In addition, students undertake a distance learning programme because they are unable for various reasons, such as geographical location, domestic and work commitments to enter into full-time education. The tutor may have to provide the inspiration for learning through support for students who are finding it difficult to combine their studies with work and family commitments as well as the promotion of the self-direction that a distance learning course requires.

The Collins dictionary definition of the word 'inspire' is 'to infuse thought or feeling into'. Applied to the educational sector, this definition could be interpreted as the role the tutor may play in the infusion of such inspiration of learning and empowerment for the student to be able to develop self-directed learning skills by the end of a course. This inspiration may occur at two levels: course level and individual level.

At the course level, the inspiration of learning may occur through the delivery of relevant course material that is applicable in practice. The modular structure of the course means that students attend the university for an introductory week per module, which enables inspiration to occur through the networking with other students. In addition, students meet their personal tutor on an individual basis. This helps to reduce the isolation that distance learning can instil, as noted by Myers *et al.* (1992). Additionally, Cookson (1989) reported that there is a reduction in the number of drop-outs from distance learning courses with the inclusion of face-to-face strategies.

At the individual level, a student-centred approach to support enables the student and tutor to plan an individual learning programme that recognises the individuality of each student and their circumstances throughout the length of a student's studies. Hayes (1990) confirmed this need to look at students on an individual basis. In the existing literature on counselling, similarities were also noted between the developmental model of counselling (Hawkins and Shohet, 1989) and the notion of a developing relationship.

Difficulties facing adult distance learners

There are certain difficulties that adults face which might cause them to lack the necessary inspiration to learn. Chiefly, the lack of self-confidence that an adult may feel on re-entering higher education may be based on one or more of the following:

- time lapse since previous study;
- age;
- perceived ability;
- concern about academic writing;
- previous educational experiences and expectations;
- the juggling of home, work and studying;
- isolation.

These factors are very much in keeping with previous studies investigating the learning needs of adults in higher educational settings (Rees and Reilly, 1990; Biggs, 1978; McGivney, 1993; Smithers and Griffin, 1986; Thyer and Bazeley, 1993). Richardson (1994) argues that the research on adult learners focuses on their needs rather than on their strengths. Perhaps the needs reported above are based on the attitudes of students themselves, rather than confirmed in research. This suggests that the confidence building that may occur in the tutor–student relationship can help inspiration to occur.

Due to the nature of distance learning and the lack of ongoing contact, some students may have concerns about their studying abilities as they begin and progress through a course. This lack of confidence might hinder the inspiration for learning throughout the course, not merely at the beginning. A review of the literature relating to drop-outs in distance learning courses undertaken by Bernard and Amundsen (1989) reported that the major variable that predicted student drop-out was the amount of contact with faculty members.

Developmental stage of the framework

A model of supportive learning would enable a structure that could be used to plan, implement and evaluate a tutorial programme for each student. Such a model could also provide inspiration by promoting the networking of students in the core weeks; to enable the student to progress through the course while balancing their other commitments. It would also offer a way of evaluating the tutorial provision offered by the academic staff, to ensure a consistent and high quality service by all members of a course team.

The notion of 'support' within higher education, and particularly within distance learning, has been interpreted in various ways by different writers. For example, the Open University defined student support as 'advice, help and support given to students to enable them to make satisfactory progress in the system' (Bailey and Moore, 1989). The Unit for the Development of Adult Continuing Education (UDACE) stated that there are seven components which should be addressed in the support of students. These are: 'informing, advising, counselling, assessing, enabling, advocating and feeding back' (Vowles, 1990). Although inspiration is not specifically mentioned, a supportive system that encompassed these elements would enable inspiration of learning to occur.

Distance learning models found in the literature focus on the prevention of drop-out of students (Billings, 1988) but the focus of this model of supportive learning would be aimed at increasing the educational experience of a student throughout their course, rather than only focusing on the potential drop-out figures. The quality of the experience is as important in the inspiration of learning as are the completion rates. However, it is agreed in the existing models that students' needs should be identified before or at the beginning of the course.

This has implications for the tutoring staff. With the devising of a student-centred model of learning support, the tutor needs support from colleagues. Although this is a particularly important concern, it is not fully addressed in this chapter. In the absence of a readily available model, a specific theoretical framework was developed followed by the devising of a model of learning support.

Philosophy of the framework

The main tenet of this framework would encompass the following philosophy:
A framework for the support of adult students should be used in a proactive way to enable students to make the most of their educational experience and thus allow for the inspiration of learning to occur. It should be flexible to meet the needs of a student group who have very varied educational and professional experiences.

The development of the theoretical framework

From reasoning gathered in the literature and ongoing personal research, a conceptual scheme emerged as described by Polit and Hungler (1991) as an inductive approach to enquiry. This led to a distinction being made between the factors potentially making distance education effective and those factors making it ineffective. This is shown in Figure 1 as the conceptual scheme.

Distance education	
Effective factors	*Ineffective factors*
	Apprehension
Confidence	Concern about academic level
Relevance of course	Time lapse since previous study
Flexiblity of programme	Sustained motivation
Ongoing support	Organisational factors
Optimism	Lack of support
	Age and ability

Figure 1 *Conceptual scheme*

The 'effective' factors are those which would enhance the conditions needed for the inspiration of learning to occur and are related to the positive experiences outlined earlier. In contrast, the negative experiences are shown as 'ineffective' factors. To enable a student to have a valuable learning experience, a model developed from the conceptual scheme would have to accentuate the 'effective' factors and support any of the 'ineffective' factors that emerged during the course of the student's programme of study.

Three phases of the model have been identified, recognising this focus on the whole programme of study.

Phase one – meeting
This initial phase focuses on the beginning relationship between the student and the tutor. It is a time to create links, and assess needs based on the 'effective/ineffective' concepts; to highlight the expectations of the student and establish a trusting relationship. The student is offered an individual tutorial during each core week which allows these themes to be raised. During the self-study phase of the course, contact is maintained between the student and tutor by telephone tutorials. The tutor may expect the student to feel fairly uncertain and to be quite dependent at this stage. Possible reasons for this dependence may relate to the ineffective factors highlighted above. The tutor may have to describe how help (however that is identified) can be offered. Peplau (1952) suggests that the way in which people feel about asking for help is dependent on how they see themselves and how they think they should be in that situation. For the student who has been used to a more formal educational setting, they may have an initial impression of their tutor as being rather distant and remote. The participation and involvement of both the student and the tutor in

goal-setting is one approach to the formation of this trusting relationship as well as the need for positive feedback. It would appear that the links with the inspiration of learning at this stage are in the development of the student's self-confidence.

However, a note of caution has to be made here. A balance must be kept between offering help and creating a dependency on the tutor or a dependency on the student. This is where the support from fellow tutors would appear to have such value. As Hawkins and Shohet (1989) suggest, it is very difficult to remain a 'vehicle' in the counselling relationship and not become totally immersed in the relationship.

Phase two – guiding
As the student progresses through the course, there are opportunities for individual student–tutor contact between modules. This is of particular relevance for the distance learning student who may feel very isolated while they work on their self-study material and begin to lose inspiration for learning. As tutors mark and return work, an opportunity to discuss ongoing issues should be maintained to continue the process of positive feedback. The tutor's role is that of guide at this stage, encouraging and 'being there' as an ear on the end of the telephone. This again shows the importance of the building of a trusting relationship so the student is able to approach the tutor without feeling that they are 'bothering the tutor'. It would be anticipated that the relationship in this part of the model would fluctuate as the student copes with the positive and negative experiences of undertaking a distance learning course. At the end of this phase of the model, the relationship, hopefully, will have strengthened, with the student moving some way to independence.

Phase three – moving on
At the end of the course, there has to be an ending of the student–tutor relationship, which might be a difficult phase for both. It suggests that the relationship has allowed learning to occur for both student and tutor, but not at the expense of one another. It may be that the relationship does not progress through these three phases, but remains at the 'meeting' or 'guiding' phase. This might be due to the fact that the ineffective factors outweigh the effective factors and the student leaves the course. Alternatively, the student may have failed the course, which will be difficult to deal with and would have an effect on the relationship. As with the other phases, it would seem imperative that the tutor has support to enable feelings to be shared with other members of the team.

Testing the model in practice

It is realised that one of the problems in the development of a model is the possibility of over-simplification of its abstract components as well as focusing on its insignificant parts (Keeves, 1988). This reinforces the notion that it is crucial to test the model in practice and be able to adapt it in the light of regular evaluation.

The implementation of the model began in the autumn term of 1994. Currently, a self-assessment form is completed by the student prior to their commencement of the distance learning course. This form asks the student to rate on a Likert-scale the various 'effective' and 'ineffective' factors identified above. This gives a basis for potential discussion points at the initial tutorial meeting regarding their perceptions of the course. The structure of the tutorial system is described to each student in detail. Following this initial meeting, the tutor records the results and the jointly devised individual plan of support for that student which is implemented and evaluated as they progress through the course. It is proposed that a similar form be completed by the student towards the end of the course, to see if they feel that they have made progress.

Evaluation of the model and the inspiration of learning

If, as has been suggested in this chapter, inspiration for learning can be enhanced by the support a tutor may provide, how would it be evaluated? Possibilities include:

- by observing the drop-out rate from a course;
- by measuring the student's success through the course;
- by measuring the student's satisfaction with the course.

The first two categories are measuring the quantifiable elements of the course and the third one is measuring the qualitative aspects of a course.

However, with reference to inspiration, the drop-out rate might not pick up those students who feel truly inspired to learn, but who are facing difficulties beyond their control and have to leave a course. The student success rate is another method of looking at student progress through a course. However, the marks that a student receives for course work may not give clues as to their level of inspiration.

The third suggestion involves asking students how satisfied they have been with their educational experience and seems to offer one way of measuring their level of inspiration. This could be through personal contact, discussion and feedback as well as self-assessment as described in the supportive model of learning outlined above.

References

Bailey, D and Moore, J (1989) 'Closing the distance: counselling at OU residential schools', *British Journal of Guidance and Counselling*, **17**, 3, 317–30.

Bernard, R and Amundsen, C (1989) 'Antecedents to drop-out in distance education: does one model fit all?', *Journal of Distance Education*, **4**, 25–46.

Biggs, J (1978) 'Individual and group differences in study processes', *British Journal of Educational Psychology*, **55**, 185–212.

Billings, D (1988) 'A conceptual model of correspondence course completion', *American Journal of Distance Education*, **2**, 2, 23–35.

Cookson, P (1989) 'Research on learners and learning in distance education: A review', *American Journal of Distance Education*, **3**, 2, 22–35.

Elwood, C (1987) 'Motivating learners', in V Hodgson, S Mann and R Snell (eds), *Beyond Distance Teaching – Towards Open Learning*, SRHE/OU Press, Buckingham.

Hayes, E (1990) 'Adult education: context and challenge for distance educators', *American Journal of Distance Education*, **4**, 1, 25–39.

Hawkins, P and Shohet, R (1989) *Supervision in the Helping Professions*, OU Press, Buckingham.

Kember, D (1989) 'An illustration, with case studies, of a linear process model of drop-out from distance education', *Distance Education,* **10**, 2, 196–212.

Keeves, J (1988) 'Models and model-building', in J Keeves (ed.), *Educational Research, Methodology and Measurement: An International Handbook,* Pergamon Press, Oxford.

McGivney, V (1993) 'Participation and non-participation, a review of the literature', in R Edwards, S Sieminski and D Zeldin (eds), *Adult Learning, Education and Training,* Routledge, London.

Myers, C, Fletcher, M and Gill, P (1992) 'Learner-centred distance education: strategies and evaluation', in B Scriven, B Lundin and Y Ryan (eds), *Conference Proceedings of 16th World Conference of International Council of Distance Education,* Thailand.

Peplau, H (1952) *Interpersonal Relations in Nursing,* Macmillan, Basingstoke.

Polit, D and Hungler, B (1991) *Nursing Research: Principles and Methods,* 4th edn, Lippincott, Philadelphia.

Rees, K and Reilly, J (1990) 'Supporting and developing adult learning', *Open Learning,* **2**, 3, 76–7.

Richardson, J (1994) 'Mature students in higher education: A literature survey on approaches to studying', *Studies in Higher Education,* **19**, 3, 309–26.

Smithers, A and Griffin, A (1986) *The Progress of Mature Students,* Joint Matriculation Board, Manchester.

Thyer, S and Bazeley, P (1993) 'Stressors to student nurses beginning tertiary education: An Australian study', *Nurse Education Today,* **13**, 5, 336–43.

Vowles, B (1990) *Educational Guidance,* Conference Proceedings of Student Learning in the Open University: Process and Practice, Open University Press, Buckingham.

Address for correspondence: **Sally Lawton**, Lecturer in Nursing, The Robert Gordon University, Kepplestone Annexe, Queens Road, Aberdeen AB9 2PG.

8. Using Peer Support: Implications for Student and Lecturer

Stuart Johnston, *School of Civil and Structural Engineering, University of Plymouth*

SUMMARY

Major shifts in attitudes held, and revisions of techniques adopted, may be required to accommodate the rapid changes occurring within higher education in the UK. Peer support for learning provides one avenue of response to the pressures for change.

This chapter outlines and reports on applications of peer support including trial 'proctoring' and 'supplemental instruction'. The implications for course delivery and hence for students and lecturers are examined.

Introduction

Higher education courses are subject to two major pressures for change. For several years student intake numbers have grown rapidly with only limited and seemingly always retrospective increases in resources; indeed, the resourcing per student continues steadily to decrease. Additionally graduates, their employers, and often accrediting professional institutions, are all pressing for courses to place greater emphasis on breadth of awareness, adaptability, creativity and communication skills. When peer support for learning is coordinated with other means of increasing student-led activity, major changes in learning methods can be stimulated. Students develop greater responsibility for their individual and peer-group studies, become better motivated and contribute more to the quality of their courses. Hence the quality of education experienced by subsequent intake students can be enhanced.

This chapter outlines a number of applications of peer support. Emphasis is placed on the need for investment in continuing professional development (CPD) to initiate a smooth transition from traditional approaches to course delivery and the need to determine to what extent students can be used legitimately as a resource in higher education.

Applications

Many agree that higher education students have much to gain from the experience and knowledge of their peers and of other students. Unstructured peer-support occurs routinely whenever students meet to discuss impressions of their course or to compare notes. Many lecturers have built on the impression that students can learn from their peers by providing opportunities for student–student transfer of experience in course contact time.

Learning should be exciting; courses should be capable of stimulating the motivation to learn through topic interest. In reality it appears often to be assumed that the motivation to study comes largely from the need to complete a work schedule and relates to the mark obtainable, ie that learning is assessment led.

Indeed, adoption of a particular assessment mode can have the effect of encouraging particular learning strategies. Use of group-based project work undertaken to a realistic industrial-style brief permits individual students to investigate the merits of peer support. Understanding of theoretical concepts and communication skills both may be enhanced if an acceptable balance between stimulation and resource provision is achieved. The potential advantages are increased if students are briefed to engage in group–group and individual–individual peer- and self-appraisal. The adoption of an open-book style end-of-course examination can encourage earlier group interaction and peer support, especially if only course notes and coursework submissions are permitted into the examination room.

Increased student numbers and decreasing lecturer–student contact have put excessive pressure on laboratory and worked example periods. In the HND course in geotechnics, peer support has been utilised to lessen the adverse effects of these pressures. Laboratory periods are considered an integral part of the first-year course. Five two-hour periods were programmed within the module's timetabled contact time. However, only one member of each group of four students was required to attend any laboratory period. The student briefed other group members on the experimental work undertaken. Unsupervised, student-led, worked example sessions ran parallel to the laboratory periods. Those attending briefed their group members on their worked solutions and the problems encountered. Time was set aside in the formal contact time for the student–student transfer of experience.

In whatever form students' coursework is submitted, it has the potential to provide others with a resource. If the work of peers, undertaken to the same brief, can first be viewed and critically appraised, self-appraisal becomes more realistic. Further, ideas and questions may be generated which can lead to greater motivation to learn. As part of their assessment of a candidate for professional status, the Institution of Civil Engineers allocated each an essay title from a pre-published list. Final-year degree students wrote essays on the same topics as part of their coursework in Construction Management. The essays were placed in a resource 'library' to be consulted by other students, and by graduates prior to their professional interview.

A programme of student-led proctoring was initiated within my department in 1990. This took the form of providing intake students with an opportunity to meet volunteer second- and third-year students during their induction period. Follow-up sessions were held in the backroom of a local hostelry! Perhaps unsurprisingly these proved popular, typically drawing 40–50 students. Feedback indicated that students appreciated and used the opportunity to make and reinforce cross-year and cross-course contact; both academic and social survival skills were discussed.

More recently a pilot programme of supplemental instruction (SI) activity has been initiated in the Faculty of Technology. Second-year students acting as paid SI leaders guide and reinforce the learning of intake students in semi-formal peer assisted study skills (PASS) sessions. Feedback from both the SI leaders and the intake students indicates that both perceive the pilot has benefited them.

Implications for course delivery

Maximum benefit is obtained if peer support is coordinated with other techniques to encourage and assist the development of student-led activity. The planned use of peer support necessitates basic changes from traditional course delivery. For it to be effective:

- both lecturers and students must be aware of, and sensitive to, the learning ethos within which peer support is to be encouraged;
- students must be prepared to investigate, or be persuaded of, potential benefits accruing from peer support;
- students should be respected and nurtured as the providers as well as the users of a resource. Their collective experience should be viewed legitimately as a potential resource of considerable value. However, its use must be carefully and sensitively managed. There are dangers that lecturer overload could become student overload or that students could be perceived as 'used' rather than 'users'.

Implications for the student

Planned use of peer support has the following implications for students.

- Student–student contact should supplement formal lecturer contact sufficiently to identify, discuss and explain minor difficulties and to identify and report major problem areas.
- Students themselves should discover the extent of the resource available within their peer group. Individuals may reveal more, both of need and of knowledge, to their peers than to lecturers.
- Students should develop their skills in identification and effective use of other relevant resources. Learning resources become facilities to be shared and debated with peers (compared to individually won). Greater emphasis on group-based activity is likely.
- Students should accept greater responsibility for their own and their peers' studies and for the perceived quality of their course. They should be prepared to offer and accept constructive criticism of their course, their peers and themselves.
- Greater emphasis may be placed on student-led activity within and outside the academic course. Programmed contact may accentuate seminars/workshops with active student participation (compared to lectures). Proctoring may develop greater contact outside the course programme.
- Students' study techniques should seek to develop topic-specific learning, contextual awareness and interpersonal skills.
- Students may become freer to manage their work programme to reflect their own rate of development. They may lose the comfort of being able to rely on a carefully constructed, rigorously structured programme of learning.

- A more open course structure may make it less likely that students will have to clear rigorously defined interim hurdles. Assessment styles are likely to become more open-ended. Problems may be set which have no single solution.
- Students may be more likely to research information relevant to their course but outside the topic areas formally lectured and assessed; their knowledge may then exceed that of their lecturers. There is a danger that formally assessed topics are perceived as being forsaken by the lecturer and left to be self-taught by the student(s) – without adequate guidance or resourcing.

Implications for lecturers

Planned use of peer support has the following implications for lecturers.

- Lecturers should be prepared to accept that student–student transfer of experience can be useful as learning support and is not 'cheating' (ie peer support does not equal cribbing nor does student cooperation equal collusion).
- Lecturers should be prepared to accept that students have an interest in maintaining the quality of their courses, and that lecturers will have less control of the way that information is acquired. They must be prepared to debate and respond to constructive criticism on style of delivery, course content, etc.
- Students should be encouraged to produce constructive criticism of their courses, their peers, themselves and their lecturers. Students should become more active partners in their own education.
- Considerable strain may be taken off lecturers if students self-diagnose, identify and solve routine problems in consultation with peers. It is likely that fewer, more penetrating, queries will result from student–student discussion.
- Considerable strain may be placed on lecturers to provide carefully planned but loosely structured and adequately resourced topic modules that will encourage student-led activity but minimise the risk of misinformation being circulated.
- Lecturers should become facilitators too; programmed contact need not be utilised to transfer knowledge in the conventional way. More emphasis may be placed on facilitating studies and informal counselling as students research and explore.
- Emphasis should be placed on determining what a student knows and understands (compared to does not know and understand). There should be less tendency to penalise students for failing to conform to a rigorously defined learning programme.

The need for continuing professional development

Many lecturers in higher education are not trained teachers but were appointed on the basis of research performance or industrial experience. Publications resulting from focused research into narrowly defined academic areas, or the potential to develop industrial contacts, or consultancy, may have counted more at the time of appointment than the perceived ability to educate others in a climate of change. Traditionally in HE the onus has been largely on students to accept existing course formats and to adjust to the modes of delivery chosen by lecturers. Planned use of peer-support is perceived as implying a different lecturer–student relationship and different approaches to course delivery and assessment. For its use to be effective many of the implications detailed above may become requirements. Lecturers have to possess skills and attitudes that many may not have found necessary in the context of more formal lecturer–student contact.

Courses are already placing greater emphasis on student-led activity, group-based work and student ownership. Typically course objectives now include developing responsibility, adaptability, free thinking, interpersonal skills and creativity in students. Adoption of peer-support as an integral part of a programme of learning underlines the need for lecturers to demonstrate these same characteristics. In a period of rapid change in HE the knowledge base for decision making and hence for course development and delivery has changed dramatically and will continue to do so. Already under pressure, courses are being revised to a modular format and the structure of the academic year is being changed to be based on semesters. The scale of change both demands and gives the opportunity for basic rethinking.

When faced with similarly dramatic changes, schools were obliged quickly to initiate programmes of staff development – presented as 'inservice training' days. All teachers and some ancillary staff were required to attend. So far the HE sector has failed to match the scale of this response.

Conclusions

- Change from traditional approaches to accommodate planned peer support is not without risk. It requires basic, carefully considered adjustments in the attitudes of students and lecturers. If these are not sensitively managed inconsistencies may develop which are incompatible with coherent learning strategies.
- Maximum advantage is gained from peer support when it is coordinated with other means of encouraging student-led activity and student ownership of their course.
- A student induction programme is of great importance in explaining the character of the course, detailing what is to be expected of students, and providing the opportunity for student–student pre-briefing (initial peer support).
- There is an urgent need for coordinating and extending the educational development initiatives being taken in HE. All lecturers in HE must be provided with recurring opportunities and *time* to identify, acquire and develop skills relevant to the introduction of peer support and other means of acceptably and sensitively utilising students as a resource, and identify and consider the constraints and opportunities presented by ongoing changes.

References

Conlon, J A and Halstead, A (1991) 'The use of project work in the assessment of engineering students', in R A Smith (ed.), *Innovative Teaching in Engineering*, Ellis Horwood, Chichester.

Fraser, D M (1992) 'Teaching engineering more effectively with cooperative study

groups', in T Duggan (ed.) Proceedings of the Third World Conference on
Engineering Education, Computational Mechanics Publications, Southampton.

Johnston, S G D and Williams, C (1992) 'Encouraging ingenuity in civil engineering
students', in T Duggan (ed.), *Proceedings of the Third World Conference on
Engineering Education*, Computational Mechanics Publications, Southampton.

Matthew, R G S and Hughes, D C (1991) 'Problem based learning – a case study in civil
engineering', in R A Smith (ed.), *Innovative Teaching in Engineering*, Ellis Horwood,
Chichester.

Stephenson, J and Weil, S (eds) (1992) *Quality in Learning. A Capability Approach in
Higher Education*, Kogan Page, London.

Appendix

Peer support objectives: student observation

A Student Perspective: N Pike, Year 2 BEng Civil Engineering

The problem with peer support and the skills that it produces is purely that a student,
who has never worked within the industry, does not recognise the need for such
skills. For most students, they have always been 'told what to do' in their education
and have never faced the situation where they themselves have to instruct others.
Most students produce work and leave the assessment up to the lecturer. This *cannot*
be done in the industry. Many students, when asked to assess their own work cannot
do so accurately without practice. If they cannot assess their work now, how can
they be expected to in the industry? They *must* realise the standards required and
must meet those standards. *Only* by self- and peer-assessment can this be achieved.

It must be spelt out that peer-assessment must be undertaken properly. Students
find it difficult to say that another's work is lacking and therefore they should lose
marks. I feel that peer-assessment should be only on a non-mark basis or slight mark
basis. But then some of the initial relevance has been lost.

Students worry about 'true assessment' losing them marks.

Peer group studies give good practice in communication and discussion. However, an individual's briefing to others may break down and hence they may suffer
academically. Alternatively one person's lack of interest could cause others to suffer
too, which is another student worry when they don't get the information straight
from the lecturer.

Also not *all* staff show their support for joint work. The students working
together in cooperation leads to worries that collusion may be suspected. Where is
the line? And how do the students know which is which?

Proctoring has worked well in more of a general 'I'm worried about how hard
the exams will be', rather than a 'How do I do this?' manner. However, first-year
surveying was based practically on proctoring from those with experience. This
worked very well but again could break down if the proctor is incorrect – therefore
danger.

The group-based projects are ideal to create skills in decision-making, delegation, communication and peer-assessment. One of the hardest things to do when
working is to tell others, often older than oneself, to do better, more or different
work. This must be undertaken in a constructive yet honest manner.

Groupwork develops skills in constructive assessment which is vital in the industry. It leads to the skill of being able to discuss points of view and accept decisions rationally, and not leading to aggressive arguments and personal insults! Such skills can only be obtained with practice and at Palace Court such practice is obtained via peer-assessment and groupwork.

CEng graduates from Plymouth are highly respected not only for their abilities in CEng but also for their common sense, communication and general approach to work. This must surely reflect on the group activities and peer work assessments obtained within the course.

The problem which I can see clearly, being a student who has already worked in the industry, is that of conveying the *relevance* of skills.

How do you tell a student that he or she must be able to tell another student how good their work is?

I know the importance of communication, self- and peer-assessment and delegation in the industry, but most of my colleagues don't. I feel that the importance of peer-assessment and the related skills should therefore be conveyed via ex-graduates and not staff. Ex-grads have the 'that will be me in a few years' and 'he knows what it's like for a student' affect on current students and therefore this is where I feel the peer-assessment message can be conveyed best.

Stuart Johnston, a qualified structural engineer, joined the then Polytechnic of Plymouth in 1974 as a lecturer on a range of topics on HND, BSc, BEng and BEng (Hons) courses. Now retired he lectures part time and has a broad interest in students' perception of study/student welfare. Since 1993 he has supervised a pilot programme of Supplemental Instruction (SI) at the University of Plymouth.

Address for correspondence: Senior Lecturer, School of Civil and Structural Engineering, University of Plymouth, Palace Court, Palace Street, Plymouth PL4 8AA.

9. Listening to Our Students Talking About Their Learning

Roger Catchpole, Hazel Fullerton and **Jonathan Smart,** *University of Plymouth*

This chapter reports on a workshop, the aims of which were for the participants to:

- consider the evidence that the students have a very wide range of learning experiences and use a wide range of methods and approaches;
- consider the implications of the points raised by the students as we move towards more flexible teaching and learning provision.

We hoped that the workshop would also:

- demonstrate the effectiveness of video as a qualitative research tool;
- promote the idea that we do need to get close to the real learning experiences of our students if we are to target the support to their learning development effectively;
- demonstrate that students could be used as valuable role models for their peers.

The 20 participants at this workshop were shown two 15-minute video extracts. In each extract a different group of four second/third year students from four different faculties at the University of Plymouth talked, with the assistance of a facilitator, about their university learning experiences.

The 16 students had been identified as being keen to talk about their learning. Having agreed to be involved, they were not primed in any way, apart from being briefed about the organisation of the recording session. They were told that the facilitator would introduce a series of key topics for the group to discuss (eg processing information, feedback, using IT). Each of the four recording sessions took about an hour and a half, the resulting material being edited to form a series of 1½–2 minute clips, each focusing on one key topic.

The workshop participants were divided into two groups, one viewing the Arts and Education and Social Sciences students' discussions, the other viewing the Business School and Technology video extracts. In small groups they then exchanged their observations, brought their ideas together and gave feedback to a plenary session.

The following extracts from the transcript of the video will give readers an idea of the contributions the students made to the discussions.

Facilitator: There are a lot of people that think that learning, or real breakthroughs in learning, occur not in a structured way but as sudden flashes of inspiration – it suddenly clicks. Have any of you had that sort of experience? What triggered it?

Student 4: I think it's during the lectures for me. If I have a lecturer that's very enthusiastic about their subject then I actually catch on quite early because I like the way the lecturer is actually teaching it. That encourages me to go and look up more things.

Student 3: Well, I think the discussion groups. The group that I have worked with all through my degree. We tend to meet up regularly. I actually found statistics relatively easy, so for my group anyone came to me with any problems.

Student 1 (part-timer): If I can fit it all in then I've won. But I really enjoy the degree. I have focused down in the third year. I was lucky enough to get the options I wanted and I can relate them to everyday life.

Student 3: I actually quite enjoy the fact that I can sit down with the people who have got knowledge in the same area as me and have a discussion over coffee. It's not a case of 'I know more about something than you'. It's a case of we have all got some knowledge. You feel you've actually learnt something.

Each workshop participant was given a sheet on which they could record their observations and each small group recorded the results of sharing them. The many points that were made included:

- relevant, formative feedback to students should be a priority;
- some students will suffer when they are not part of a continuing, cohesive group;
- the opportunity to give mutual support is important for personal development;
- IT is seen by some of these students as a means to an end – they manipulate it effectively to their own advantage;
- the students seem to be worrying about delivering what is expressly wanted by tutors, rather than 'taking risks' or following hunches;
- the 'do it your own way' message came across strongly – the students recognise that they have different learning styles;
- the students are very coherent and articulate in the way they talk about their learning.

Hopefully each participant left the workshop with some positive personal outcomes. Four bought a copy of the video and several showed interest in making similar videos in their institutions. Certainly this video is going to be valuable for the University of Plymouth and, since the conference, copies have been distributed widely.

Hopefully, senior management will 'listen to their students talking about their learning' and take heed of the real student learning experience as they direct future developments. Also, departments now have another valuable resource for staff development events. Learning Skills support staff will have valuable models and quotes to use to support students in their learning skill development. Already at the University of Plymouth we are making another video which will follow the experience of a group of Access students from the end of their course, through the initial induction period and into the first months of their higher education learning experience.

Address for correspondence: **Roger Catchpole**, Development Officer, **Hazel Fullerton**, Manager, and **Jonathan Smart**, Development Officer, Educational Development Services, University of Plymouth PL4 8AA.

10. A Computer-Based Introduction to Learning Skills

Paul Bailey, *University of Plymouth*

SUMMARY

The learning skills package is a screen-delivered interactive computer-based learning application, running under Microsoft Windows on a PC. The learning skills package is designed to be used as a flexible learning aid, in conjunction with existing learning skills material.

Introduction

The content of the learning skills package is designed to help the users explore and evaluate their own approaches to learning and to encourage them to become more effective and efficient learners. The emphasis of the package is on the user finding their own strategy, as well as giving positive ideas and approaches to develop skills. The user is required to participate actively when using the package, by answering questions, completing activities or selecting options based on their own experience.

Modules included in the package are:

- Studying in higher education
- Managing your time
- Learning from lectures
- Improving reading effectiveness
- Planning and writing essays
- Preparing for assessment.

(See Figure 1.) Further modules are being written to look at 'Researching materials for an assignment' and 'Writing skills'.

Customisation

To be wholly effective the package needs to be flexible in its design as well as its use. The following features are being included which may be customised as required.

- Information on further support available in the university (see Figure 2), this will include details of forthcoming skills workshops.
- Skills development resources available.
- Text file versions of skills leaflets, etc which can be copied to a disk (to be printed later) or viewed online and annotated by the user.
- Further development exercises which can be copied and printed by the user.

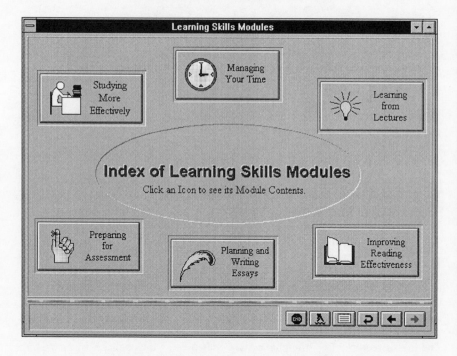

Figure 1 *Index of learning skills modules*

The package also needs to be made widely available and accessible to everyone. There is no reason why the package can not be made available to students to run on their own PCs as well as being networked throughout the university.

Integration and application

The package will be fully integrated into the university in September 1995 and we have identified a range of ways the package will be used.

- Integration into existing learning skills modules within departments.
- As an open learning resource for students entering higher education.
- As the basis of a learning skills module for departments introducing skills development for the first time.
- To support tutorial programmes looking at skills development.
- As an open access resource for all students at the university.

Evaluation so far has given us valuable feedback and we are pleased at the positive response from both staff and students at the university. This has helped shape the package and will continue to do so in the future.

The workshop gave an opportunity to see the package and evaluate its potential as a learning resource for students in higher education. Although it was recognised that the package is not yet complete, some positive feedback was received from the evaluation:

'The interaction is good, holds attention.' (see Figure 3)

'Easy to use. A friendly package.'

'I'd like to see this available to my students.'

'It's an excellent package with content that *all* students and lecturers should be aware of.' (see Figure 4)

The future success of this package will be dependent on its availability to students, method of delivery and being able to adapt the material in response to staff and student feedback.

Address for correspondence: **Paul Bailey**, Educational Development Services, University of Plymouth, Drake Circus, Plymouth, Devon, PL4 8AA. e-mail: p1bailey@plymouth.ac.uk

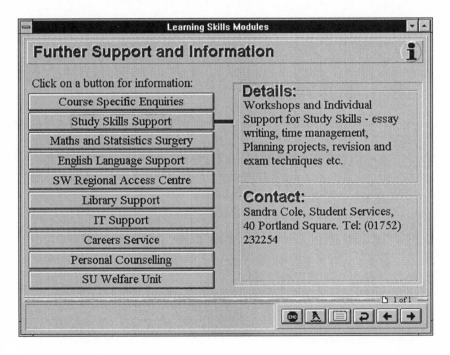

Figure 2 *Further support – customisable information*

Figure 3 *Interactive study base screen*

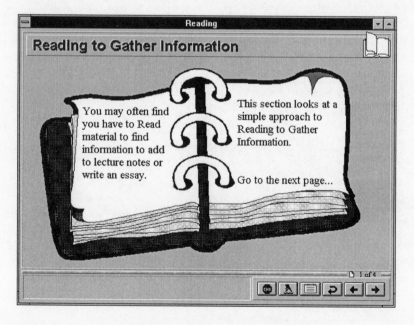

Figure 4 *Reading to gather information*

11. Adopting a Student-Centred Approach to the Management of Learning: Songs of Praise and Lessons

Jenny A Hall and **Mark N K Saunders**, *Cheltenham & Gloucester College of Higher Education*

SUMMARY

This chapter explores the issues associated with developing and teaching information technology to first year undergraduates using a student-centred approach. This approach is contrasted with the traditional methods used previously. Using findings from their action research process, the authors discuss both the advantages of this approach to teaching and learning, and the lessons they and their students have learnt.

Introduction

Pressure to increase staff–student ratios has hastened the need for lecturers to move away from a traditional approach and adopt more flexible strategies to manage student learning. This has been particularly so for practical-based subjects such as information technology (IT) which have traditionally had greater lecturer–student contact. Such subjects necessitate incremental learning to enable students to develop their understanding and build on their skills. At the same time the need for students to feel secure remains (Raadheim *et al.*, 1991). A flexible student-centred approach where much of the responsibility of managing learning is given to the student provides one possible solution.

Research reported in this chapter shows that a combination of innovative teaching and assessment approaches can enable a student-centred approach to succeed. Differences between the use of these approaches to teach IT to undergraduate Business Studies students are highlighted. Detailed student evaluations, together with other data such as attendance levels and student results, are used to draw out the praiseworthy aspects and associated lessons of adopting a student-centred approach.

The research on which this chapter is based follows the action research process widely used in educational research (Robson, 1993). This involves a cycle of planning, acting, observing and reflecting (Lewin, 1946, cited in Robson, 1993). More specifically, the process is concerned with planned intervention to improve a situation and involves practitioners in the research. The results of this intervention are subsequently monitored, the situation re-evaluated and the cycle continues.

The traditional approach

For the past five years we have taught a first year undergraduate 12-week compulsory Business Information Technology module. In the first year it was planned as a traditional lecture followed by practical class programme (Table 1). The objectives were:

- to enable students to gain a sound knowledge base in the subject;
- to allow the students to develop the understanding and skills to enable them to use IT in a wide range of practical day-to-day situations in college and the workplace.

Delivery was through a weekly one-hour lecture based on a topical case study and a two-hour 'practical' tutorial using suites of 20 microcomputers, one computer per student. Practical work was taught using a word-processing workbook we developed and weekly handouts for a spreadsheet and a database package. The workbook was designed to be used by the students on their own and included a series of linked graded exercises. Demonstrations and explanations were carried out for each topic. Students were also expected to undertake three hours of private study a week. The degree to which the students met the module objectives was assessed by a case study-derived assignment incorporating much of the practical work, and an examination (Table 2).

Table 1 *The traditional and student-centred approaches*

Traditional	Student-centred
Lecture: 1 hour a week	*Seminar*: 1 hour a week
Delivery: lecture	Delivery: variety including student presentations; quiz; discussion groups
Support materials: reading list	Support materials: study notes; reading list
Practical session: 2 hours a week	*Practical session*: 2 hours a week
Support materials: weekly handouts	Support materials: self-paced workbooks

Once the module was under way we quickly became dissatisfied. There was no 'buzz'. Student attendance at classes became sporadic and the lectures did not appear to be well received. A questionnaire was devised to explore student perceptions of the module.

Table 2 *Contrast of the pattern of assessment between the traditional and student-centred approaches*

Traditional	Student-centred

IT skills and application:
    Assignment towards end (50%)
	IT skills and application:
	    6 mini assignments at 2-week intervals (50%)

IT theory and application:
    Exam at the end of module (50%)
	IT theory and application:
	    2 objective tests, mid-way and end (40%)

	Student-assessed presentation (10%)

The questionnaire was given to students in class time and completed while the lecturer left the room. Due to low attendance this only achieved a 65% response rate. While responses were probably biased, as it was only completed by those who attended, it still provided pointers to likely problems. Students found the lectures 'boring', the case study was 'too long', 'boring' and 'complex', and they were unclear about their progress in the practical work. Apart from the lack of clarity about their progress, feedback from the students regarding practical teaching was reasonable – the handouts were adequate, the staff were knowledgeable, developed their understanding and the staff–student relationships were good (Table 3, p.90).

When assignments and exam scripts were marked it became obvious that for many students the module objectives had not been achieved. Students were not computer literate – many of them had done as little work as possible in order to gain a bare pass (or fail). Students were rarely seen near the computer rooms between practical classes and were not transferring the skills learnt to other modules. Informal discussion with groups of students suggested that they had not received feedback as quickly or as regularly as they required to enable them to develop their skills or to realise the standards expected. In addition, the students were voting with their feet, with sometimes over 40% not attending lectures.

Impetus for change

At the same time, pressure was increasing to raise staff–student ratios. Student feedback had confirmed that the word-processing workbook had worked reasonably well, providing the necessary security in the early stages of learning (Table 3). However, inexpensive off-the-shelf distance learning material that provided a sufficiently strong business element was not available. (Although such material is now available such as through the DP Publications *Promoting Active Learning* Series; for example Muir (1992), it is still relatively expensive and it soon becomes dated.) By this time we had written a spreadsheet workbook, and the handouts could be developed into a database workbook. It was felt that they could be developed into the basis for practical teaching. A more detailed introduction and a series of graded self-assessment questions were included in addition to the practical exercises. These, it was hoped, would provide students with the necessary support and confidence to develop their skills outside formal classes; to help them to identify their own strengths and weaknesses and thus where their learning needs lay. They would also reduce the need for formal teaching time.

Student feedback (Table 3) and attendance levels suggested that the lectures were not well received. A series of college seminars on dealing with large classes and associated material suggested alternative ways of using the lecture time, in particular using student-centred approaches (Gibbs *et al.*, 1989). This it was felt could overcome the problems with the lectures. Further reading (for example, Rogers, 1983; Edwards and Sutton, 1991) indicated that giving students responsibility for their own learning and choice paid dividends in terms of successful learning and skills development.

The student-centred approach

Since 1991–92 the module has been offered using a student-centred approach. The objectives of the module have remained the same; but the method of delivery has changed (see the comparisons in Tables 1 and 2). Student response to each 'run' of the module has been monitored through a questionnaire and through informal discussions. Delivery of the student-centred module, although essentially the same as in 1991–92, has evolved in response to the action research as well as advances in IT. Lectures have been replaced by a range of student-centred sessions called 'seminars' (Table 1). These are based on business applications of IT and stress links with other modules in their degree programme. They include individual and group activities and are supported by the study notes and appropriate video material. The module now consists of one hour per week of seminars and two hours per week of practical work. Typically, 120 students attend the seminar sessions; practical work is now conducted in a large computer room with groups of 60 students. Students are still expected to undertake an additional three hours of private study each week.

All students purchase their own support materials, charges being sufficient to cover photocopying and associated costs. Each set consists of a Module Handbook, Study Notes and three Self-Paced Workbooks introducing word-processing for business, spreadsheets, and databases. Students realise quickly that in order to complete the assignments successfully they must engage with the tasks set out in the study notes and work through the workbooks. Lecturers are not available to answer questions in the way that they might have been in small lecture groups, and during the practical sessions they are mainly engaged in providing individual help. Students are encouraged to work more collaboratively, and the introduction of peer-assessed group presentations helps to provide interaction and social cohesion.

Large practical classes necessitate workbooks that are designed to support independent learning. The tutor's role in these classes is largely confined to helping the weaker and less experienced students, and developing the more advanced students' skills. Practical skills are assessed through six graded mini-assignments based on a business-related scenario (Table 2). Students are expected to complete all six, but only three are assessed: the students do not know in advance which will be assessed. Marking sheets with clear criteria and checklists have been devised, and typically a mini-assignment will take less than five minutes to mark. The theory element of the module is tested using two multiple-choice tests. This pattern of assessment has had the effect of markedly improving levels of attendance and quality of work.

Group presentations provide students with choice, the chance to explore an aspect of the business context of IT in reasonable depth and share their knowledge. Each group of four or five students has to choose a topic from a list and plan their work. Peer assessment is employed using a closely prescribed marking scheme but staff attend about 20% of the presentations. Students are encouraged to approach their presentations in a business-like manner and use this opportunity to further develop their presentation skills. All are expected to produce a summary handout and a tape-recording of their presentation to hand in to their tutors.

Songs of praise and lessons

Praise

The move from a traditional to a student-centred approach has resulted in improvements in students' learning, both in terms of assessment grades and in softer areas such as their use of IT in other modules. Failure rates have declined from 12.6% in 1991 to 5.2% in 1994. Modules such as Quantitative Methods and Financial Accounting no longer need to teach spreadsheet skills as the students are already prepared. In the most recent student evaluation questionnaire, over 66% of students responded positively to the question 'Do you think that the (student-centred) module has proved to be as helpful as you originally hoped it would?' compared with 54% for the traditional module. Similarly 94% of students who took the student-centred module would recommend the module to others.

Similar proportions of students feel that the student-centred teaching method is more appropriate than the traditional approach for practical classes and a greater proportion rate the educational value of seminars more highly than that of lectures (Table 3). Students like the practical work; personal achievement when finishing certain assignments; and regular assignments to reduce exam pressure. Comments also demonstrate an awareness of the implicit nature of the student-centred approach in the module design: 'builds confidence, encourages the students to work constantly hard'. However, they also highlight problems with the design of the module and facilities available: 'work load' and 'lack of computer availability for long periods'. The problems have continued to be raised despite substantial improvements to the facilities available. These and similar comments when combined with our experiences provide evidence for the lessons which accompany the praise.

Table 3 *Student scores for various aspects of the student-centred module (responses for the traditional module are given in brackets)*

Aspect	Percentage of students rating								
	Good/reasonable			So-so			Room for improvement/poor		
	'90/91	'91/92	'93/94	'90/91	'91/92	'93/94	'90/91	'91/92	'93/94
Clarity and quality of support material									
– Module Handbook		82	79		9	9		9	12
– Study Notes		72	71		13	16		15	13
– Word-processing Workbook	(74)	86	79	(13)	11	15	(13)	3	6
– Spreadsheet Workbook		82	68		13	16		5	16
– Database Workbook		76	61		20	21		4	18
Educationsl value of Seminars (Lectures)	(46)	69	70	(26)	25	22	(28)	6	8
Ability of practical to develop student understanding	(67)	72	58	(220	20	31	(11)	8	11
Appropriatness of teaching methods used in practical	(72)	78	68	(18)	15	26	(10)	5	6

Note: In 1991 the groups for the practical work were small (20), in 1993/4 there were 60 students in a group.
Source: survey of traditional module students 1991 – 65% response rate and student-centred module students 1992 and 1993 – 96% response rate.

Table 4 *Proportion of students agreeing or disagreeing with statements about the student-centred module (responses for the traditional module are given in brackets)*

Statement	Support		
	'90/91	'91/92	'93/94
The module was over-taught	(-37%)	-49%	-57%
The module lacked intellectual coherence	(-45%)	-70%	-51%
The module was a total disappointment	(-56%)	-82%	-78%
The amount of work for the assignments was far too great	(+43%)	+64%	+46%

The support is given as a percentage: a + signifies agreement, a – signifies disagreement.
Source: survey of traditional module students – 65% response rate and student-centred module students – 96% response rate.

Lessons

Lesson 1: attendance may fall with student-centred learning

Attendance at both practical and lecture/seminar sessions has improved and remained high with the adoption of the student-centred approach. Average attendance for the traditional method was 65% compared with between 80% and 96% for the student-centred approach. However, in the last year attendance levels for the practical workshops have fallen. Reasons for this are unclear although discussion with students suggests that the practical sessions are increasingly viewed as 'guaranteed access to computer' and 'individual problem-solving' sessions rather than classes in the traditional sense. It seems probable that our students are becoming more flexible learners, using the materials provided and only attending practical workshops when necessary. This causes problems when students attempt assignments without working through the workbooks.

Lesson 2: workbook development is continuous and very time consuming

The workbooks have been revised and developed over the past four years. Rising student expectations mean that, in addition to being correct and up to date, workbooks must now be well produced. Student feedback (Table 3) indicates that this is the case, although further improvement is possible. Each practical class of workbook material takes between 20 and 30 hours to develop and requires careful proofreading, preferably by novices. As new versions of software are introduced (almost annually) and better ways to explain topics are discovered, the workbooks need revising. Close liaison is needed with regard to new software introduction. Updating the spreadsheet and database workbooks in 1993/4 was undertaken to very tight deadlines.

Lesson 3: good workbooks free up lecturer time, but...

Workbooks have freed up lecturer time in the practical sessions to assist weaker students as well as to help more experienced students to pursue more advanced ideas. They have also enabled lecturers (with demonstrator support) to cope with practical class sizes of 60 as opposed to the original 20. This represents a substantial resource saving. Students following the student-centred approach have helped each other more with the theory and the practical work. While this is of educational benefit, we have also seen an increase in cases of plagiarism (two cases were proved this year, and more were suspected but not proved due to large numbers).

Lesson 4: not all students cope well with the student-centred approach

Teaching methods used in the practicals are felt to be appropriate and to develop understanding by the vast majority of students (Table 3). However, those who had previously studied IT, and in particular the computer software used, still feel insufficiently challenged despite the inclusion of additional exercises. In contrast, students who have never used computers are frightened at the beginning of the module and still want more support in the practical sessions. The latter has been overcome partially by extra staffing in the practical classes when new software packages are introduced. Despite this there are still students who require more help.

Lesson 5: students like variety

Replacing formal lectures with seminars provides opportunities to use interactive teaching methods and feedback indicates they are more enjoyable to students. Typical student comments include 'these were enjoyable' and '… good and informative'. Students have rated the educational value of seminars significantly more highly than their predecessors rated lectures (Table 3). However, a note of caution must be added. Other modules have adopted student-centred approaches, so what was considered innovative four years ago is increasingly commonplace. In the past year a minority of students have requested more lectures as these are unusual!

Lesson 6: assessment encourages students to work

Individual students' comments are illuminating, indicating that regular assignments encourage them to keep up with the work. A typical comment is 'At the time I disliked handing the work in on a weekly basis, however it gave me an idea of how I was doing'. However, students' concern over the assessment load increased (Table 4, p.90). Nearly two-thirds of students are now concerned about the assessment load compared to just under half with the traditional assignment and exam. This is despite reducing the number of mini-assignments from nine to six. Analysis of students' comments suggests that they find the first Objective Test frightening, and in general work hard at their presentations. The results overall are better than for the traditional approach, but of equal importance, students are using their skills and are pleased with their success.

Lesson 7: assessment methods impact upon lecturers' workloads

Increased practical class size and number of assignments have also increased the lecturers' workload considerably. Initially all mini-assignments were marked but, with large class sizes it proved impossible to return them to students quickly enough to provide useful formative feedback. For this reason it was decided to only assess three and provide ideal solutions for the remaining mini-assignments. By contrast, multiple-choice objective tests are quick and easy to mark. To date this has been undertaken manually, although it is hoped to automate the process fully, and provide immediate student feedback using the Question Mark software.

Lesson 8: self- and peer-assessment require lecturer planning

Use of self-assessment for three of the six assignments and peer-assessment for the presentations has had costs as well as benefits. Students need considerable encouragement to be constructively critical of their peers' work. For presentations a clear marking proforma is required. Mini-assignments require model answers, with clearly annotated indications of likely mistakes. Initially student feedback supported this approach, although recent discussion has suggested that students feel this is not acceptable.

Lesson 9: too many assignments cause resource problems

When there are frequent deadlines for 240 students, printers are under intense pressure. This problem is exacerbated towards the end of the semester by other students needing to use the computer rooms for their assignments.

Future developments

In order to address the last two problems, we are considering reducing the number of submitted assignments to three, thus cutting down the printing and administration caused by the collection of such numbers of assignments. In addition, students will need to complete at least certain compulsory exercises in the workbooks. This method should improve learning as there will be immediate feedback; it should improve attendance as completion of tasks will be part of the criteria for passing the module; it may cut down on plagiarism, and improve the staff–student relationship.

Plans for the future include the possible use of multimedia initially to support the lectures and study notes for weaker students. Eventually it could replace some of the lectures. Work has started on a package using Asymetrix Toolbook.

Conclusions

Praise for student-centred approaches is justified by improved student learning and their enjoyment of the learning process. The approach outlined allows student flexibility in the choice of presentation topic and practical class attendance. To achieve this it relies heavily on a range of teaching methods (including lecturer prepared workbooks) and a variety of sequentially graded assessment methods to ensure that students cover and understand the module content. Lessons learnt from the adoption of this approach reflect the heavy investment required in workbook preparation and assessment time. In addition, they highlight students' desire for a variety of approaches, their ability to teach each other and the fact that not all students cope well with this approach to learning.

References

Edwards, R and Sutton, A (1991) 'A practical approach to student-centred learning', *British Journal of Educational Technology*, **23**, 1, 4–20.

Gibbs, G, Habeshaw, S and Habeshaw, T (1989) *53 Interesting Things To Do In Your Lectures*, 3rd edn, Technical and Educational Services, Bristol.

Lewin, K (1946) 'Action research and minority problems', *Journal of Social Issues*, **2**, 34–6.

Muir, J (1992) *dBase for Business Students*, DP Publications, London.

Raadheim, K, Wankowski, J and Radford, J (1991) *Helping Students to Learn*, Society for Research into Higher Education/Open University Press, Buckingham.

Robson, C (1993) *Real World Research*, Blackwell, Oxford.

Rogers, C (1983) *Freedom to Learn*, Merrill, New York.

Jenny Hall is the Field Chair of the Business Information Technology Field of the Undergraduate Modular Degree Scheme at the Cheltenham & Gloucester College of Higher Education. Her main research interest is teaching and learning strategies for IT-related courses.

Address for correspondence: Faculty of Business and Social Studies, Cheltenham & Gloucester College of Higher Education, PO Box 220, The Park Campus, The Park, Cheltenham, GL50 1QF.

Mark Saunders is a Senior Lecturer in Research Methods and Business Studies at the Cheltenham & Gloucester College of Higher Education, whose interests also include teaching and learning strategies. Mark and Jenny have worked together for the past four years developing new teaching methods for Business Information Technology.

Address for correspondence: Faculty of Business and Social Studies, Cheltenham & Gloucester College of Higher Education (as above).

12. Providing Flexible Opportunities for Overseas Students at Masters Level

Dr Robert Kowalski, *The University of Wolverhampton*

SUMMARY

There has been a change within the management of overseas aid, moving away from free-standing training awards towards project-related training. This means that students coming to the UK have more clearly defined objectives for their training which relate to their role in projects back in their own country. Thus traditional fixed-content courses are no longer appropriate, and every student needs to be treated uniquely on a very flexible programme.

We have sought to create such a programme with our MSc in Development Training and Education by providing access to technical training at Masters level; by enabling students to develop their ability to pass their skills and knowledge on to others; by ensuring personal development through the process of learning; and by giving all aspects of the curriculum a project focus through negotiation with the student and their sponsor.

This chapter explains the nature of the provision, the salient characteristics of the students, the process that the students experience and the problems we have encountered in seeking to achieve our objectives. Our responses to these problems will also be outlined as a case study illustrating the provision of a flexible and progressive curriculum.

Introduction

The Centre for Rural Development and Training (CRDT) at the University of Wolverhampton has been receiving overseas students from developing countries and sponsored by the Overseas Development Administration for over 20 years. During this time and particularly in the last few years, there has been a noticeable switch from Technical Cooperation and Training Department (TCTD) awards to scholarships directly linked to projects, and a growing emphasis is being placed on the identification of training needs (Iredale, 1992). Increasingly these are being expressed as objectives for the study fellow, against which the success of the training is evaluated.

As recipients of such scholars we are both challenged and frustrated by this system. To meet the challenge we have developed a number of programmes that are flexible and responsive to the individuals concerned and their contexts. This chapter sets out details of one such programme, the MSc in Development Training and Education. The frustration will also be explained by describing the difficulties we have faced in providing a flexible experience and the ways in which we are surmounting those difficulties.

The MSc is the latest in a series of programmes that have been developed to respond to the needs of this client group (both scholars and their sponsors). 'Projectisation' has led to a welcomed emphasis on the outcomes of education by specifying objectives for each scholar. However, this creates problems in the construction and delivery of a programme that is appropriate to those objectives while at the same time meeting the scholar's aspirations for an MSc qualification and the university's academic requirements for awards at Masters level.

Hulme (1990) emphasised the problems of creating relevance in courses for overseas students delivered in the UK. From the experiences of the staff of the CRDT in working as consultants on projects all over the world it is clear that this is a real issue which has several causes.

Firstly, the courses chosen are often at Masters level because of prestige and career development for the scholar rather than the need for Masters level outcomes. The projects require 'can do' people, but degree holders are unlikely to want to come and take diploma level practical training.

Secondly, the receiving institutions may require the scholars to join technical programmes primarily designed for UK graduates where the level and focus are inappropriate for the situation in the scholar's own country, especially in regard to the availability of technical equipment.

Thirdly, the programmes and objectives of the scholar do not cover the sustainability of any technical updating; the scholar is not required to address the need to transfer knowledge, skills and attitudes achieved to others in their home country.

The programme

The CRDT has set itself the aims of creating a programme that is capable of addressing technical needs, communication and sustainability needs, self-development needs and a project orientation in line with a curriculum design approach advocated by the Further Education Unit (FEU, 1989). The MSc programme achieves this by pursuing a two-pronged approach within a Modular Credit Accumulation system. Half the taught modules are a compulsory core dealing with issues of training, development and communication skills, and the remainder form a 'modular space' which can be filled in a variety of ways. The whole programme is then integrated and drawn together by a major dissertation project which bridges the taught modules (see Figure 1).

The modular space of optional elements can contain modules on technical subjects, management modules, information technology, media and many more as appropriate. The flexibility this creates is considerable, and modules are available in the university which enable students to pursue tailor-made programmes. In addition, it is possible for students to study technical subjects that are not available at the university by attending other institutions and bringing credits so obtained to their award.

Part of the philosophy underpinning the programme is that the content of the modules must be delivered through a practical, applied approach involving learning by doing (Gibbs, 1988). This is achieved by the scholars undertaking assessed assignments. The theme of these are negotiated with the scholar within a framework for the module. This is a further aspect of flexibility that enables the scholar to focus upon their prespecified outcomes.

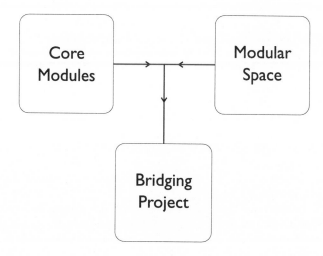

Figure 1 *The structure of the MSc programme in Development Training and Education*

Programme management
The MSc award is part of a larger Professional Development Programme, managed by the School of Education at the university. The management structure is responsible for the quality assurance of the Award and for conferment of the qualification. Each individual scholar's programme of study is considered and agreed through the committee structure of the school's programme and the credits necessary for completion are brought to that programme's examination board. Individual modules are taught within subject areas of the university and assessment is overseen by examination boards at that level, who will have their work scrutinised by external examiners. The MSc in Development Training and Education has an overall coordinator, the route leader, who is responsible for tracking each scholar through the system and ensuring that individual programmes are negotiated and achieved in line with the objectives specified by the sponsor, by liaising with the subject tutors who run the modules.

The participants
The students are invariably mature and from an extremely wide ethnic and cultural background. The gender mix is two to one in favour of males. Perhaps the most complex issue is the educational experiences of the scholars which are very varied. South American scholars, for example, are much more used to active learning approaches than are scholars from the Indian subcontinent (Avalos and Haddad, 1979).

The sequence of events
The process for the students is as follows:

1. Application and initial proposal of a set of modules.
2. Negotiation of a set of objectives between scholar and project manager.

3. EFL test and where necessary a pre-course programme of English.
4. Arrival and induction, including study skills and computing.
5. Negotiation of first semester modules, registration and allocation of a personal tutor.
6. Classes, self-study, tutorials and assignments.
7. Attachments to industry, other institutions and organisations, as necessary.
8. Identification of dissertation topic and allocation of supervisors.
9. Negotiation of second semester modules and registration.
10. Classes, self-study, tutorials and assignments.
11. Project development.
12. Project field work.
13. Dissertation preparation and submission.

This process follows the curriculum principles outlined by Shackleton (1989).

The problems

In addition to the problems of 'culture shock' affecting the students, as described by Krizmanic and Kolesaric (1991), a number of other problems arise because of mismatches of perceptions. Figure 2 sets out the relationships between the various parties involved, and these generate the following problems.

1. The purposes of the programme do not conform to those of more traditional Masters degrees. In the terms of Warren-Piper (1985) it is designed from a 'functional' approach to education where traditional ones are from a 'cultural' one. Quite frequently there is no initial contact between the project manager and the receiving institution.
2. In many cases what the programme has to offer is not understood by the project manager and so the training objectives set for the scholar are not sufficiently well articulated to enable the scholar to negotiate effectively.
3. The scholar may be unused to dealing with teachers as equals and so has problems in specifying what their needs are and responding appropriately to the heuristic methods. Their perception is often that it is the role and responsibility of the route leader to decide what has to be studied.
4. The scholar is unused to taking responsibility for learning and so shows signs of dependency. The heuristic approach underpinning the whole process causes the scholar difficulties manifested as a demand for spoon-feeding and frequent lobbying of the tutors to pre-mark assignments. The tutor who is not used to working with overseas students has difficulty in explaining what is required. Many skills of presentation of analysis and evaluation are learned by UK students over a long period of having their work marked, throughout their higher education, and are not easily acquired in a short period.
5. The route leader has difficulty in communicating to some tutors the project context and specific objectives of the scholars, which are necessary for the assignments to be well focused. Tutors are frequently socialised in a cultural approach to education which makes it difficult for them to respond as flexibly as necessary.

6.   The school management structure does not take account of the demanding nature of working with overseas students (eg there is no means of gaining credit for the many unscheduled contacts with the students).

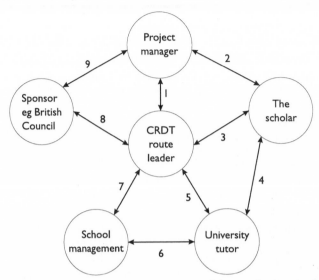

Figure 2 *Mismatches of expectations of the parties involved*

7.   The bureaucratic procedures for administering programmes can inhibit the flexibility needed to deal with a small number of full-time overseas students. In addition, the very nature of a credit accumulation system fosters the adoption of a banking education metaphor which runs counter to the self-development philosophy of the work we are doing (Freire, 1970).
8.   The procedures of sponsoring agencies often make it impossible to begin the process of negotiation about outcomes and programmes before the scholar arrives. These often make it impossible to overcome the problems outlined in 1, 2 and 3 above. In addition, the sponsor's requirements for progress reports are often founded on the more traditional term-based courses, rather than a modular semester-based programme.
9.   The length of bureaucratic chains within the sponsoring agency and the project can also make it difficult to involve the project manager in timely negotiation about modules to be studied, the focus of assignments and making all the necessary arrangements for the project field work.

Successful strategies

Despite the long list of difficulties outlined above, the programme is a very successful one. The objectives of the scholars, their projects and the CRDT are to a very large extent achieved through this provision. This success is due to the efforts and dedication of the staff involved, and to a number of strategies and techniques that have been developed and employed in the realisation of the programme over the last five years.

1. An induction programme for the students dealing with a range of issues from study skills and time management, through cultural transitions, to computing and information technology.
2. The allocation of personal tutors who give strong pastoral support and who lead the process of dialogue towards self-discovery of the scholars.
3. The consultancy work of the CRDT enables close contact between project managers and the route leader. Involvement of the CRDT in the training of many project managers for ODA is also proving most helpful.
4. The possibility for the scholars to return to their own country to conduct the field work for their dissertation projects is a very valuable mechanism for ensuring an applied focus for the studies.
5. The timetabling of formal classes is heavier at the beginning of the year, and is gradually reduced. This provides both support and incentive for the development of the scholars' independence as learners.
6. In addition to inducting the scholars onto the programme, a number of staff development events have been organised both for university staff and for those of other institutions who receive these scholars. There is also a liaison committee which acts as a forum for tutors from across the programme to meet and exchange views and to respond to specific issues.
7. Students are required to maintain a tutorial logbook to document each meeting with tutors. Students are at liberty to consult with a wide range of tutors, and this helps each tutor to see what other consultations have been taking place and to ensure that the current one fits in with the overall pattern of development.
8. Efforts are made to publicise the programme as widely as possible, drawing particular attention to the advantages of its flexible approach and emphasising the role of negotiation and objectives setting. This chapter represents just such a measure. Recently a newsletter has been launched for alumni of the CRDT in which they are encouraged to report on developments in their projects resulting from their studies.
9. Because the scholars are mature students, quite usually in positions of seniority in their own countries, they are welcomed and treated as colleagues by the staff of the CRDT. This is particularly manifest in the many social events that take place with the staff over the duration of the programme.

Conclusion

The challenges facing those providing education and training for scholars from development projects across the world are considerable. The time is past when they could simply be fitted in to existing courses. Now we must provide flexible opportunities for them to study what they need in ways that develop their independence as learners.

At the University of Wolverhampton we have sought to achieve this through a modular programme in which the student has a large say in what is to be achieved. This is undertaken in a supportive environment based upon a dialogue of equals.

The future holds a number of further challenges in the shape of more credits being made available for studies undertaken outside the UK, distance learning approaches and distance teaching opportunities.

Acknowledgements

I would like to thank all my colleagues at the CRDT who work so hard to provide exemplary student experiences. In particular I would like to thank Dr Christine Cottam for reviewing this chapter and providing me with helpful comments.

References

Avalos, B and Haddad, W (1979) *A Review of Teacher Effectiveness Research in Africa, India, Latin America, Middle East, Malaysia, Philippines and Thailand*, International Development Research Centre, Ottawa.

Further Education Unit (FEU) (1989) 'Towards a framework for curriculum entitlement', in M Preedy (ed.), *Approaches to Curriculum Management*, Open University Press, Buckingham.

Freire, P (1970) *The Pedagogy of the Oppressed*, Continuum, New York.

Gibbs, G (1988) *Learning by Doing: A Guide to Teaching and Learning Methods*, FEU, London.

Hulme, D (1990) *The Effectiveness of British Aid for Training*, Manchester University.

Iredale, R (1992) *The Power of Change: Part 1. A Review of Training: Needs and Criteria*, ODA, London.

Krizmanic, M and Kolesaric, V (1991) 'Cultural determinants and implied values in international education', *Higher Education Policy*, **4**, 32–6.

Shackleton, J (1989) 'Planning for the future in further education: beyond a curriculum-led approach', in M Preedy (ed.), *Approaches to Curriculum Management*, Open University Press, Buckingham.

Warren-Piper, D (1985) 'The changing role and status of post secondary teachers', *Higher Education in Europe*, **10**, 6–11.

Address for correspondence: **Robert Kowalski**, Senior Lecturer, Centre for Rural Development and Training, University of Wolverhampton, Walsall Campus, Gorway Road, Walsall WS1 3BD.

13. Workshop on Assessment of Groups of Students

Mark Lejk, *School of Computing & Information Systems, University of Sunderland*

SUMMARY
This report describes a workshop on assessment of groups of students. The workshop comprised an examination of delegates' attitudes to group assessment followed by an investigation of a number of methods of assessing groups that have been reported in the literature. Delegates were encouraged to feedback their views on group assessment and their opinions of the methods presented.

Aims of the workshop

- To examine the attitudes of delegates to group assessment.
- To examine a number of methods used to derive individual grades from a group assessment and establish some advantages and disadvantages of each.

Process of the workshop

Attitudes to group assessment
The workshop began with delegates examining their own attitudes to group assessment by completing the questionnaire given in the Figure 1. In groups of three, they then picked the statement on which there was most agreement, and the one on which there was the least and reported these back to the rest of the delegates.

Methods of group assessment
Delegates were supplied with details of six methods of deriving individual grades from a group assessment. These methods are described very briefly below.

Method 1: Group mark x individual weight (Goldfinch and Raeside, 1990; Conway et al., 1993; Goldfinch, 1994)
The tutor arrives at a group mark and the students, through peer assessment, arrive at a weight for each member of the group. An individual's mark is then found from:

Individual's mark = group mark x individual weight

Method 2: Distribution of a pool of marks (Habeshaw et al., 1993)
The tutor arrives at a group mark and this is multiplied by the number of students in the group. The students then divide this total up as they see fit.

Attitudes to group assessment

Below are some statements about group assessment. Please indicate by placing a tick in the appropriate box the extent of your agreement with each statement.

	Strongly agree	Agree	Uncertain	Disagree	Strongly disagree
It is more important to expose students to learning in groups than to assess them in groups					
Automatically granting each group member the same grade for a group assessment is unfair					
Group assessments save time in marking					
Group assessment should be used *only* to measure an individual's ability to work in a group					
Group assessment tends to 'bunch' the marks for a given cohort of students					
Peer assessment methods are a valid way of distributing marks in a group assessment					
Group assessments should be concentrated in Years 1 and 2 of a course					
The Final Year of a course should contain a large amount of group assessment					
Group assessments allow students to 'hide' more easily than with individual assessments					
Group assessments tend to penalise able students					
Group assessment methods are not as reliable as individual assessments					
Before undertaking a group assessment students should learn how to work in a team					

Figure 1 *Attitudes to group assessment questionnaire*

Method 3: Group mark plus or minus contribution mark (Habeshaw et al., 1993; Gibbs, 1992)

The tutor arrives at a group mark. The students then peer assess each other according to predefined criteria and marks are added to or subtracted from the group mark to reflect an individual's contribution. Different importance weightings can be attached to the criteria.

Method 4: Separation of process and product (Falchikov, 1988; 1991)

The tutor arrives at a mark for the group product and all students receive this. Using peer assessment the students allocate individual marks for each person's contribution to the assignment. The two marks are then combined to give the final individual mark.

Method 5: Yellow and red cards (Lejk, 1994)

Each group member receives the group mark unless the rest of the group has awarded a yellow card (reduction of 20% for that member) or a red card (mark of zero for that member).

Method 6: Assessment of the information systems group project

This project is run at the University of Sunderland with large groups of students (up to 12). It has several interesting features including extensive peer assessment based on precise criteria. These peer assessments are entered by the students on to a computer disk and these disks are then input into a spreadsheet program which calculates the individual marks.

Delegates, in groups of three, examined three of these methods and fed back one positive feature and one negative feature about each method.

Results of the workshop

Attitudes to group assessment

The results of this exercise varied considerably between the groups with the most controversial statement being the first one: *it is more important to expose students to learning in groups than to assess them in groups.* Two of the groups found this statement led to the highest consensus whereas the other two found it led to the least consensus. The presenter found this result surprising as he felt most people would agree with the statement.

Methods of group assessment

The following table summarises the feedback from examination of the methods.

Method	Positive features	Negative features
1	Logical. Ability to select criteria. Good for assessing professional issues.	Dangerous if criteria are vague. Mathematically slightly complex.
2	Quick and simple.	Can be superficial.

3	Good to be able to attach importance to criteria.	Example included negative marking.
4	Good to be able to separate product and process. Falchikov's questionnaire attractive.	Too many categories in the questionnaire. Students need to be sophisticated at assessment.
5	Very clear and 'punchy'.	Could be regarded as Draconian and negative.
6	Criteria very comprehensive and clear.	Complicated to administer. Tutor needs to be very computer literate.

References

Conway, R, Kember, D, Sivan, A and Wu, M (1993) 'Peer assessment of an individual's contribution to a group project', *Assessment and Evaluation in Higher Education,* **18**, 1, 45–56.

Falchikov, N (1988) 'Self and peer assessment of a group project designed to promote the skills of capability', *Programmed Learning and Educational Technology,* **25**, 4, 327–39.

Falchikov, N (1991). 'Group process analysis: self and peer assessment of working together in a group', in S Brown and P Dove (eds) *Self and Peer Assessment,* Standing Conference on Educational Development, Paper No 63.

Gibbs, G (1992) *Booklet 4: Assessing More Students – The Teaching More Students Project*, The Polytechnics & Colleges Funding Council, 26–30.

Goldfinch, J (1994) 'Further developments in peer assessment of group projects', *Assessment and Evaluation in Higher Education,* **19**, 1, 29–35.

Goldfinch, J and Raeside, R (1990) 'Development of a peer assessment technique for obtaining individual marks on a group project', *Assessment and Evaluation in Higher Education,* **15**, 3, 210–31.

Habeshaw, S, Gibbs, G and Habeshaw, T (1993) *53 Interesting Ways to Assess Your Students,* 3rd edn, The Cromwell Press, London.

Huddersfield (1992) *Draft School Quality Handbook,* School of Computing and Mathematics, University of Huddersfield.

Lejk, M (1994) 'Team assessment, win or lose', *The New Academic,* **3**, 3, 10–11.

Address for correspondence: **Mark Lejk**, Senior Lecturer, School of Computing and Information Systems, University of Sunderland, Langham Tower, Ryhope Rd, Sunderland SR2 7EE.

14. Computer-Assisted Assessment: Benefits and Pitfalls for Flexible Learning

Christine Ward, *Guildford Educational Services*

Objectives

The objectives of this workshop were to introduce participants to a wide range of potential and actual uses of computer-assisted assessment (CAA), to identify the advantages and potential pitfalls of CAA and to assist participants to think about ways in which CAA could be used in their own field. The format of the workshop comprised an initial presentation, opportunities for discussion and questions and the opportunity for hands-on exploration of a number of software packages that exemplify different uses of CAA.

Computer-assisted assessment can be used to assess a wide range of knowledge and skills. Suitably used, CAA can provide flexible assessment, with a saving in marking and recording time. However, it is essential to ensure the quality and appropriateness of assessment.

The term 'computer-assisted assessment' can be used to refer to any use of computers in assessment, including computerised recording of student achievement, but the workshop concentrated on computer-delivered assessment in which the student or candidate takes the assessment on the computer. This normally means that the computer 'marks' the responses, although some applications have used simulations in which a human assessor is present to monitor the student activity.

Computer-delivered assessment can be used to assess knowledge in almost any subject and occupational area. The examples on show related to accounting (*Basic Accounting* from Ivy Software Ltd) and security guarding (by Infosound Ltd for National Vocational Qualifications in Security Guarding). Also on show were two examples of 'shell' software, *Question Designer for Windows* (Question Mark Computing Ltd) and Interactive Assessor (EQL International). Shell software allows the user, whether awarding body or institution, to create their own objective tests. The software provides the storage and delivery mechanism. Another product on show relevant to the testing of knowledge was *Better Testing* (jointly published by Question Mark Computing Ltd and Guildford Educational Services Ltd). This is a CBT guide to writing good quality objective tests and which includes a wide range of examples of their use.

CAA can also assess a range of skills, both computer related and general. *Type Quick* (Comprix Ltd) is one example of a test of keyboarding accuracy and speed. *Qwiz Software* produces a much wider range of options, from basic keyboarding through data entry and letter layout, to software which tests the candidate's skills in using particular applications, (eg a word processor or database package). Computerised assessment has also been used in simulations to assess fault finding skills or skills in controlling complex processes. One example quoted was a simulation of candidate's skill and understanding in adjusting the controls of a plastics processing operation to eliminate the cause of a faulty component.

CAA has a number of potential pitfalls including issues of security and hardware problems. The most significant, however, is the importance of ensuring that the assessment content is of good quality. Computer-assisted assessments need to observe the normal principles of good assessment, especially those of validity and reliability. This means, for example, that CAA should be used only where it is appropriate for the skills and subject matter being assessed, that it should consistently assess the right skills and knowledge, that it should not require irrelevant skills and that the content should be technically accurate.

When used appropriately, CAA can provide a flexible assessment mode, able to offer assessment on demand, with immediate feedback to the student or candidate. It can assess skills which are difficult to assess by other means, for example through simulations. Finally it offers savings in the time spent on marking and on recording students' results.

The discussions by participants identified three main areas of concern.

1. The potential for cheating was thought to be greater in computerised assessment. For example, it is very easy for a student to print off a second copy of a spreadsheet exercise for use by another student. Rigorous computer security is needed to prevent unauthorised access to files. One possible way of overcoming the problem is to set slightly different assignment tasks to different students. Another is to question each student orally to ensure that they have understood the work submitted. Both of these are difficult if student numbers are high.
2. Some students may be terrified of using computers. Measures that can overcome this problem include user-friendly software and plenty of opportunities to practise with similar material before the actual test. In extreme cases, including some cases of physical disability, an alternative assessment method may be needed.
3. The effort of writing questions and assessment tasks is not reduced when computers are used as the method of delivery. Cooperation between teams, either within the institution or between institutions, offers one possible way forward. This is better than 'buying in' assessment material since tutors usually like to feel 'ownership' of the material.

Address for correspondence: **Christine Ward**, Consultant, Guildford Educational Services Ltd, 32 Castle Street, Guildford GU1 3UW.

Workshop Report

15. Automated Assessment of Basic IT Skills

Tony Pedder, The University of Humberside

SUMMARY
A recent development at the University of Humberside is the Skills Aquisition Programme. The aim of the programme is to equip new students with both generic study skills and basic IT skills. This brought together newly produced paper-based open learning materials, a new support system and newly developed automated assessment methods for IT skills. The last is the focus for this chapter.

Introduction

The aim of the workshop was both to describe the approaches used in the assessments and to provide participants with the opportunity to try out the assessments that have been developed.

At the outset, the programme development team decided that as much automation as possible should be attempted in the processes of assessment and processing of results. Our aim was to test if skills had been acquired, and to attempt to give the student immediate feedback together with an immediate pass or fail result. One method we have adopted is to set specific tasks to be completed in an application, which have a known outcome which can then be evaluated for a measure of success. However, we discovered that this approach was not always feasible and certainly not suitable for assessing whether basic concepts had been understood. For this type of assessment we resorted to multiple-choice questions. After researching the market for suitable delivery software it was decided to develop our own. This inhouse development has given us full control and the potential for further development to best suit the institution's requirements.

The assessments developed

Multiple-choice question software

This system comprises four Windows applications:

1. **AqDesign:** This provides the means by which libraries of questions can be developed. It is interactive and somewhat like a drawing package in as much as you move and place elements on the screen. In this application you also establish a marking scheme. Version one supports the following types of question:

   - selection of correct item from a list
   - true or false questions

- matching of items
- sorting of items.

It is also possible to place graphics on the screen; one use of this feature can be asking students to label diagrams.

2. **AqBuild:** A small application to assemble a specific assessment by selecting questions from various libraries.
3. **AqRun:** The 'engine' that delivers the questions to the student.
4. **AqMS:** This is a management system that both produces reports and controls access to the assessments in space and time.

Direct assessment software

Where we have been able to use this it has been our preferred assessment method. To date this has been possible in assessing use at two levels of Word and Excel. Also under development are direct assessments of SPSS and Foxpro. The form of these assessments varies but both the Word and Excel ones are based upon quite sophisticated macros which examine a document or spreadsheet when the student submits them for assessment.

To give an idea of these assessments in practice some of the outcomes we are currently evaluating in an intermediate Word assessment include:

- use of bullet points and numbered lists;
- use of section breaks and page orientation;
- use of margins;
- ability to format tables;
- use of page headers and footers;
- use of columns.

Evaluation

The evaluation of the process is at an early stage. One questionnaire survey has been conducted on a sample of 200 from the target population of 800. Early indications are promising; we are also pleased with the assessment criteria, pass rates and student feedback on the process of assessment. This precedes a more detailed evaluation planned to be conducted towards the end of the second semester.

Conclusions and future actions

As with any new venture there have been problems and we have learned a great deal since the project commenced. For instance, it became apparent that additional automated informal or self-assessment tests should be provided prior to the formal accredited assessment. I am sure that this initiative will proceed successfully, most probably enhanced as above, into its second year of operation.

Address for correspondence: **Tony Pedder**, IT Manager, The Computer Centre, Humberside University, Cottingham Road, Hull HU6 7RT.

16. The Learning College: An Holistic Approach to Institutional Development

Lyn Oates and **Les Watson**, *Cheltenham and Gloucester College of Higher Education*

SUMMARY

This chapter summarises developments in response to pressures for change in styles of learning and teaching at Cheltenham and Gloucester College of Higher Education (CGCHE) and outlines the strategies employed to promote the change from a teaching-driven organisation to a learning-driven one.

In common with other institutions in higher education, CGCHE places learning at the centre of the college's three main areas of activity: teaching, research and commercial activity. Recent developments towards becoming a 'learning college' have focused essentially on a learner-centred approach for deep learning, rich in structure and meaning. The college recognises that the prerequisites for such developments include appropriate beliefs, values, attitudes and perception among college staff and is now starting to address these issues.

The Faculty of Information Services' work to promote change in these areas has involved the development of strategic alliances to ensure the promotion of effective learning-centred policies and strategies. Developments implemented by the faculty have included a range of elements, each equally important to providing the infrastructure necessary to support student learning. The components of this jigsaw include the establishment of a Flexible Learning Design and Development Unit, the formation of a Flexible Learning Area to promote and accommodate flexible delivery and independent learning activities, the installation of college-wide network facilities, and the integration of Information Technology and Library Services within recently established Learning Centres.

This holistic approach views each element as essential and complementary to developing the learning college. All parts must be present to complete successful change in support of learning. However, tackling the difficult human resource issues is central to the strategy's success.

The college

CGCHE has a student population of 7,000, including 5,400 full-time students. Approximately 80% of undergraduates follow a modular degree course. CGCHE is a university-sector college with undergraduate and taught postgraduate accreditation. There are three teaching faculties within the institution: Business and Social Studies; Environment and Leisure; and Arts and Education. In addition there is a fourth faculty, the Faculty of Information Services, which provides support for both staff and students. The scope of this support encompasses library, academic computing, flexible learning development and delivery, reprographics, design services, audio-visual support, administrative computing and networking.

The need for change

Throughout higher education, issues of efficiency have been high on the agenda for some time, with reductions sought in the 'costs' of teaching and learning. The difficulties and urgency of change from teaching towards learning has increased, along with student numbers and as continuing reductions in funding per student stretch both academic staff and the available unit of resource. Assessment of quality and quality issues generally are also of increasing influence as institutions seek to enhance the entire student learning experience (Freeman and Thorne, 1994) and especially the learning environment. The key forces promoting and inhibiting change in styles of learning and teaching at CGCHE are presented elsewhere as a force-field diagram (Oates and Watson, 1995). The influential human elements inhibiting change identified included fear, technophobia, suspicion of motives and adherence to organisational culture and tradition.

Information Services, in conjunction with the College Professional Development Centre (PDC) conducted an institutional audit of teaching, learning and assessment (ATLA) in 1993 (O'Connor *et al.*, 1993). This overview showed that much of the teaching of the institution was of a traditional nature, based largely around lectures and making little use of new technology to promote independent student-centred learning. It did, however, provide a discussion point for learning and teaching issues and a base against which developments in learning and teaching can be measured.

Purpose and potential benefits of change

The College policy refers to the promotion of deep learning as described by Biggs and Moore (1993). Consequently the Faculty of Information Services has adopted a 'learning centred' approach which recognises the centrality of learning development to the future of the College (CGCHE, 1995). Changing styles of learning and teaching are promoted through systems and services which encourage the adoption of student-centred approaches to learning. The aim is to involve students and staff in active engagement with information, ideas and concepts, and promote deep learning. The faculty works to develop closer working relationships with academic colleagues as partners in learning.

The adoption of this approach is aimed at developing in students:

- a sound base in their chosen subject area;
- effective reflective independent approaches to learning;
- high levels of transferable skills;
- commitment to lifelong learning;
- employability.

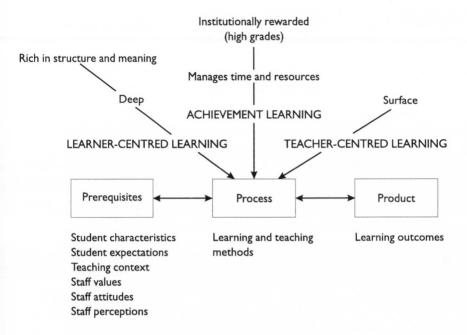

Figure 1 *Styles of learning*

Developing the infrastructure for learning

Developments at CGCHE in support of learning and teaching have incorporated distinct but equally essential components, all vital for success. The importance of information technology in promoting changing styles of learning and teaching at CGCHE was acknowledged by senior management. IT resource provision has formed an important part of the strategy to develop and support student-centred and flexible learning.

The following changes have taken place in parallel over the last four years.

- Development of an appropriate IT infrastructure.
- Integration of traditional library, IT and audio-visual support services at managerial and operational levels.
- Establishment of a Flexible Learning Design and Development Unit.

Distinction should be made between the three mainly physical resource developments above and the more intangible changes in beliefs, values, attitudes and staff perceptions, highlighted by Biggs and Moore (1993) as essential ingredients for successful change. In retrospect, addressing the 'hard' physical resource aspects of change was relatively easy. Strategies for tackling the intangible elements, which must fundamentally involve people, are infinitely more complex.

Two developments at CGCHE to promote the *climate* for change are:

- strategic alliances to develop cooperative working relationships between the College Professional Development Centre, Enterprise in Higher Education, and Information Services;
- formation of a College Teaching, Learning and Assessment Committee.

While strategic alliances and the formation of committees in themselves are not solutions, they provide a framework for debate and have the potential to promote a wider understanding of the issues.

Development of an appropriate IT infrastructure

An IT strategy was implemented to provide individuals with the tools and skills required to become productive knowledge workers. This included the installation of a college network linking staff on all sites and the provision of a networked computer for each member of academic staff. Of central importance to the success of this strategy has been a programme of free IT training for all staff on the hardware and integrated software package supplied.

Integration of traditional library, IT and audio-visual support services

In recognition of the changing role and function of learning support, the first step towards integration amalgamated the management of the library, support for academic information technology, and audio-visual support. Although done primarily for reasons of cost-efficiency, the momentum of the learning and teaching debate soon indicated the potential benefits of the merged service developing a more proactive role in the support of learning and teaching. The college decided in 1992 to promote Learning Support Services to faculty status. This represented an important signal to staff within the service and those working elsewhere in the college, indicating that the developing role of the renamed Faculty of Information Services had the college management's full support. Information Services (IS) emerged as a change agent moving the emphasis from teaching as the primary activity of the institution, towards learning.

There are enormous implications of this changing role for all IS staff. Communication has been most important for understanding and airing individual fears and concerns and enabling a consensus to develop. Training and continuing development for all IS staff, has been viewed as the essential ingredient to the management of this process of change. Staff development was given high priority at an early stage, backed by significant investment, as explained elsewhere (Edwards *et al.*, 1993), and later. In addition, concerns of academic staff centred on the issue of disempowerment are acknowledged by IS. Communication, cooperation and the development of a partners in learning approach are seen as effective tools to overcome these concerns.

It is now the mission of IS to be proactive in learning and teaching developments, with increased responsiveness to customer needs assisted by further integration of services. As a result of the changing role of the faculty, the management structure was reorganised in 1994 into three sections: Learning Centres, Learning and Teaching Support, and Technical Services. Learning Centres provide an integrated focus for access to information, expertise, and technology supporting the independent learner. Developments in learning materials and their use are managed by Learning and Teaching Support to ensure a continually developing and improving service to its users. Technical Services underpin delivery and access ensuring systems are integrated, technologically stable and reliable. This new integrated structure places learning firmly at the centre of all faculty activities.

IS structure to support learning activities

Learning Centres

Library and computing resources were physically integrated in 1993 to establish learning centres for the combined delivery of traditional library and IT services to promote and encourage student-centred learning. Further development of the learning centre environment is planned which will encourage and facilitate more student-centred active learning. Information on the use of space and resources and student and lecturer opinions are being obtained and evaluated. Quality assurance procedures, course committees and customer perception surveys provide a steady stream of input to this evaluation process. The intention is for Learning Centres to provide a place where all students can work using a range of learning styles and resources, individually or in groups and independently at their own pace and level.

A Flexible Learning Area was created in 1994 to develop an accessible information rich learning environment for independent and flexible approaches to learning, with integrated support for the student at an operational level. Former Library and IT staff work here in close cooperation as Learning Centre professionals. Located within the main College Learning Centre, this area provides study spaces equipped with networked computers. The following resources are available:

- Networked CD-ROM
- Internet
- Remote databases online
- Print-based and computer-based flexible learning materials
- Flexible learning development collection
- Open Study Centre
- Language laboratory.

Flexible Learning Area staff have a range of skills in information and its associated technologies. Their developing role as facilitators is being supported by considerable investment in staff development. IS closes for one hour per week to provide training time for all IS staff to develop the necessary skills to respond to the changing information needs of lecturers and students. An additional investment equivalent to 2% of payroll supports further staff development activities.

To ensure an informed programme supporting continuing staff development, it has been decided to follow up the academic staff ATLA previously mentioned with an audit of the perceptions, skills and practices of Learning Centres staff. Informal discussions and observations suggest that a number of staff within the Learning Centres either see themselves as 'traditional' librarians or IT staff who require encouragement to adopt the new role as key promoters of active learning in partnership with academic staff colleagues. Many are keen to embrace this role but are uncertain about their 'new' relationship with academic staff. The audit aims to explore these issues more systematically and provide data on individual training needs. It is expected that the audit will also clarify practical implications for promoting active student learning.

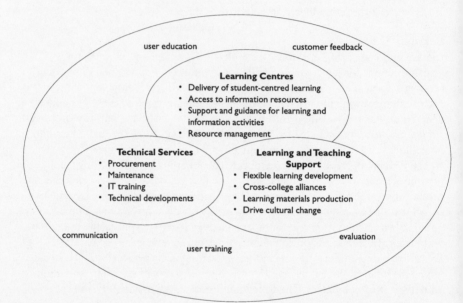

Figure 2 *IS structure to suppport learning activities*

Flexible Learning Design and Development Unit (FLDDU)

Joint college and Enterprise in Higher Education (EHE) funding enabled the establishment of this unit in 1994, with the role of coordinating and stimulating cross-college learning and teaching developments. The FLDDU provides central support for the development of learning materials, including project management, editorial advice, courseware design, material production and technical expertise. A budget is available to second academic staff to write learning materials. During the last year, 14 projects have been undertaken, the majority of which are now being piloted for student evaluation.

Further extension of these activities will include the evaluation and research phase, shown in Figure 3, for which resources have still to be made available.

The unit aims to disseminate good practice, publicise developments in multimedia and other learning materials and encourage innovative learning.

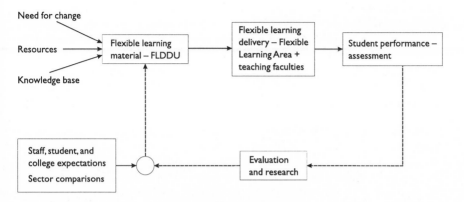

Figure 3 *The feedback loop*

A close and cooperative working relationship with staff in the Flexible Learning Area has proved essential to this proactive role, not only in ensuring appropriate support for learning delivery but also for the initiation and publicity of new developments. Of particular success has been the recent production of flexible learning materials designed especially to support independent student learning, covering research and information skills, study skills and bibliographic skills.

Tackling the real issues

In order to become a learning organisation as opposed to a teaching one, it is necessary to challenge the values and beliefs of students and staff within a framework that does not disrupt the stable nature of the organisation. Two powerful tools to be used to achieve this are strategic alliances with other institutional change agents and the college committee structure.

Strategic alliances

The close working relationship developed between Enterprise in Higher Education, the Professional Development Centre (PDC) and IS has been the most important enabling factor for learning developments at the college. These three units recognised that successful change is best achieved through cooperation. This cooperation has linked the resources of EHE, with the developmental role of the PDC and the implementation role of IS to produce successful results.

In 1990 the college was successful in obtaining £1 million of EHE funds over five years. This funding has played an important role in college-wide flexible learning developments. Initially EHE provided financial support for individual projects to develop learning and teaching materials, but this proved to have disappointing results and produced little in the way of widely applicable learning resources.

Cooperation between IS and EHE resulted in a successful bid for substantial funds to set up the FLDDU mentioned above. The EHE continuation strategy ensures that important activities it has initiated will be carried forward embodied within the college infrastructure. The college Professional Development Centre was established to address learning and teaching issues across the institution. IS and the PDC have cooperated widely to promote learning. There is now an established culture of cooperation which has encouraged the joint design and delivery of specially tailored staff development programmes and events and the joint delivery of courses.

Teaching, Learning and Assessment Committee (TLAC)

The college Teaching, Learning and Assessment Committee was formed in 1994 as a subcommittee of the Academic Board. The previously established FLDDU steering group was given a reporting function to the TLAC to embed it within the institution. The TLAC's role includes the promotion of college policy on teaching, learning and assessment, consideration of learning and teaching issues in general, the coordination of flexible and open learning initiatives, policy development, and dissemination of good practice both inside and outside the institution. The committee is also a forum for IS staff, academic staff and students to work together as partners. To assist dissemination and as part of its communications strategy, the Faculty of Information Services produces *Information News*, a newsletter which promotes learning and publicises information developments. IS is also participating in the production of the *Journal of Learning and Teaching* (*JoLT*). Other recent outcomes include cross-college discussion of assessment and the observation of teaching. A learning and teaching development programme for college staff, which can be linked to formal qualifications if desired, is planned.

Conclusion

The strategies adopted so far have primarily addressed the need for a supportive resource infrastructure to encourage changes in learning and teaching. There is now a firm foundation for the future. The material issues have been acknowledged and continue to be addressed. IS continues to develop an information-rich environment with easier electronic information access, increased workstation availability for independent study, and resources to support active learning. It is recognised that change is necessary in the way courses are delivered but that the only way forward is through the development of shared perspectives. The intention is actively to encourage debate through both formal and informal channels throughout the institution.

The clear institutional commitment to independent and flexible learning at the strategic level and the newly formed TLAC establishes a new phase of college-wide cooperation. The emphasis is now firmly focused on the more complex and difficult human resource issues, stressing the importance of a shared understanding of the need for change. Staff development and the collective action of internal change agents (IS, PDC and EHE) are seen as vital in the continued promotion of organisational and cultural change for the development of learning. The key elements of this development process are summarised in Figure 4.

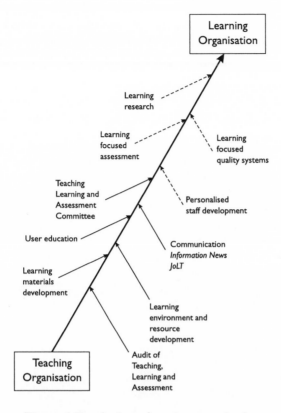

Figure 4 *Developing a learning organisation*

References

Biggs, J B and Moore , P J (1993) *The Process of Learning*, Prentice Hall, Hemel Hempstead.

Cheltenham & Gloucester College of Higher Education (1995) *Strategic Plan*, Faculty of Information Services, CGCHE.

Edwards, C *et al.* (1993) 'Key areas in the management of change in higher education libraries in the 1990s', *British Journal of Academic Librarianship*, **8**, 3.

Freeman, R and Thorne, M (1994) 'First steps towards the virtual university', International Symposium for Independent and Flexible Learning, University of Sunderland.

O'Connor, K Mason and Watson, L (1993) *Audit of Teaching, Learning and Assessment*, Cheltenham & Gloucester College of Higher Education.

Oates, L and Watson, L (1995) 'Providing the institutional infrastructure to support flexible learning', in G Wisker and S Brown (eds), *Enabling Student Learning*, Kogan Page, London.

Address for correspondence: **Lyn Oates**, Learning and Teaching Support Manager, Cheltenham and Gloucester CHE, PO Box 220, Park Campus, Cheltenham, GL50 2QF.

Workshop Report

17. Designing Flexible Learning Materials

Fiona Campbell and **Siân Bayne**, *Napier University*

SUMMARY

Are there any rules when it comes to the graphic design of flexible learning materials? How can the layout and 'feel' of materials be used to enhance student learning? What is the value of an institutional house-style?

In discussing the details of these design issues, participants in this workshop were able to articulate some of their ideas about what constitutes a good and effective design and what doesn't. By bringing these ideas together, the group was able to clarify some of the issues that need to be considered when designing a house-style for flexible learning materials.

The Napier house-style

In evolving our house-style we concentrated on clarity and legibility, in order to stimulate student interest and confidence and in this way to encourage understanding. We sought to create materials with a professional appearance, which could be clearly identified as a quality Napier product. In developing a simple and easy-to-use design which minimised visual noise and maximised space for interactive input, we aimed to create materials that looked professional and authoritative without appearing daunting or over-formal. To this end, we chose a 'classic', serif font (Times Roman) which could be used in a certain set number of emboldened point sizes for headings. For figures we decided to use a sanserif font (Arial) in a smaller point size. We decided to justify the text, which we found made it look more 'serious'. Any over-formality which this created was countered by leaving space for fairly large margins (3cm each side) to allow room for notes.

We chose to stress the Napier identity by using a reduced version of our triangle logo for bullet points and for signpost markers indicating activity panels. A clear break between the body of the text and an activity was created with a black line spanning the page, and ample space was left for students to fill in their answers to self-assessment questions and other interactive tasks.

The structure of the material was clarified by using a simple hierarchy of headings, as an alternative to paragraph numbering which we thought looked too formal. Figures and illustrations were kept as plain as possible – we found that the general simplicity of the layout meant that scruffy or over-elaborate figures stood out too much, making high-quality figure reproduction essential.

We decided always to use paper of good quality and reasonable weight, in order to avoid a budget feel. Our materials are heat- or ring-bound into booklets with a standard cover incorporating the Napier University logo. The cover can be over-printed to include the course or module title, and, if the materials have been sponsored or produced jointly, other logos can be included as required.

The workshop activity

In preparing for the workshop, we had taken a page from a flexible learning bridging course aimed at HND students (a level 1 module), and redesigned (and rewritten) it in three different ways. The participants divided into three groups, and each group was given one of these versions. Since straight comparison of the different designs seemed too easy, each group was asked to come up with as many arguments as possible in favour of the design and then to present their own version to the rest of the workshop, as though they were designers selling their ideas to a client. After each presentation, the other participants were given time to challenge their ideas and to develop them further.

Aspects of the design that participants looked out for included:

- the effects of the typeface(s) used;
- the effects of the alignment used (justified or unjustified, indented or aligned left);
- the effectiveness of the figure;
- the clarity of the structure;
- the use of space and 'visual noise';
- the use of upper- and lower-case letters;
- the tone and style of the writing (the tone in which the material is written informs the design of the page, and vice versa);
- its appropriateness for its target students.

Version 1

In presenting this design to the workshop, the members of the first group claimed that this version had a lively and friendly overall effect. It tempted students into the page, with its energetic use of different typefaces and its clear visual markers indicating the activity and clearly stressing an especially important point. The unjustified, sanserif text made the page seem approachable and informal, reflecting the liveliness of the writing – all of which added up to give an appropriately 'youthful' feel to the material, making it very suitable for its target students. The figure was clear and easy to understand quickly.

In response, the other participants were critical. They said that the page looked messy and annoyingly 'jolly', to the point of being patronising. The rounded typeface made the material look childish and, like the style of the writing, was inappropriate to the nature of the material being taught. It was also less easy for the eye to read than a 'quieter' typeface would have been. They did agree, however, that the figure as a graphic representation of some dry statistics was more effective and approachable than the tables used in the other versions.

Version 2

The group asked to promote this version had a hard time thinking up many points to recommend it! They did claim that the heavy marking of the task gave a helpful emphasis to the need for some serious student activity, while the structure of the material was clarified by the shaded area marking the beginning of a new section. The numbering of section, task, figure and paragraph made it easier to understand the structure. The figure and the boxed areas provided clear breaks in the text which, with its quiet, justified typeface made the page formal but open and easy to read.

Discussion of the defects of the design went on for far longer. It was suggested that it looked wordprocessed and messy. Because they were of the same weight, the shaded boxes marking the task and the section heading confused the structure of the material, rather than clarifying it. Similarly, attempting to number each section and paragraph caused further confusion, since the system quickly became illogical when combined with numbered tasks and figures. The figure was clumsy and hard to use, obscuring the important information with excessive boxing in and shading. While no one objected to the typeface, it was suggested that upper case letters were over-used, making it hard to read the text smoothly and easily.

Version 3

The group speaking for the final version of the page claimed (this time with some conviction) that this was a very clear and comprehensible layout. The separation of headings into the margin meant that the whole page was understood at a glance, while it also allowed room for students' own notes and input. The separation of the task and the beginning of the new section were gently stated to give the correct degree of emphasis, and did not compete for attention with the body of the text. The figure was reduced in a way that made it easy to read – it flowed with, and was part of, the text rather than a gratuitous attempt to illustrate the material merely as a break from heavy reading. The formality of the typeface and justification contributed to the impression that this was an authoritative and reliable piece of text.

The rest of the workshop agreed that this design was 'the best of a bad lot'. The main complaint was that it was over-formal, and too much like a textbook. Like version 2, it did not seem to make much attempt to function specifically as material for flexible learning – it was felt it might be a bit too dry and dull-looking for its target students.

Conclusions

The workshop highlighted some of the difficulties involved in designing flexible learning materials, rather than providing clear answers. It was felt that the layout of the page should be considered *during* the writing of the materials, so that the look and feel of the design was integral to the subject matter, rather than something which was tacked on afterwards. Having said this, the workshop acknowledged that the creation of a consistent house-style, which can be applied to all materials, gives an impression of professionalism and integrity while also helping to ensure consistency of quality.

The general conclusion drawn as to the design of materials was that simplicity and careful use of space, avoiding complicated structuring and overdone graphics, helps to create a clear and accessible look which should enhance student interest and confidence in the materials, and therefore also enhance learning.

Version 1

So you can see that we need a really effective competition policy within the EU to keep up (and hopefully increase) competition within the union. Do you remember that we talked about this kind of policy in Unit 9?

Oh no, not another

 Task
I'd like you to try your hand at a bit of research now! Go to your college library and try to find some examples of state aids and subsidies which have been used to give ailing national industries a boost over the years. What do you think the EU competition authorities thought about these goings on?

Here's a hint for you – try looking at some back copies of the *Financial Times* and the *Economist* as a good starting point.

Regional economic integration and 'international' companies.

So now we know that customs unions and common markets cause dynamic effects. They may even make member states restructure the ways in which they produce things. As we know (at least we should do...!) firms facing increased competition will do their best to cut their costs. They will have to if they want to survive in the market, won't they? At the same time, a much bigger market means that firms can take on really large scale production. And they can enjoy the economies of scale which come along with it. We already know (I hope!) that all this is likely to occur **within** national economies; but here's what's **new**.

 Restructuring also takes place **across** national frontiers between member states.

In this section we're going to look at this new idea. We'll even check out some examples from Europe. First of all though, have a quick look at this figure. It shows us where we can find the top 50 industrial companies in the world.

Figure 12.3 **The World's Top 50.** Source: Times 1000 (1995)

I have discussed the fact that the EU needs an effective [...]
is going to maintain (and even increase) the competition of fi[...]
this sort of policy in **UNIT 9.**

TASK 12.2
Try finding out some more information about subsidies yourself by using your college library to find examples of state aids used to prop up ailing national industries over the years. What has been the attitude of the EU competition authorities to this?

NOTE Back copies of the FINANCIAL TIMES and the ECONOMIST publications will give you a good starting point.

SECTION 12.4 REGIONAL ECONOMIC INTEGRATION AND 'INTERNATIONAL' COMPANIES.

12.4.1 As I pointed out in the sections above, Customs Unions and Common Markets generate dynamic effects. They may cause restructuring of production in member states. I also discussed the fact that firms faced with increased competition will aim to cut their costs in order to survive in the market. At the same time, the enlarged market created by integration allows large scale production to take place, and firms can benefit from economies of scale. I have already pointed out that these effects are likely to occur WITHIN national economies – I would also like to look at the possibility that restructuring also takes place ACROSS national frontiers between member states. In **SECTION 12.4** I will highlight such possibilities, drawing on examples from the European Union.

In **FIGURE 12.3** below I show the location of the top 50 industrial companies in the World, according to their sales turnover data.

GEOGRAPHICAL AREA	NUMBER OF COMPANIES
JAPAN	19
USA	16
EU	14
EFTA	1
TOTAL	50

FIGURE 12.3 The World's top 50 industrial countries: Geographical Distribution (based on Sales Turnover) Source: TIMES 1000 publications (1995)

Version 2

Version 3

This point highlights the need for an effective competition policy within the EU in order to maintain (and increase) the competitive process within the union. Competition policy was discussed in unit 9.

Task

Use the college library to find examples of state aids and subsidies which have been used to support failing national industries over the years. What has been the attitude of the EU competition authorities in such instances?

note

back copies of *The Financial Times* and *The Economist* will provide a good starting point.

Regional economic egration and nternational' countries

Previous sections have described the way in which customs unions (CUs) and common markets (CMs) generate dynamic effects, possibly causing restructuring of production in member states. Firms faced with increased competition will aim to cut their costs in order to survive. At the same time, the enlarged market allows large-scale production with its inherent economies of scale. As already discussed, these effects are likely within national economies, but the possibility also arises that restructuring may take place   *across* national frontiers, between member states. This section highlights such possibilities, drawing on examples from within the European context.

Figure 12.3 shows the spatial location of the top 50 industrial companies in the world, defined as such by their sales turnover data.

geographical area	number of companies
Japan	19
United States	16
European Union	14
European free trade association	1
total	50

figure 12.3 The world's top 50 indust
source *Times 1000* (1995)

The Napier House-Style

Human Resource Management | Unit 7

 Activity

Go back to your previous list of performance indicators and reorganise the list in light of the following three questions.

 What are the most important measures?
 How do these measures relate to one another?
 What measures truly predict l ong-term financial or other success in your business?

The last exercise may have helped you focus upon aspects of your performance measures which you had not previously considered. It is important that all measures should be challenged in order that the organisation is aware of the potential for change, especially change for the better.

Activity

With regard to performance measures, do you or does your organisation undertake any or all of the following?

Do you agree objectives with your boss?	Yes	No
Do you agree objectives with your subordinates?	Yes	No
Are your objectives quality-based?	Yes	No
Are your objectives time-based?	Yes	No
Are your objectives output-based?	Yes	No
Do you have training/learning targets?	Yes	No
Do you use work group targets?	Yes	No

According to a national survey (IPM (1992), *Performance Analysis in the UK: an analysis of the issues*, Institute of Personnel Management, London), the above type of targets are being used in more performance measurement schemes. According to the findings of the survey, a performance measurement system is in place when the following conditions are met by an organisation.

7

18. Designing Open Learning for Occupational Competence

Joyce Walmsley, *Employment Department, Sheffield*

SUMMARY

The basis of National Vocational Qualifications (NVQs) and Scottish Vocational Qualifications (SVQs) is occupational competence. Love them or loath them, S/NVQs are here to stay. We need therefore to consider how best to deliver them for people who aspire to them. That means examining how we enable the learners to achieve competence. This chapter looks first at the definition of 'competence' and at what that implies for the learning we must design in order to help its achievement. It then looks at open and flexible learning (OFL) and what it has to offer for competence-oriented learners. Finally, it looks at work, sponsored by ED in the last few years, on learning design to help the development of competence. There is no recipe for open learning designed for competence. There are in fact a lot of questions and challenges for OFL designers and developers if they are to get the best from OFL, and realise its potential for developing competence in the widest sense.

What is meant by competence?

'Competence' can be simply defined as 'the ability to perform work activities to the standards required in employment'. A more meaningful definition in today's workplace is:

> '...a wide concept which embodies the ability to transfer skills and knowledge to new situations within the occupational area. It encompasses organisation and planning of work, innovation and coping with non-routine activities, It includes those qualities of personal effectiveness that are required in the workplace to deal with co-workers, managers and customers.' (Department for Education and Employment, DfEE, 1991)

The latter is a much more complete description of the DfEE's and NCVQ's vision of competence and is the one on which my argument is built. The Job Competence model developed by Mansfield (1991) identifies four aspects of competence:

1. Task or technical skills.
2. Task management skills (ie, the planning, decision making, prioritisation, etc, which go into managing a job).
3. Contingency management skills (ie, the management of the unexpected, dealing with breakdown or events beyond the scope of routine instructions, etc).
4. Role and environment skills (ie, understanding, working within and using the physical, organisational and cultural environment of the job).

Implicit within the contingency management and role and environment skills are those abilities to analyse, understand and assess situations and available options and to act upon that analysis, taking responsibility for one's own actions, often referred to as personal autonomy. Also included in this area are the skills of personal effectiveness. The definitions used by NCVQ and awarding bodies in assigning a level to an NVQ are briefly:

- *Level 1*: competence in a range of varied but largely routine work activities.
- *Level 2*: competence in a significant range of varied activities, including complex and non-routine ones, carried out in a variety of contexts. A degree of individual responsibility or autonomy; also a need for collaboration and/or group and team working.
- *Level 3*: a wide range of varied activities, most of which are complex and non-routine, carried out in a wide range of contexts. Considerable responsibility and autonomy and (frequently) a requirement for control/guidance of others.
- *Level 4*: complex, technical or professional work activities; a wide variety of contexts; considerable personal responsibility and autonomy. Frequently, responsibility for the work of others; allocation of resources.
- *Level 5*: the application of a significant range of fundamental principles and complex techniques across a wide and often unpredictable range of contexts. Substantial personal autonomy and accountability; significant responsibility for the work of others; allocation of resources.

There is more scope for personal autonomy at levels 3, 4 and 5, where the standards become broader in their approach, allowing for the greater conceptual content of work and for the greater discretion allowed to workers in supervisory, management and professional grades. This makes it more imperative at these levels that learning is designed to help learners achieve the breadth of competence, including personal effectiveness and autonomy, which the standards require.

Open learning for competence

Successful implementation of competence-based learning and assessment demands flexible approaches to delivery of education and training. Jessop (1991), among others, envisages learners on individualised learning programmes, and the recently introduced Modern Apprenticeship, which has as its centrepiece a level 3 NVQ, calls specifically for the learners to have individual learning plans. Over recent years many colleges have taken steps to make their provision more flexible and for most this has meant the use of some form of 'open learning'.

What is open learning?

Definitions of open learning have two foci: extended and developed access to learning by the removal of barriers; and the philosophy of learner-centred provision in which learner choice is key and which extends beyond access issues to the way learning is approached once access has been gained. The following definition, synthesised from a number of publications, attempts to include both. An open learning system is one which:

- tries to remove or reduce barriers to access for the learners by offering choice in when, where, and how quickly the learner can learn; and
- tailors the provision as far as possible to the needs of the individual learner by offering negotiated programmes and support options that seek to balance the learners' needs and preferences with what is reasonable and possible for the providers/sponsors to offer.

Balancing of needs and preferences with the reasonable and possible represents an acknowledgement of both the resource constraints and the fact that some learners may have inconsistent needs and preferences, which cannot all be met within the same learning experience. As in most systems, the ideal is modified to a working compromise.

Openness and competence-based systems

It should not be assumed that current open learning materials and systems will adapt to competence-based learning without further development. The main areas where open learning systems need to adjust to competence-based goals are highlighted by considering Lewis's (1986) table of eight 'dimensions of openness'. It should be remembered that no currently available system would score as 'fully open' in all respects, and indeed most OFL provision would score differently at different times and in relation to different learners' needs.

The impact of competence-based systems on Lewis's table appears to be as follows.

Why learn

The reasons which motivate people to learn are not, certainly in the short term, likely to be affected by the competence movement. People will still be driven by a need for qualifications, a desire to prove themselves, a love of knowledge or an urge to keep up with their peers. The greater flexibility offered by S/NVQs may, however, encourage more people to return to learning.

What to learn

For S/NVQ candidates, the required outcome of learning is given in considerable detail and *all* performance criteria must be satisfied. There is the option of unit accreditation for those who wish to concentrate on specific areas rather than a whole S/NVQ, while ideally those who undertake successful accreditation of prior learning (APL) should be able to start their learning at a point appropriate to their needs. The standards, however, are not a syllabus. They are arranged in functional groups and often do not represent the order in which a job might be done, let alone learned. It is for learning providers to establish, with the learner, what needs to be taught in order to achieve the required outcome and how the content should be structured and presented.

How to learn

Methodologies will be influenced by the availability of APL, by the requirement for workplace assessment and by the need to integrate contingency management and role/environment skills into the learning. The need to address the new objective of competence will in many cases change, but not necessarily narrow, the choice of approach available and appropriate to the learner. The good teaching/learning practice that has developed over the years has not suddenly become irrelevant. It needs to be applied and extended to include the new objectives.

Where to learn

The requirement for workplace assessment tends to suggest that in some cases more of the learning will be done in the workplace. For some this will be an added option. For others, especially those whose employers are not supportive, it may present difficulties and reduce openness. OFL providers will need to consider how best to utilise workplace support and how alternatives may be provided for those who have no, or limited, access to workplace practice.

When to learn

Study times will remain a matter for negotiation between learners and providers, employers, sponsors, etc. However, the insistance on workplace assessment means that often this at least will now be done in working time and may in turn help some learners to gain more support from their employers and line managers for relevant learning in working hours.

How learning will be assessed

S/NVQ assessment is described in the (then) Training Agency's Guidance Note 5 as: 'a process of collecting evidence about [the candidates'] capabilities, and judging whether it is sufficient to attribute competence.'

Methods of assessment for competence are prescribed by the awarding bodies, often as 'observation' supplemented by relevant questioning and workplace simulations. Many of the issues surrounding assessment concern control. Mitchell and Stourton (1993) identify 11 stages in the assessment process at which the candidate makes a contribution. They show clearly that the benefits to candidates from the fullest possible participation at each stage of the process are considerable, including the development of autonomy, reflectiveness and self-assessment skills. They also point out some pitfalls and areas where further research is needed on how *best* to involve candidates. In field research they found considerable support from tutors for the involvement of candidates in all stages except summative assessment. Providers of open learning systems must consider how to empower candidates to participate in the assessment process to the best of their ability.

Who can help

The introduction of competence-based goals and systems does not lessen the potential pool of supporters available to learners. Indeed, it may widen it if workplace assessment draws line managers more effectively into the learning process. Providers of open learning systems must consider how workplace support might be provided, to what extent it can realistically be relied upon and what support workplace contributors may themselves need.

Open learning for competence

The main components of an open learning system are its materials, media used, and the support that it offers learners by human and/or by technological means. The division into materials and support commonly seen will be used here, but it is to some extent misleading since the two elements must be integrated and used appropriately together. The quality of both is important to student success.

OFL relating to S/NVQs is beginning to appear in some quantity, often prefaced by the words 'this pack will give you the underpinning knowledge required for assessment against the — standards'.

I have two problems with this statement. First, certainly OFL can be a good vehicle for providing knowledge, and certainly there are some occupational areas where the underpinning knowledge is so substantial that whole OFL packs could well be devoted to it. But the provider does the learner a disservice if no attempt is made to link that knowledge to practice – and there is no indication in the words used that such an attempt is being made, although perhaps the publishers are underselling their product.

Second, I believe that the statement underrates considerably what OFL has to offer to learners, especially at the higher levels of competence where breadth is most important.

What does OFL have to offer, over and above the delivery of knowledge? In order to help learners become competent as well as knowledgeable, open learning materials and systems have to integrate subject knowledge with the learning of task skills, role skills and contingency management skills and ensure the transfer of the whole from theory into practice. This raises a number of issues.

Encouraging active learning and autonomy

Jessop (1991) notes that the whole model for S/NVQ acquisition encourages and calls for individualised and autonomous learning, although he discusses this at the surface level of access rather than at the level intended by Boud (1981) and Elton (1991) in their work on autonomy in learning. Boud says that autonomy: 'implies responsiveness... creative and unique response to situations as they arise rather than patterned and stereotyped responses from one's past.'

Elton refers to the ability to select appropriate learning modes, either alone or in consultation with others. Approaches designed to improve learning autonomy should help learners to acquired the kind of personal autonomy that the competence model requires. The same approaches can help learners extend their autonomy to other situations. OFL uses many techniques to foster autonomy.

Use of projects and portfolios

One important approach to individualising activities and assignments is the project. Morgan (1987) identifies two types of project: those which directly utilise the skills learned and those which use interdisciplinary approaches such as problem solving.

Also, the project may provide the candidate with evidence for assessment, either because the activity itself can be observed and assessed or by including the work in a portfolio.

Portfolio building, especially where it is an acceptable form of evidence gathering for assessment purposes, offers many opportunities for the learning designer. Mitchell and Stourton (1993) demonstrate that it can involve the candidate in self-assessment, planning, gathering, summarising and collating, and writing activities, most of which will contribute to the development of role skills and autonomy as well as to the learning of subject matter. Care must be taken, however, to ensure that the demands made are not disproportionate to the candidate's level.

Reflection

Activities need to be followed up with encouragement to reflect on both the process and the outcome of the exercise. The use of reflective techniques serves two purposes. It enables the learner and tutor to consider the role or 'people skills' involved in the activity, which may affect the process rather than the eventual outcome and which may be overlooked if feedback is limited to whether or not the outcome conforms to a specific model. In addition, Mooney (1993) points out that reflective methods can be shown to promote the deep and holistic learning approaches desirable for the development of real understanding and therefore of autonomy and contingency management skills.

Role of support

OFL providers have already accepted the change in their role from instructor to facilitator and guide. One of the main differences in using the workplace as a learning resource is that support must come to a far greater extent from workplace personnel. OFL needs to harness the help of peers, supervisors and others whenever possible. We need to ensure that workplace supporters are themselves properly supported by the materials and by preparatory briefing and training.

Self-assessment

Self-assessment skills are an important element in autonomous learning and are essential for the learner participation in S/NVQ assessment discussed by Mitchell and Stourton (1993). OFL has long used self-assessment questions as a means of helping learners to measure their own progress. This approach should be extended to help the learner develop the autonomy required for competence at higher levels and to prepare the learner for the assessment regime used in S/NVQ assessment.

Recent developments

The third element in this chapter is the work recently done on designing learning to encourage competence development. People become competent by doing, by putting into practice what they have read or been told or seen demonstrated, etc. Learning designers can build in features that will help the learner to make the switch from theory to practical application, and we can help people to learn how to solve problems, to deal with those contingencies. Mitchell and Stourton's report on the candidate's role in assessment includes some very useful thoughts on encouraging learner autonomy.

Other reports of value include *Teaching Thinking Skills in Vocational Education* (1993), prepared by Rebecca Soden, and *Development of Transferable Skills in Learners* (1993), by Nigel Blagg Associates. Both projects were conducted in the context of 'conventional', ie classroom-based learning. Neither makes reference to OFL and it will be up to developers to translate the findings into the OFL context.

The main message of the first is 'make the implicit explicit'. Most people learn more easily if we help them to understand the thought processes used for solving problems; most never analyse the process they go through to arrive at an answer. The report demonstrates that such understanding takes practice and OFL designers will need to apply some of the techniques themselves in order to develop them for OFL use.

The second report looks at how to encourage the transfer of learning from theory to practice. It points out that there are two sets of skills involved:

- transferable skills such as maths and communication which the learner acquires in the classroom and which then need to be transferred to working situations;
- transfer skills which will help them to do this.

Transfer is also divided into 'near' and 'far' transfer. Near transfer is where there is little difference between the learning situation and the transfer situation. Far transfer is where there is greater dissimilarity, either in the activities to be done using the learned skills or in the context in which they are done, or both.

Near transfer can be facilitated by using similarity (role-play, simulation, etc). Far transfer has more often been left to chance but again the technique is to make the implicit explicit, such as teaching learners to be aware of their problem-solving processes. The report recommends using whole complex tasks for learning; tasks with more than one answer and more than one level of understanding and application. It also recommends the process of 'cognitive apprenticeship'. This includes modelling the problem-solving process by demonstration and discussion, supporting the learner with coaching and expert advice which is then slowly withdrawn as the learner becomes more competent and confident. This encourages learners to describe and reflect on their thinking and conclusions, as well as explore similar and dissimilar problems and the strategies they can develop for themselves to deal with them.

Again all this was explored in the context of conventional learning. How are we going to build it into OFL? That is the challenge, but I believe that much of it can be adapted for OFL presentation. And when it is, OFL will be able to go much further towards helping learners to become competent, rather than simply supplying 'underpinning knowledge'.

Bibliography

Nigel Blagg Associates (1993) *Development of Transferable Skills in Learners*, DfEE, London.

Boud, D (1981) 'Towards student responsibility for learning', in D Boud (ed.),

Developing Student Autonomy in Learning, Kogan Page, London.

Elton, L (1991) 'Conditions for learner autonomy', in P Raggett and L Unwin (eds), *Change and Intervention: Vocational Education and Training*, Falmer Press and the OU, London.

Department of Education and Employment (1991) *Development of Assessable Standards for National Certification*, E Fennell (ed.), HMSO, London.

Jessop, G (1991) *Outcomes: NVQs and the Emerging Model of Education and Training*, Falmer Press, London.

Lewis, R (1986) 'What is Open Learning?' *Open Learning*, **1**, 2.

Mansfield, R (1991) 'Deriving standards of competence', in E Fennel (ed.), *Development of Assessable Standards for National Certification*, DfEE, London.

Mitchell, L and Stourton J (1993) *The Candidate's Role Project – Final Report*, DfEE, London.

Mooney, N (1993) 'Outcomes and Autonomy', Abstract collected at a conference in April 1993. No publication data given in the abstract.

Morgan , A (1987) 'Project work in open learning', in M Thorpe and D Grugeon (eds), *Open Learning for Adults*, Longman Open Learning, Harlow.

Rowntree, D (1992) *Exploring Open and Distance Learning*, Kogan Page, London.

Soden, R (1993) *Teaching Thinking Skills in Vocational Education*, DfEE, London.

Thorpe, M (1987) 'Student assignments', in M Thorpe and D Grugeon (eds), *Open Learning for Adults*, Longman Open Learning, Harlow.

Wolfe, A (1989) 'Can competence and knowledge mix?', in J W Burke (ed.), *Competency Based Education and Training*, Falmer Press, London.

Address for correspondence: **Joyce Walmsley**, Employment Department, Room W645, Moorfoot, Sheffield S1 4PQ.

19. Open Learning in Support of Vocational Training and Economic Regeneration

Susan Clayton, *Open University*

Vocational training is often the poor relation of academic education. The needs of urban dwellers may take precedence over those of people living in sparse rural areas, particularly where it is more expensive to provide courses for the latter. Educational organisations may find it more financially secure to focus on the needs of students for whom substantial government grants are available rather than on students who have to pay their own fees. State-funded and privately funded educational organisations sometimes have false images of one another, hindering the development of high quality collaborative ventures.

The South West Region of the Open University recognised these difficulties and has sought to develop an innovative, flexible project aimed at tackling some of the problems and prejudices outlined above. It also seeks not only to train individual students but to promote economic regeneration in the far South West of England.

The starting point of the scheme was a recognition by the Open University that it had a large number of free-standing 'study packs' on sale or for use by other education providers. These study packs typically comprise printed correspondence units plus supporting video and audio cassettes. They are sent to students through the post but, unlike normal Open University courses, no tuition or assessment is provided.

While these study packs provide valuable training, the Open University has difficulty making potential users aware of the educational opportunities that they offer. Until relatively recently little effort was placed by the university's regional office for the South West of England on the sale of these study packs. No regional infrastructure existed to promote the full range of study pack materials.[1] It is not a particularly cost-effective use of time to promote study packs and many staff find it more rewarding to focus on supporting people who undertake substantial programmes of study with associated tuition, counselling and assessment. It was, however, recognised that this lack of promotion of distance learning vocational study packs was disadvantageous to the people who could have benefited from the materials. It particularly disadvantaged those who were unable to access the alternative of face-to-face tuition provided by conventional public and private educational organisations.[2]

It is well documented that there is an urgent need to enhance provision of vocational training in Cornwall and the rural parts of Devon and West Somerset (Government Office of the South West, 1994a and 1994b). These areas have below average GDPs per head, higher than average unemployment and some of the UK's worst unemployment blackspots. Earnings and levels of vocational qualifications are well below the national average. Women are under-represented in full-time and senior positions. Many key industries are in decline or in need of restructuring. Many people experience difficulty obtaining vocational training as a consequence of the nature of employment in the area of rurality. Sparse populations make local training expensive to provide while low incomes and the poor transport infrastructure act as a barrier to access. Conventional training courses may be difficult for seasonal, part-time or shift workers to attend, while prospective adult trainees may lack confidence in their study skills or be put off by courses geared to the needs of young people.

It was also recognised that there are many people who want to improve their job-related skills and knowledge but only wish to take a relatively short course. Others do not have the time or desire to undertake assessed work. Some people want to use distance learning materials and others need to study at home as a consequence of travel difficulties, unsocial hours of employment, family responsibilities or disability.

It was felt that many of these problems could be overcome if a new way of providing quality supported distance education to people in sparsely populated rural areas could be developed. This would enable people to study short courses at a time, and in a location, that is convenient to them. It was also felt desirable to forge close links between vocational training and the students' employment circumstances.

A problem for the Open University is that it does not have the resources necessary to promote each study pack that is available to all potential users, including those working in small businesses or living in sparse rural areas. Moreover, some study packs focus on skills and knowledge of relevance to a wide range of employment situations and do not attempt to provide detailed guidance on the application of the knowledge to a specific occupational setting.[3] While this type of education is very valuable, the learning experience can often be enhanced if personal tuition is provided and assistance given with the task of linking theoretical learning to the trainee's own work situation.

The Open University recently identified a new approach to the provision and support of open learning vocational training and was most fortunate to obtain support for the idea from Devon County Council, Devon and Cornwall Training and Enterprise Council, The Rural Development Commission, Somerset County Council, The West County Development Corporation and the West Country Tourist Board. This group of organisations, the 'strategic partners', raised £125,350 to develop the scheme and also put a bid for additional resource to the government's Single Regeneration Budget programme. The partners received a grant of £232,000 from this source to support the scheme between April 1995 and March 1998. It is hoped that European Union and private money will also be obtained. While these grants are essential to develop the scheme, it is hoped that it will continue without such support when the external funding runs out in 1998.

The strategic partners are now developing the details of the scheme, drawing on their knowledge of vocational training and the needs of the local economy. The approach adopted will make extensive use of existing Open University printed vocational training materials and their associated video and audio cassettes.

Trainees will be sent these through the post and encouraged to study them at times and in places which are convenient to them.

Trainees will be supported in their learning by a new group of 'operational partners' who will be involved in the provision of workshops aimed at facilitating learning. The workshops will offer face-to-face tuition and guidance. However, where it is difficult for trainees to reach workshops the alternative of telephone tuition will be offered. The operational partners will also help trainees to see the relevance of their study to their own, or intended, field of employment and help them to link into existing employment-related networks and support services.

The 'operational partners' have yet to be identified but is likely they will include a number of private training agencies, community organisations and professional bodies, as well as other educational organisations and the Workers Education Association. The 'strategic' and 'operational' partners will also help to publicise the training opportunities to their members and contacts, reaching communities and employers who are traditionally difficult and expensive to inform of local vocational training opportunities.

One of the strengths of the Open University working in partnership with local operational partners is that trainees will get access to high quality distance learning materials together with assistance in making the course content relevant to their own work situation and the needs of their geographic locality.

The trainees will be encouraged to put themselves forward for vocational qualifications. It is, however, recognised that NVQs do not exist for all the work-based competencies required in the locality. Furthermore, many adults in employment wish to update their knowledge and skills but do not want to obtain a formal vocational qualification.

Trainees will also be helped to link into relevant local and national networks and to develop their own informal support groups. A sample of the trainees will be given access to a networked computer and the Internet, thus helping them to liaise not only with their tutor and the other students on the courses, but also all free networks and databases around the world.

The topics to be studied by the trainees have primarily been selected to meet the needs of the locality as defined in development plans prepared for the European Union by the Government Office for the South West (1994a, 1994b). These include the development and growth of small and medium-sized enterprises, information technology, scientific and technological updating, training for the provision of caring services, environmental conservation and management, community and human resources development, study and career progression skills.

The scheme will be carefully evaluated, including in terms of enhancing the development of the project, ensuring its objectives are met and helping to extend the lessons learnt from the project to other parts of the country and Europe. Statistical analysis, postal questionnaires and qualitative interviews with trainees, employers, project partners and other key stakeholders will take place. The evaluation will be both formative and summative. The formative evaluation will primarily seek to analyse the scheme's implementation and recommend how its modes of operation might be enhanced. The summative evaluation will assess the overall impact of the scheme and the way it has met trainees' and project sponsors' objectives. If the scheme is successful in developing new ways of providing quality open learning in support of vocational training and economic regeneration then good practice guides will be written aimed at helping other vocational training providers to replicate the scheme or develop further flexible approaches to vocational training.

Notes

1. The Open University does, however, have a section at its headquarters in Milton Keynes, dedicated to promoting the sale of the university's study packs and some regional staff promote certain of these materials.
2. There have been some collaborative projects with further education colleges, the Workers Education Association, etc, but these have primarily focused on access to undergraduate programmes, not access to training which is very directly vocational in nature.
3. It should be stressed that there are some study packs which provide vocational training of direct relevance to a specific field of employment.

References

Government Office of the South West (1994a) Single Programming Document, South West Region, Objective 5(b) Programme Cornwall & the Isles of Scilly; Devon and Somerset, 1994–1999.
Government Office of the South West (1994b) Single Programming Document, Plymouth Objective 2 Area 1994–1996.

Susan Clayton is Director of the UK Open University's South West Region with responsibility for the support of over 11,000 students. Susan taught secretarial skills before taking a degree with the Open University and a Masters degree at Durham University. This led to a lectureship in Social Policy at Lancaster University and to becoming Head of the Corporate Policy Unit of a London local authority. In 1991 she joined the Open University as a Regional Director. Throughout this time she has been involved with the voluntary sector, carrying out social policy research and writing academic articles.

Address for correspondence: **Susan Clayton**, Regional Director (South West), Open University, Portwall Lane, Bristol BS1 6ND.

20. The Mixed Mode University

Dr Stephen J Fallows and Professor Kate Robinson, *University of Luton*

SUMMARY

UK higher education has traditionally followed a rigid course delivery system in which the student attends classroom-based teaching activities held at predetermined times and places on campus. The exception to this rule has been the Open University, which relies on flexible learning to reach students who are geographically dispersed and who learn at times and locations convenient to themselves.

Numerous universities offer both campus-based courses and distance teaching, thereby creating 'dual mode' institutions with little overlap between the two modes of delivery and little chance of flexible exchange of students between these.

A fourth approach is the 'mixed mode' university in which materials and methods developed for distance teaching are also utilised for on-campus students. The mixed mode commonly applies as dual mode universities seek to maximise benefits from their own distance learning materials. A second mixed mode model applies when a conventional university adopts a flexible approach incorporating materials prepared elsewhere (for distance use) within its on-campus programmes. This chapter focuses on the special issues in this second mixed mode and examines these in the context of the experience gained within the University of Luton.

The University of Luton has used open and other flexible learning approaches in a low-key manner since the early 1980s. A significant expansion in student numbers during the 1990s has led to a re-evaluation of teaching and learning strategies to focus on student-centred approaches. The university recognises the shift in the nature of university students away from 18-year-old school leavers to mature individuals with family and, often, work commitments.

The justifications for this strategy include: a need to maximise return on staff resources (especially in shortage areas); a need to broaden the available expertise; a need to use limited space most efficiently; a desire to enhance access to higher education for those who may be limited by their social, physical or employment circumstances; and an opportunity to extend the effective geographical catchment area.

One strategy adopted is to use 'off-the-shelf' flexible learning materials. The materials are a major and essential part of the teaching process, being interspersed within and beside conventional teaching. While 'off-the-shelf' learning materials have been adopted, they have been subjected to the university's validation and quality assurance procedures. Furthermore, the materials have a much greater level of face-to-face support than could be offered by a distance teaching institution.

Introduction

Mainstream higher education has a traditional focus on campus-based activities. The traditional university has provided an education for its students through a mixture of lectures, seminars, practical classes and tutorials, each of which has involved the use of the timetabled resources and people. In general the student has had little or no flexibility in times of attendance. The system is predominantly an institutionally managed and lecturer-focused model.

The principal alternative is the distance-teaching university (DTU), in which the curriculum is delivered through a variety of media to students who are remote from the institution and who generally have considerable personal flexibility in their times of study. The distance teaching universities, typified in the UK by the Open University, are facilitators of learning (rather than deliverers of teaching), chiefly targeted at adult learners.

The DTUs rely for their success on quality learning materials which are utilised by mature individuals with considerable drive, determination and good study skills. The quality of the learning materials is ensured by the establishment of production teams who are able to draw on a wide range of pedagogic skills as well as subject knowledge. Curriculum content is, to some extent, limited by the need for materials to have a 'fixed' content that will have utility over a number of years; by contrast the lecturer presenting the curriculum face-to-face may update materials constantly to keep abreast of developments within the discipline.

Similarly, curriculum may be limited to topics of 'national' importance and the opportunities to include courses which focus on 'local' examples (particularly relevant in subjects such as history, geography, etc) are minimal. Many DTUs therefore offer flexibility of study time and place but may be less flexible in terms of curriculum content than the conventional university.

The production of distance teaching materials is expensive and can only be sustained by the combination of longevity and relative generics referred to above. Investment in production of materials is also countered by the avoidance of many of the usual infrastructure costs associated with a campus-based university.

The third model of university education is the dual mode model in which a single institution offers both conventional campus-based courses and distance teaching. In most instances these two approaches are separately delivered with minimal synergy between them. In general, the dual mode university carries forward the flexibility limitations of each of its constituent approaches:

- The distance mode is flexible in time and space but may have limitations on curriculum content.
- The campus mode can be flexible in curriculum content but is restricted by timetabling and the demands of face-to-face delivery.

A fourth approach is to be found in the mixed mode university. This model is characterised by the use of materials originally prepared for distance learning with otherwise mainstream (campus-based) students. Most mixed mode institutions have previously operated in the dual mode; in these instances the shift is one of consolidation rather than innovation. Priorities are being re-evaluated in the context of increased student numbers, demands for ever higher quality and externally imposed financial constraints.

An alternative approach to the creation of the mixed mode university applies where an institution which previously concentrated on conventional face-to-face on-campus activities adopts materials prepared elsewhere (for open or distance learning). This model of the mixed mode university has been adopted by the University of Luton and this chapter discusses the mixed mode concept by drawing upon the experiences gained.

Open learning pedagogy

The key pedagogical difference between open learning and traditionally taught courses is the use of interactive materials (which may be low-technology or high-technology using the latest computing systems) as the primary teaching and learning resource. The lecturer supports the students' use of these interactive materials and complements the learning process through tutorials and other activities. Open learning is characterised by the student's learning becoming an independent activity rather than a class activity.

Open learning cannot be considered a cheap option since the production of learning materials requires considerable investment at all stages of development. Inhouse production can only be justified where groups are large and the expected curriculum content is unlikely to change for several years. Commitment of the necessary investment will be limited to a few institutions and there can be little or no justification for duplication of courses that cover the essentially generic areas of study, which are perhaps the most cost-effective for use of the open-learning methodology.

It is a recognition of the need to pool resources that has provided one justification for funding of the Teaching and Learning Technologies Programme (TLTP) to develop computer-based open learning materials for use across the higher education sector.

A mixed mode university

The University of Luton (previously Luton College of Higher Education) has utilised open learning as part of its academic provision since the early 1980s. Initially the approach was dual mode and small scale with a unit given the responsibility for the production of open learning materials. The unit was intended to work with colleagues from a variety of disciplines in order to extend the delivery of courses to those outside the institution. The unit was minimally resourced and was not embedded within the academic disciplines it was intended to support. The impact on the academic provision at the time was minimal and the initiative faded away as the college rapidly expanded its mainstream higher education provision. For some years open learning was a marginal activity with interest only maintained within a few professional courses, particularly those offered by the Faculty of Management.

A re-evaluation of the benefits of open learning came in the early 1990s as the college progressed towards its transition into a university. At this time, expansion in student numbers was phenomenal and a rethink about teaching and learning strategies essential. Open learning was judged to offer a range of benefits to the institution, its staff and the student population, as follows.

- As an institution relatively new to higher education, the emerging university had limited staff resources compared to other institutions. Absolute numbers were less and, furthermore, the range of expertise was limited. Open learning was seen as a method by which the benefits derived from existing staff could be maximised while also offering the opportunity to draw upon the wider educational resource. These interrelated factors are of key importance while the university is developing its staff resource through both recruitment and staff development.

- A second major resource which was limiting within the emerging university was space for teaching and learning. This was particularly the case with respect to lecture theatres. The use of open learning provides a valuable shift in the space requirements away from expensive teaching space (lecturing in particular) to the relatively cheaper areas needed for self-directed study. Furthermore, for many students the adoption of open learning moved the principal learning activity off the university's premises and into their own homes. Flexibility in personal timing of learning was thereby maximised.

- The increased flexibility was also considered to offer new opportunity to certain classes of actual or potential students. The ability to study at a time, place and pace to suit personal circumstances and requirements can widen the option to participate. This is particularly the case for those students whose family circumstances impose heavy demands and for those with disabilities that limit attendance. Increases in flexibility can make a substantial contribution to improving educational opportunities. The practical benefits of the flexibility associated with being able to choose where and when to study are of key importance to many.

- The university seeks to incorporate diversity in its range of teaching and learning methods, with the aim of preparing students for life after graduation; a link to vocational training techniques is judged to be desirable as students move towards a lifetime of education and periodic retraining. Open learning is increasingly utilised in staff training and its use within the curriculum provides students with the opportunity to gain competence in the use of this methodology.

- Open learning can be used to extend the catchment of potential students in respect of both their geographic location (often an occasional visit to the university is feasible while day-to-day attendance is problematic), and available time (the university's portfolio of courses includes several which relate to the in-service and developmental needs of specific professions – practitioners within these professions may require the avoidance of time constraints that open learning offers). Again open learning is seen as a means to enhance the flexibility.

The justifications listed above are principally concerned with managerial aspects rather than pedagogy. They mostly seek to maximise the returns from the investment of resources by the institution, its staff and the students. However, although managerial concerns are of major importance, it is recognised that an extra and powerful teaching and learning methodology is on offer.

The approach adopted by the University of Luton has been to utilise off-the-shelf open learning resource materials purchased from other institutions. The principal supplier so far has been the Open University, which is by far the UK's major producer of university-standard open learning materials, although materials have been acquired from higher education institutions from as far away as Australia.

The materials are a major and essential part of the teaching process, used within and beside conventional teaching. This strategy was greatly facilitated by the concurrent adoption of modularisation for all undergraduate courses, since this offered an ideal opportunity to re-examine course structures and delivery methodologies.

While off-the-shelf learning materials have been adopted, they have been subjected to the university's standard course approval and validation processes. Furthermore, the materials are supported by a much greater level of face-to-face support than would normally be offered by a distance teaching university such as the Open University.

Once the mixed mode strategy had been accepted by the university's senior academic managers, a target of 10% of course delivery by open learning was set for academic year 1993–94. The target for 1994–95 was 20%. Implementation of such a strategy raises issues for the institution, its teachers and the learners. These are considered in turn.

The institution

The University of Luton has rejected the separatist approach in which a distinct department takes responsibility for open learning. Open learning is considered as a core teaching methodology to be applied to certain modules within courses in all faculties. Open learning is therefore placed on the agenda for each department and hence for each member of staff. The mixed mode approach adopted requires that all the university's systems (quality assurance, finance, management information, etc) be capable of servicing the needs of either a conventional or open learning module or course. In addition, all staff need to understand the concept and practice of open learning as applied within the university. This means that institutional policies, on matters such as staff selection, induction of new staff and the continuing professional development of both new and existing staff, must take full account of the mixed mode strategy.

The university's quality assurance processes are of key importance; groups charged with the validation of new courses and review of older ones need to be fully aware of the application of the mixed mode strategy. Since an additional teaching and learning methodology has gained corporate acceptance and encouragement, course teams need to question even more closely the teaching and learning methodology to be utilised. Questions need to be asked to elicit clear and unequivocal justification of the chosen methodology (be it open learning or face-to-face delivery). Each methodology has its positive attributes and its difficulties and these need to be weighed against each other. Similarly, those responsible for selection of the learning materials will need to address quality assurance issues through well thought out and transparent evaluation protocols.

The teacher

The institutional commitment made by the university to use mixed mode delivery brings open learning potentially within the role of every teacher. Conversely, in those institutions where a separate open learning specialist or team is designated there is a division of expertise. It is essential to consider what is of importance if teachers are to be able to support open learners effectively.

- Tutorial skills must be enhanced; there is a need for teachers to maximise the effectiveness of feedback given to the open learning student. This skill, while initially developed to facilitate support for the open learner, will no doubt bring benefits to conventional learners as well.
- Open learning students may need support at times different to those required by conventional students. If open learning facilitates a return to study for those with employment or family commitments, then an out-of-hours service may be needed. This clearly has implications for conditions of service.
- Teachers with mixed commitments (to both open and conventional students) need to ensure that resources are not biased towards one or other group. The needs of all students differ over their time with the university and all teachers of necessity develop skills in balancing resources between cohorts and between individual students.

For the mixed mode university, the overwhelming advantage of integration at staff level is flexibility. Staff can move between modes of delivery according to student enrolments; this is particularly important within modular courses with a high degree of student choice. The advantages to the teaching staff are also significant. Each teacher has the opportunity to develop a full portfolio of teaching skills depending on the balance of needs of the learners, the curriculum and their own personal preferences. For many teachers, a commitment to openness represents a considerable expansion of opportunity and may yield the space and time necessary for professional upgrading, personal study and research.

The students
Individual students experience higher education in a variety of ways and the mixed mode strategy allows flexibility which is not possible in other approaches. Normally, once the choice of institution has been made, there is no further choice of mode of learning; but a choice of methodology within a single institution can be attractive to many students. The expanded resources for learning inherent in a mixed mode institution allow students to 'mix and match' within their programmes.

The distance teaching universities face limitations which occur because open learning *production* is essentially an industrial process and relies for cost-effectiveness on large numbers of students. Open learning courses will always, therefore, tend towards the most popular or the core subjects of a discipline. The economics of the production system prohibit specialist courses with limited student 'pulling power'. Neither can there be much room within a large-scale industrial production system for courses related to local issues and circumstances.

Conversely, the local university has the capability of offering more idiosyncratic course programmes. Conventionally taught courses can be cost-effectively taught (with care) with a student population of less than 20 and put on at short notice. Each local university has good teachers, but cannot have national experts in more than a few subjects. By contrast, an open learning course used nationally, or internationally, will draw upon a range of experts either within the course team or working as associate authors. The individual student at a mixed mode university may have additional considerations:

- As with a conventional university, other resources are available, such as the library or the sports facilities.
- Compared with study at a distance teaching university, additional contact with both teacher and fellow students will be available because they are not at a distance from each other. A resource-based course within a mixed mode university offers more face-to-face support and group work than is possible for a distance teaching university.
- A student may want to move to other courses offered in the conventional or open learning mode within the university. It may be that open learning is particularly attractive to the student at the start of study because of work or domestic constraints, but there is an easy opportunity to switch to conventionally taught courses in the future. The same principle applies to students who begin their study on conventional courses but need to change their mode of study due to changed circumstances.
- The development of an ability to work within both the conventional and open learning mode equips students with additional skills for lifelong learning. In higher education there is increasing emphasis on transferable skills, and perhaps the most important of such skills is the ability to become an independent learner, able to cope with a range of different teaching and learning approaches. Many employers adopt open learning in their training programmes and it is therefore important to equip graduates with an understanding of the methodology, its strengths and weaknesses.

Conclusion

A chapter such as this inevitably provides more questions than answers. The answers can only be found within a specific institution by examining its resources in the context of its portfolio of academic disciplines and educational mission. We have sought to raise points for discussion and debate and have provided some insights on these debates with reference to our own university. The shift to a mixed mode of operation is not simple and straightforward – it requires a change to the academic culture of the institution. Students need to develop personal autonomy; teachers and lecturers need to move away from the 'not invented here' syndrome and embed the 'off-the-shelf' materials with imagination and skill; and, not least, higher education managers must not be tempted to judge open learning solely by costs and resource requirements, but rather must also recognise the opportunity for pedagogical transformation and development.

Address for correspondence: **Stephen J Fallows**, Reader, Educational Development, and **Kate Robinson**, University of Luton, Park Square, Luton, Bedfordshire LU1 3JU.

21. The Importance of Managing Student Expectations on an Undergraduate Programme

Janette Davies, *University of the West of England*

SUMMARY

How students perceive the quality of their learning experience is dependent on the degree to which their expectations are met by their experience on the course. This chapter presents a case study evaluation of a Year 2 undergraduate marketing programme which relied heavily on directed private study (DPS). The focus of this research was to test the hypothesis that if efforts are made to manage students' expectations, all students will perceive DPS as a quality learning experience.

This chapter highlights that students expect a quality learning experience to be challenging and practical, characteristics that can be delivered by a DPS programme. Findings indicate that students' responses to DPS are intrinsically linked to the learning strategy they adopt on a course. If students perceived that they were being overworked they readily adopt a surface approach to learning, which is not sympathetic to the successful implementation of a DPS programme.

Findings also suggest that it is essential for students to understand the objectives of a DPS approach and how it can facilitate their own learning process. This involves proper preparation by utilising basic marketing techniques to promote DPS in a way that is relevant and appealing to students. In addition, a course team must manage students' expectations by clarifying what is expected of them and by developing an academic climate which is supportive of the demands of a DPS programme.

This chapter concludes by suggesting that even if every attempt is made to manage students' expectations, students can be segmented into three types: *enthusiasts*, who perceive DPS as a quality learning experience; *satisficers*, who perceive DPS as a good way to learn, but no better than didactic methods, and *sceptics*, who perceive DPS to be a poor learning experience for them, one which places too much emphasis on the student being responsible for their own learning. With higher education increasingly relying on flexible independent forms of delivery, this chapter poses the question: what should we do with the sceptics?

Background to the study

Researchers and managers concur that service quality involves a comparison of expectation with experience. Delivering a quality service means conforming to customer expectations on a consistent basis. In line with this thinking Gronroos developed a model of Perceived Service Quality (1982), in which he contends that the quality of a service as perceived by the customer is a result of a comparison between the expectations and the real-life experiences. If the experience exceeds the expectations, the perceived quality is positive. If, on the other hand, the experience does not meet the level of expectations, the perceived quality is low.

Gronroos also states that quality is not an objective phenomenon: the same objective quality may be perceived in different ways. What is good for one student may be less good for another depending on their expectations, hence the importance of setting expectations prior to the service encounter through advertising and selling the service.

Defining quality when investigating a product is straightforward, Crosby (1979) defines quality as 'the conformance to requirements'. Defining service quality is more difficult due to its characteristics of intangibility, heterogeneity and inseparability.

What is meant by a quality learning experience?
Here is the CNAA definition:

> 'the development of students' intellectual and imaginative powers; their understanding and judgement; their problem-solving skills; their ability to communicate; their ability to see relationships within what they have learned and to perceive their field of study in a broader perspective. The programme must aim to stimulate an enquiring, analytical and creative approach, encouraging independent judgement and critical self awareness.' (Gibbs, 1992)

This is taken to mean the need to learn by understanding and applying, not by memorising and regurgitating. This is characteristic of a 'deep approach' to learning as described by Entwistle (1988) who maintains that students who adopt this approach start with the need to understand, they question and evaluate content, they relate content to previous knowledge and past experience and they learn through understanding and applying.

What is meant by directed private study?
There is a litany of terms used to describe flexible learning in higher education, such as DPS, student-centred learning, independent learning, self-directed learning and private study. The CNAA definition of student-centred learning is as follows:

> 'a style of learning where the student is responsible for their own learning. They, with direction from the tutors, decide on the content of their learning, the pace at which they can learn and how they should be assessed.' (CNAA, March 1992)

I agree with this definition but prefer the term DPS because it more adequately describes the learning strategy adopted on the programme which formed the basis of this study. Learning was directed by the lecturer through the provision of frameworks, discussion in seminars and assignments set. Learning involved private study by designing the course so that it depended on students completing the DPS activities. Learning was not totally student-oriented, otherwise the student would have been able to influence all elements of the course, which in this instance they could not. An increasing dependence on DPS was the direct result of the following constraints and challenges facing the lecturer: pressure on resources conflicting with the desire to deliver a quality learning experience; an increasing student–teacher ratio resulting in larger and more diverse classes; and the need to develop students' interpersonal skills. The above led to a desire to promote an academic climate that emphasised a deep approach to learning, one where the student takes responsibility for their own learning.

How directed private study was implemented

Because there are so many different models of DPS, it is necessary at this stage to clarify exactly how the DPS was delivered, and to point out that these students would not have been used to such a dependence on DPS (which resulted in a reduction in contact time), or on having a lot of responsibility for their own learning.

The programme was structured as follows.

- No lectures took place.
- A course handbook supplied the framework; it included an outline of what would be covered on the course, the assessment strategy, topics for discussion in the seminar sessions, references for further reading and practical exercises that tested knowledge. The handbook was not prescriptive (although some exercises were compulsory) and students were encouraged to find their own path through the material.
- Contact time was reduced to fortnightly sessions of two hours with 25 students in each session. Students were expected to come to the sessions having completed the reading and the exercises set. Student study groups were responsible for presenting the first 30 minutes of each session, which was peer, tutor and self assessed.

The stages involved in managing student expectations on the programme were as follows.

Stage 1: Selling the benefits of a DPS programme
The first time the lecturer met with the students, they were asked to identify the key characteristics of a good learning experience. This information was then used by the lecturer to explain that the DPS programme was designed to deliver the characteristics they had identified – a learning experience that was practical, challenging, developmental, disciplined and fun. Two key issues emerged here. The first was that a lecturer relies on the students to identify 'practical learning' as a key characteristic of good learning experience; the second was that the students must believe that the DPS programme is designed to achieve 'practical learning'. It was evident at this stage that a minority of students were sceptical about the benefits of DPS and would have preferred a more didactic approach.

Stage 2: The DPS strategy was promoted to the students
At this stage the lecturer needed to defray any suspicion that this teaching strategy is a way of the lecturer doing less work and the student doing all the work. Time must be spent convincing students that it takes a lot of time and effort to prepare suitable DPS materials. In addition, a carrot was needed to ensure that the students took the DPS approach seriously. Because of this some of the work they had to do was linked to the course assessment criteria. Students were self, peer and tutor

assessed. This subsequently proved critical to the success of the DPS approach.

Stage 3: Groundrules were implemented on the course

In order to discipline the students to complete the DPS activities a groundrule was agreed in the first session. This rule stated that students who did not complete the DPS work would not be allowed to attend the session, unless they had exceptional circumstances for not completing the work. Several key issues emerged (all of which were confirmed in the findings of the research). Firstly, most students felt strongly that it was their right to attend even if they hadn't prepared. Secondly, it had to be explained to them that it would be the quality of their learning that would suffer if they did not do the work. Thirdly, they had to be reminded that they said that they needed discipline to make them do the work. Finally and probably most importantly, mutually agreeable 'exceptional circumstances' were identified that would permit students to attend when they hadn't completed the work. What was obvious was students were reluctant to accept having a groundrule, until the impact on their learning of not having one was spelt out.

Stage 4: Students were given a say in how the course was run

Students were informed that they would be given an opportunity to change how the course was designed after the first term if they felt it was not meeting their expectations of a good learning experience.

The importance of managing students' expectations

The research was designed to test the hypothesis that if efforts are made to manage students' expectations, they will perceive DPS as a quality learning experience.

Stage 1: In the first session of the course

The objective of this stage of the research was to identify what students expected of an undergraduate course, in particular to identify how they expected to learn on it. The data collection mechanism was a semi-structured discussion.

Stage 2: At the end of the first term

A questionnaire was administered to all students which asked them if they wanted the delivery method to change to a more didactic approach. In addition, focus groups took place among a sample of students to see how they perceived the DPS learning approach to be working.

Stage 3: After the completion of the course

A semi-structured questionnaire was administered at the end of the course to a sample of the students, in order to evaluate if the DPS approach met students' expectations of a quality learning experience.

It is suggested that generalisation of the findings in this study may be limited to similar interpretations of DPS. In order to maximise validity and reliability, sample sizes used were large and representative of the whole cohort of students. Also, discussion guides and questionnaires were pilot tested to ensure their completeness and accuracy.

Discussion of findings

Stage 1: Students' expectations of an undergraduate course
General expectations. Students' expectations influence their beliefs about the outcomes of attending an undergraduate programme. Included in this are how they expect to be taught and how they expect to learn. Students' primary focus is the end result, 'a good recognised degree', not the process of obtaining the knowledge. Some of them admitted they didn't care how they got the degree as long as they got it. In this particular course students expect it to build their understanding and knowledge of business concepts. They expect to enjoy the course and have '*fun*'. They are aware that key interpersonal skills such as communication, team-building, time-management and problem-solving skills are important and should be encouraged on the course.

Expectations of good and bad learning experiences. The findings suggest that students do not think about their learning process. Most of them found it quite difficult to come up with spontaneous examples of a good learning experience. When they did the illustrations came from the past and from outside the academic arena, for example 'learning to drive a car'. It appeared that for most students good learning equated to a good grade, which makes them concentrate all their efforts on work that is assessed and on developing a learning strategy to cope with the demands of the assessment requirements on the course.

Students believe that good academic learning is 'practical and challenging'. However, in reality, challenging, practical DPS work will never be perceived to be as important as assessed work. Students weigh up the perceived benefit to them of completing the work, which they primarily measure according to the contribution it makes to their assessment grade. Another factor that may come into account (depending on the student) is the desire not to be embarrassed in front of their peers if they are asked a question and cannot contribute in class.

In an academic sense students identified practical learning as 'learning through doing' (eg, case studies, field visits, projects). They were aware that some subjects were more suitable to this approach than others.

It was evident from the findings that students do not see themselves as responsible for their learning. All their citations of poor learning experiences were directly attributable to the lecturers. The key characteristics they identified were: unstructured lectures, boring lecturers or where there was no discipline in lectures. Very few students identified that a lack of student motivation played a part. A lecturer's image and how they deal with the students is significant in a students' learning experience. Students do not like to feel intimidated by the lecturer. A collaborative rather than an aggressive approach is necessary to ensure that the learning experience meets their expectations: 'Lecturers must be approachable... willing to explain difficult concepts'. Students know they should attend, prepare for and contribute to sessions, in order to maximise the quality of their learning experience, but they also admit 'students are inherently lazy, they will look for the easy option'. They recognised that if a course is going to depend on them being responsible for their learning, they needed to be 'encouraged' to prepare by the lecturers.

Stage 2: Mid-year evaluation of the programme

Students confirmed that the DPS teaching strategy was more challenging and practical than didactic approaches because of the reliance on them to prepare and participate in sessions: 'You have to be able to explain, come up with examples... be able to answer questions'. However, students confirmed that the amount of work they put into completing their DPS was influenced by the demands of the course, and in particular assessment requirements. Students indicated that although they could see the benefits of completing the DPS work, they will always put assessed work before DPS work which is not assessed. DPS was perceived to be harder work than other forms of delivery because it required students to work continuously: 'otherwise you would be lost in the seminars... you could not answer questions'. Where there was a very noticeable difference in the workload required by different modules on a course, students who preferred learning to be made easier for them resented the lecturer who was implementing DPS: 'It's not fair... it's the lecturer's job, that's what they are paid to do'. No recognition was given to the amount of time and effort lecturers put into preparing the DPS materials. These students immediately reverted back to the attitude that 'it's the lecturer's fault that I am not learning'.

Two key issues emerge here for a course management team that wants to promote an academic climate supportive to DPS. Firstly, consideration must be given to an appropriate workload for each module on the course. Lecturers should be encouraged to make sure that students are only required to spend a certain amount of time on their work. Secondly, courses should not develop assessment strategies that are conducive to students adopting a surface approach to their learning.

It was surprising that in this mid-year evaluation only 7% of the students wanted the delivery method to be changed to a more didactic approach. What was less surprising was that if the students were given the opportunity to have all the DPS materials combined with a didactic delivery method, most of them would have opted for this approach. This reinforces the view that students want learning to be made easy for them: 'It is far easier to have it all handed to us on a plate'. What was evident was that a proportion of students did not want to accept the DPS strategy, and no matter how much effort was put into convincing them that it would lead to a quality learning experience, they would not change their minds.

Stage 3: Students' overall evaluations of the DPS programme and how it was implemented

Findings confirmed the need to advertise and sell the objectives of DPS so that students can understand how they can benefit from it. A DPS approach to learning is different and threatening to students when they first learn of it. The idea that the course depends on them doing the work is frightening: 'It's frightening at first, but it's nice to know what is expected'. Personal selling of the benefits of DPS takes time, which is often at a premium at the beginning of a course. It is important, therefore, to make students aware of the demands of a DPS programme prior to the service encounter. This can be achieved through course literature and handbooks. It was evident, though, that a lecturer cannot rely on the written word: personal selling of the benefits of DPS is key. This can be achieved on a course in the induction period and when lecturers first meet the students. If the requirements of the DPS programme are emphasised it should help to instil a culture where students will expect to be responsible for their learning.

It was obvious from the research that students needed to be disciplined to complete a DPS programme, as illustrated by comments such as: 'I think a lecturer has to force students to work well and motivate them, otherwise it is easy to take a back seat'. In this particular programme groundrules helped facilitate this process. A very important part of this process was that students were given a say in setting the groundrules. To force a groundrule on them would have aggravated them and made it more difficult to persuade them of the benefits of a DPS programme. But by discussing why the groundrule was required, allowing them their say which, in the main, was 'it's our right to decide whether or not we should prepare', and reaching a compromise, they agreed with the rule. Groundrules are not sufficient on their own to ensure the success of the DPS programme because, as stated earlier, assessment work will always take precedence over DPS work which is not assessed. Students identified that the most effective incentive is to link DPS requirements to the assessment strategy on a course. Assessment, they indicated, was the primary motivator for students to do any work.

The findings reveal that students can be segmented into three types according to whether DPS meets their expectations. Each segment represented one third of the students.

1. Enthusiasts

DPS is their preferred method of delivery; they adopt a deep approach to learning. They will actively contribute in class and will often go beyond the requirements set. In their overall evaluation of DPS, comments like the following were typical: 'I learn better this way... I remember it'; 'It's hard work but fun'.

Interviews with these students showed that they are self-motivated and they can cope with being responsible for their learning.

2. Satisficers

These students recognise the benefits of DPS, but they are not sufficiently self-motivated to do all the work set. They recognise that they need the lecturer to encourage them, to provide the carrot to make them get on with it. In their overall evaluation of DPS, the following were typical: 'There's an awful lot of work, I can't do it all'; 'I could see the benefit, but it's hard work'.

For them DPS is no better or worse than didactic methods of delivery.

3. Sceptics

These students do not buy into the concept of DPS from the beginning. From their point of view it is (and always will be) the lecturers' responsibility to decant the material; they should be allowed to act as a sponge if they want to. They often don't turn up and if they do they don't contribute. In their overall evaluation of DPS, the following remarks were typical: 'Lecturers get paid to teach us'; 'The lecturer was awful, only interested in you if you did the work'.

In the main they just hate the whole idea of being responsible for their learning. DPS is a big disappointment and often puts them off the subject. Interviews with these students indicate that they perceive DPS to be far too hard work, confusing, and 'a lecturer's cop-out'.

Conclusions

This chapter demonstrates that if students are to perceive DPS as a quality learning experience, their expectations must be taken into account. A course team should attempt to set expectations by proper preparation prior to the service encounter. The requirements and benefits of a DPS approach should be advertised in all course literature and sold to the students in induction sessions and when a lecturer meets with the students for the first time. This will instil a culture where students know what is expected of them from the beginning of the course. This knowledge will help them meet the demands of a DPS programme and accept the idea of being responsible for their own learning.

Successful implementation of a DPS programme also requires that a course develops an academic climate that is supportive and sympathetic to the demands of a DPS programme. Finally, even by setting and managing students' expectations a DPS approach will alienate the sceptics: those students who prefer learning to be made easy for them and who do not want to take responsibility for their own learning under any conditions.

References

Crosby, P B (1979) *Quality is Free: The Art of Making Quality Certain*, New American Library, New York.

Council for National Academic Awards (CNAA) (March, 1992) 'Improving Student Learning Project', CNAA, London.

Entwistle, N J (1988) *Styles of Learning and Teaching: An Integrated Outline of Education Psychology for Students, Teachers and Lecturers*, David Fulton, London.

Gibbs, G (1981) *Teaching Students to Learn*, Open University Press, Buckingham.

Gibbs, G (1992) *Improving the Quality of Student Learning*, Technical and Education Services Ltd, London.

Gronroos, C (1982) 'Towards a third phase in service quality research: challenges and future directions', *Advances in Service Marketing and Management*, Vol 2.

Hodgson, V E, Mann, S J and Snell, R (1989) *Beyond Distance Teaching: Towards Open Learning*, Open University Press, Buckingham.

McGill, I and Beaty, L (1995) *Action Learning: A guide for professional, management and educational development*, 2nd edn, Kogan Page, London.

Paine, N (1988) *Open Learning in Transition: An Agenda for Action*, National Extension College Trust Ltd.

Race, P (1991) *Developing Competence: Educational Development*, The Polytechnic of Wales, Pontypridd.

Parasuraman, A, Zeithaml, V A and Berry I L (1990) *Delivering Quality Service, Balancing Consumer Perceptions and Expectations*, The Free Press, London.

Address for correspondence: **Janette Davis**, Senior Lecturer, Bristol Business School, University of the West of England, Coldharbour Lane, Frenchay, Bristol BS16 1QY.

22. Education and the 'Dark Side' of IT

Robert J Siddall, *University Glamorgan*

SUMMARY

Such a melodramatic title may be eye-catching, but what does it mean? It is a phrase I use to refer to the potential *disadvantages* of IT in education.

First may I declare that I am not a Luddite: I believe that IT is part of our world, and that we must make proper use of it in education. However, I fear that we are riding an uncritical wave of enthusiasm without properly considering the implications of what is happening.

My concern lies in several areas:

- Plagiarism has become much easier with the advent of wordprocessors, photocopiers, and, most recently, e-mail.
- How much are we blinded by the technology into teaching the use of software packages to students, rather than showing them how to analyse and understand the underlying problems?
- How can we ensure that students understand the principals, rather than merely use trial and error techniques with published software?
- What is the significance of knowledge to a student, when so much information is available online?
- Do we know what computers are doing, and can they be trusted?
- Do we need mental exercise for a healthy mind, in much the same way that we need physical exercise for a healthy body?
- Computer fraud is generally accepted as a serious problem in industry, but what is the threat to academia?

Introduction

Many researchers are working extremely hard to develop IT applications within education, but most people seem to be oblivious to the fact that IT, like all other radical improvements in this world, must have its side effects. This chapter is an attempt to redress the balance by highlighting areas which I believe to be drawbacks to IT.

None of the ideas outlined is particularly original, but they are brought together to try to assess their implications. Some of the fears expressed may, and hopefully will, prove to be groundless, but if the academic world does not pause to seriously address the implications, both to academia and the world in general, we are going to create problems for future generations.

Plagiarism has become much easier

The dictionary defines the verb to plagiarise as 'to appropriate (ideas, passages, etc) from (another work or author)'. The traditional view of plagiarism implies theft of work or ideas, but in the current academic environment, cooperation with intent to cheat may be a more serious problem. Plagiarism is most certainly not a new problem: it has been around since mankind first invented formal education. It is, however, probably an increasing problem for two reasons:

- more people are competing for higher education;
- some aspects of IT appear to have made it easier than ever before to cheat successfully.

Perhaps it should be said that these judgements are subjective and based on inference, rather than solid evidence. If a particular crime becomes increasingly difficult to detect and its possible benefits are simultaneously becoming more obvious to an increasing number of people, it seems logical that more people will be tempted to try it.

Why is plagiarism becoming easier? Let us consider the background for a moment: the motivation, to deceive the examiners, is presumably the same now as it ever was, but the technology of preparing and submitting coursework is changing in ways that make cheating easier.

Consider first the hand-written essay. If one has to write out sections of a manuscript long hand, it is almost as easy to rewrite it using one's own words, and what, therefore, is the temptation to cheat? The development of the typewriter made it technically easier to copy verbatim, without analysing the contents, but, as relatively few people mastered the keyboard, this never became a real problem. The photocopier can be used to copy complete documents, but the results are relatively easy to spot, which significantly reduces the perpetrator's desire to cheat.

The advent of the cheap wordprocessor has raised the scope for such dishonesty quite considerably for several reasons. First of all, each hard copy is an original, so if two people wish to cooperate all they have to do in the most blatant case is to modify the front cover and each can submit otherwise identical copies in their own name. Such subterfuge can be spotted in a conventional small class situation, but who can guarantee to spot identical submissions when trying to mark perhaps 100 essays or projects on the same topic? The simple fact that a wordprocessor file does not decay compounds the problem even further, as exactly the same essay could be submitted by several students over a series of years, which would be extremely hard to detect. This of course assumes that the titles of essays required for coursework are not changed significantly from year to year.

The position has been further undermined by the most recent developments in communications technology which allow files to be transferred from one place to another. For example, an essay written by a student at one university could be e-mailed to a student at another institution and submitted there at the same time as the original. This fact alone should be sufficient to force academics to reconsider the whole *raison d'être* of coursework and especially its role in assessment. But consider the more traditional deception whereby a student quotes wholesale from a published document without credit to the original author. Such plagiarism has been made infinitely easier by development of the Optical Character Reader with its associated software, and such software libraries as *Encarta*, both of which almost encourage text to be copied wholesale, for use in other wordprocessed documents.

However, if technology has *created the problem*, it is quite simple, if expensive, for technology to *provide the solution*. A simple program to analyse, record and compare text, with a library of other texts on related topics should be sufficient to detect, and therefore deter, such relatively crude plagiarism. The level of detail of the comparison would naturally depend on the significance of the work being undertaken. It is reasonably easy to hypothesise a series of tests which should expose the problem, provided that the institutions concerned made it a requirement that all students who submit wordprocessed texts should also submit a file copy of the work for such comparison.

Another closely related bag of worms is the theoretical market of a national or even an international dimension which could develop, where people agree to cooperate remotely via e-mail. A student of one institution might agree to write an essay on a local, or specialist, topic from their own area of interest in return either for money, or for one written by another specialist at some other institution on a totally different subject. Such a market is technically quite feasible on the Internet and could prove far harder to counter than the one outlined above.

How much are we blinded by the technology?

'Never mind the quality, feel the width.'

Are we genuinely attempting to assess the quality of a student's answer, or merely the quality of their presentation of that answer?

Traditional coursework assessment has always given some credit to students for the quality of the presentation of their work, but modern software packages have enabled them to improve this so much that there may be an argument for reassessing the position. Could there now be an unconscious tendency to discriminate against an able student who has developed a well-reasoned solution to a problem, in favour of a simpler, perhaps poorer quality answer from another student, who has taken the trouble to master one of the 'professional' presentation packages?

Let us consider just one example that could be applicable to many disciplines: network analysis. Network analysis is an extremely valuable planning technique which can be used for controlling any type of project, but which only really comes into its own when applied to large complex projects.

The basic concepts and conventions of network analysis are straightforward and easy to grasp. We used to teach it using rudimentary networks of perhaps 10–30 activities which could be solved manually. We now tend to ask the students to master the semantics of a full blown commercial networking package and then use it in their attempt to solve one of the fairly simple examples that their comparative inexperience will allow them to tackle successfully. Do they benefit significantly from being forced to master the software?

One argument often used to justify this approach is that, out there in the 'real world of work,' employers make full use of such aids. This may well be true, but it disregards the simple fact that any employer requiring someone to undertake such tasks will train their new recruit in the company's chosen package, which may, or may not, be the same as the one in college.

How can we ensure that students understand the principles?

I trained as an engineer, and my colleagues and I spend a lot of our time teaching different aspects of design and analysis. In the past, this had to be done manually with the aid of pencil and paper. It was slow, time-consuming and only allowed students to consider a couple of simple cases. The advent of cheap computing has in one sense liberated the teacher, by enabling the students to consider more realistic, complex situations. However, in another sense, it may have harmed the quality of education, as it allows some students to make use of simple trial-and-error procedures with the software to produce quite reasonable solutions, which may hide their basic lack of understanding.

One could fairly ask 'What does this matter?' The initial answer is probably 'Not a lot', provided that all the tasks subsequently attempted lie within the parameters assumed in the software, but what happens when the problem falls outside this defined range? Will the young designer have the basic understanding to appreciate the fact?

Who will be held responsible for the subsequent failure, however minor or catastrophic it may be? Will it be the designer, who did not know enough to appreciate the problem? Will it be the software manufacturer, who never envisaged that their software could be used under these circumstances, or will it be us, the teachers, who let ourselves be conned into passing an inadequate student?

What is the significance of knowledge to a student?

Consider how you use your watch. Do you know the time, or do you, like me, tend to look at your watch perhaps five times in five minutes and still not *know* the actual time? Is this perhaps due to the fact that we can check the time so easily that we do not bother to comprehend (ie, know) the information?

Human beings have a natural tendency not to retain knowledge, unless they possess a particular interest or have a specific need to acquire it. The recent commercial availability of simple encyclopaedia-type programs such as *Encarta*, which contain information about almost any subject, could perhaps remove the need for the student to acquire any basic information because it can be discovered so easily. The use of such software presents us with a distinct dilemma. On the one hand, it must be beneficial to have all the information available on a particular problem, but, on the other hand, it denies students the motivation to digest such information and learn from it.

The big question is: How much do we need to know in order to be able to make effective use of the tools which IT offers us?

Do we need the mental exercise of learning to produce a healthy mind?

It is said that babies learn through play and so presumably can the rest of us, but what basic skills do we need in order to benefit from such play?

The athlete who practices specific motions required for a sport is probably doing two things simultaneously:

- developing the relevant muscles;

- programming appropriate control reflexes, so that they can come into their own when called, as a computer program can call up its subroutines.

It has long been known that practice of mental tasks improves the performance in those tasks, in much the same way that the physical training of an athlete improves his or her physical performance. It has only relatively recently been realised that our physical well-being is also improved by judicious exercise. Is it fanciful to suggest that our mental well-being, or at least our ability to perform everyday mental tasks, may be dependent on proper mental exercise?

If this hypothesis can be accepted for a moment, consider how it affects our perception of IT.

Consider IT as entertainment. The various broadcast programmes on both television and radio are often referred to as mental wallpaper because they provide a soothing background. A soothing background does not impinge on the foreground and therefore discourages mental effort. Could this lack of stimulation in turn actually encourage mental degeneration?

Consider artificial reality. This can be a useful or perhaps vital aspect of training people to face some tasks, as in the world of artificial reality they can do things without risk, which are either difficult, prohibitively expensive, or physically impossible, in the real world. This is highly laudable, but might not the social or recreational use of artificial reality tend to produce people who cannot socialise or react properly to the real world? Could the lack of risk factor actually remove the user's perception of cause and effect associated with risk? It is generally acknowledged that simple computer games can be addictive; how much more addictive will the world of artificial reality be?

Do we know what our computers are doing? Can they be trusted?

The question is: are these logical derivatives of the original hypothesis valid and if they are, what can and should education do to minimise the damage? This question may appear to be little more than a nuisance, but I suggest there are some aspects of it that should be considered:

- Most of us are naturally credible and tend to believe what we read in the paper, or see on the television. This is not a problem as long as the media themselves are responsible and endeavour to publish only the truth, but computers are not troubled by such ethical concepts as 'truth' and only say whatever their program dictates. How can we persuade our students to show a healthy degree of scepticism to these answers when we ask them to trust computers implicitly in so many other aspects of their daily life? How many of us have met students proposing ridiculous answers to simple calculations, merely because their calculator shows the answer and they have not actually considered if it was realistic?

'Garbage in, garbage out!

- Some conventional software packages are now so large and complex that it is impossible to test them fully and it is only realistic to use other software to test them with dummy data to see the response.

- Who can claim to understand fully how a neural network selects its solution or identify all of the restrictions that must apply if such an expert system is to function properly? We are using machines to infer rules that we cannot identify in ways that we do not properly understand. Is that wise?

Computer fraud is a serious problem in industry – what is the threat to academia?

The various IT professionals within our places of employment are well aware of these problems and doubtless have their own horror stories, views and means of tackling them. This section is just an attempt by one layman to explain to others some of the problems that may occur.

Hacking presents the same four threats to academia as it does to any other organisation:

- There is the possible theft of money.
- There is the possible theft of confidential information.
- There is the possibility of information being accidentally corrupted by the intrusion.
- There is the possibility of records being altered fraudulently.

These bald statements may appear to be a little over-dramatic, but the problems are very real and we have the added disadvantage of allowing or even encouraging intelligent, playful adolescents to use our systems.

Let us consider the possible problems one at a time.

Direct theft of money. It would be extremely complacent to assume that the funds available would not justify the effort. A potential thief might feel that probable level of financial control in the academic world was so low as to minimise the chances of detection. This view might make the effort worthwhile.

Theft of information. Any information held on file anywhere on a network, such as research results, personnel records, or even future exam papers, which could be worth money to interested parties, might be stolen.

Accidental corruption. This is where no actual malice is intended but the mere act of intrusion can sometimes be enough to garble files, which can make them useless. Does the institution have adequate means to monitor and back-up damaged files? The effort expended on this problem will naturally depend on the importance of the information contained in the files.

Unauthorised amendments. Any files kept on a network are vulnerable. It is quite possible in theory to hack into a file and change the data stored there. There are stories, hopefully apocryphal, about disgruntled hackers who have hacked into one of the police computer systems in the United States and placed false driving convictions on the computer records of people who offended them. It does not take much imagination to appreciate the chaos that could be caused if such a person tried to change academic records.

This is not intended to be a horror story. Simple good housekeeping routines can detect and therefore deter such maliciousness, provided that everybody is aware of the problem and does not lapse into complacency. However, if it does happen to an institution, it could destroy the credibility of all the qualifications which it awards.

Conclusions

This chapter is an attempt to spark discussion of the possible disadvantages that IT is bringing to education. It is not intended to stop or even to delay the application of IT, but to encourage others to consider intelligently its claimed benefits. Nothing in recorded history has been all for the good. Every revolution, however beneficial, has its own dark side and the IT revolution is just the same.

Our generation sees IT as a valuable gift from science and accepts it unquestioningly. The Trojans once thought that they had received a valuable gift from the Greeks and accepted that equally unquestioningly, but look what that gift did for them. Could our gift prove as destructive?

Address for correspondence: **Robert J Siddall**, Senior Lecturer, Building, Civil Engineering and Building, University of Glamorgan, Pontypridd, Mid Glamorgan, Wales CF37 1DL.

23. Face-to-Face at a Distance

Ray Winders, *University of Plymouth*

SUMMARY

Education and training can be delivered in three modes, any of which can be combined.

1. *Face-to-face*: tutor, students and learning materials are all in the same space at the same time.
2. *Distance learning*: the tutor is at a distance from the students. Normally study materials and guides are prepared beforehand and study time and place is variable.
3. *Face-to-face at a distance*: students and learning materials are together at the same time but the tutor communicates with them through electronic links. In addition, there may be several locations linked together simultaneously.

The third mode is the subject of this chapter, with a particular emphasis on the use of satellites to deliver education and training to a distributed audience using terrestrial links for a return path to the tutor. The addition of desktop video-conferencing also allows experts at a distance to contribute in vision to the content of the programme. Recent developments in compression technologies are reducing the costs of both terrestrial and satellite transmission. The final part of this chapter looks forward to the next five years of activity in what is now being called *telematics* – the combination of computing and communications technologies.

Introduction

Keegan (1986) reviewed theories and practice in distance learning. He distinguished between an industrial and an interpersonal mode. Attributes of the industrial mode were listed as 'rationalisation, division of labour, mechanisation, mass production and standardisation' – a mode which was initially adopted by the UK Open University when large course teams produced programmes and learning materials for a long-term market. More recently in many institutions, programmes are more flexible. There is, however, still a strong element of preparation in advance. Few programmes have sufficient flexibility to allow the student to travel beyond what the designers thought appropriate.

Keegan (1986) quotes from Peters who described face-to-face teaching as a situation in which 'There is little distinction between teacher and taught; they are both participating in the shared experience of exploring a common world'. This is Socratic dialogue at its best. Students in present-day UK universities sitting at the back of a 150-seat lecture theatre may not readily recognise Peters' ideal. The live face-to-face session can, however, be more responsive to student needs, more up to date and more interactive than most distance learning.

The use of telematics to supplement both live teaching and learning packages adds a third dimension. Traditionally distance learning has been time and place independent. At present there are many potential students who are unable to travel far because of personal commitments and lack of finance but who are available at set times of the day. The use of video-conferencing and satellite conferencing allows groups to meet at a local centre and take part in learning sessions with similar groups anywhere in the country and potentially anywhere in the world. The use of telematics to provide or support education and training to dispersed groups is developing as both satellite and terrestrial networks become more reliable and less expensive.

Satellite transmission

Communication satellites are positioned above the equator at an altitude of 23,000 miles. Each satellite can 'see' a section of the earth and has a number of transponders with varying areas of coverage (footprints) and transmitting at varying frequencies in order to separate programmes. In order to transmit full bandwidth television, transponders use a bandwidth of 30 MHz. An important current development is the digitisation and compression of this broadband analogue signal; this will significantly reduce transponder costs to the user. It is this cost which has been a major inhibitor of satellite-delivered training.

Olympus

In July 1989 the European Space Agency (ESA) launched an experimentation and demonstration satellite – Olympus. Time on its transponders was made available free of charge for a range of experiments and for the transmission of educational programmes. In the UK the Space Agency also provided two transmission stations, one at the University of London and one at the University of Plymouth. Over the four years of its life an opportunity was provided to develop techniques and markets and to plan for self-sustaining operations. In addition ESA rented a commercial satellite transponder for a further year to September 1994 (ESA, 1994).

The bulk of transmissions for education and training were asymmetric, ie transmissions were from a studio to a large number of receive sites. In Spain a symmetrical system using small transmitters at a number of sites was developed (ETSIT) providing joint sessions at eight universities. The major providers of education and training were EUROSTEP (a consortium of European educators) and the University of Plymouth. EUROSTEP organised a daily schedule of tape broadcasts together with some live events. The University of Plymouth concentrated on live transmissions and to date has transmitted over 800 live programmes for a range of clients. The impetus to these transmissions was given by STARNET, a Department of Trade and Industry-funded project at Plymouth. Three basic advantages of satellite transmission were examined:

- **Up to date:** Since transmissions are live, current news and developments can be included.
- **Interactive:** Questions can be put to experts in the studio by telephone and by e-mail.
- **Penetration:** Since no cabling is required, satellite transmissions can reach remote locations.

These are still the main advantages for satellite transmission though two developments in technology have strengthened the position. The University of Plymouth's Satellite Research Centre has developed a data modem for direct reception of data from satellite to a card in a standard IBM-compatible PC. The system operates at 128 Kbits/sec in parallel with terrestrial ISDN2 systems. The transmission occupies a small part of the television transmission channel and can be independent of the programme. A particular application is the delivery of course notes to large numbers of dispersed students.

The second development is the use of a mediator which enables a computer output to be transmitted directly from the studio. This has been very effective in the transmission of computer training series since the operator can be seen pressing a key or using a mouse followed by the movement of the cursor on the screen and the resulting display.

During evaluations of transmissions two important factors emerged (Laurillard et al., 1991). First, it is important that the students at a distance have with them a 'facilitator' who ensures that the room is prepared, the television is tuned and that during the programme the students are encouraged to ask questions. Responsibility for the effective operation of the receive site is essential. Second, most problems that have been encountered relate to the telephone questions. On occasions 'howl-around' has been introduced as a result of the retransmission of the speaker's voice via the television to the microphone. Practice is also required in the use of the telephone, particularly if a microphone system is being used via a conference bridge. The use of e-mail on the studio floor is valuable for a large audience in that questions can be grouped, basic questions answered directly, and only the more complex questions discussed using the telephone. The recent introduction of ISDN video-conferencing offers a third option.

ISDN

Integrated Services Digital Networks (digital telephony) now reach 90% of England and Wales. The use of two 64 Kbit ISDN (ISDN2) enables video-conferencing to take place. A range of manufacturers are now supplying software, a small camera and a digital telephone. For about £3000 a full terminal can be installed using a 486 computer. More limited video-conferencing using a window in the screen is already included in new AppleMac desktops and in Windows 95. The standard ISDN2 systems enable participants at a distance to send a television picture of an individual or small group, alternated with prepared graphics. An interactive 'whiteboard' is also available. For tutorials, a mixed screen can be used with the tutor continuing to appear in a corner of the screen while support graphics are displayed. A small number of sites can be linked using a bridge which is either directly controlled by the tutor, or in a discussion mode, transmits the picture from the site at which a student is speaking. ISDN is limited in that movement is sampled rather than continuous and though high quality still images can be transmitted video is not yet possible.

ISDN and satellite

A new feature of satellite transmissions is the use of ISDN feeds to the studio. The ISDN signal can be either transmitted directly or, in order to improve apparent picture quality, can be used as a window in the studio transmission. An ISDN link can be used to bring the live image of an expert to the studio. The composite picture can then show the 'host' interviewing the expert who appears in a screen window. The whole screen can be used for still images from the remote site. As expertise becomes increasingly specialised the facility to create a composite programme is valuable. Since the transmission can then cover the whole of Europe costs can be recovered.

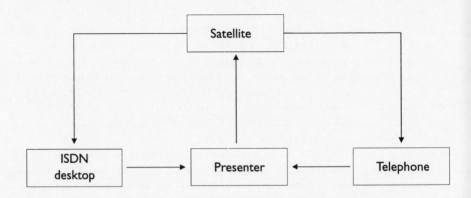

Figure 1 *Satellite and terrestrial interactive links*

Costs and transmission

It should be noted that live transmission from an existing studio is very cheap in television terms. A complex programme might take a half-day for preparation and rehearsal and a further half-day for dry-run and transmission. There is no post-production editing. The University of Plymouth is producing programmes including some location video at about £1000 per hour transmission. A more straightforward programme in lecture mode with supporting video and graphics can be created for £200 per hour.

In addition to the studio costs there are charges for transmission and for the rental of a satellite transponder. The major variable is satellite transponder cost. For occasional use this can be as high as £2000 per hour in the UK but regular bookings reduce the charge to £800–£1000. This makes a total cost of about £2000 per programme for studio, transmission and satellite. This can be recovered if 200 viewers pay £10 or indeed if 2000 viewers pay £1.

For most students, the cost must be reduced. This will be achieved by digitising and compressing the television signal. Since this would enable satellite entertainment companies to transmit ten separate programmes on one transponder there is strong commercial pressure on manufacturers to develop a digital receiver at less than £500. The University of Plymouth has just completed a research project for the European Space Agency to determine the degree of compression that might be acceptable to students in education and training.

Twelve live programmes and 12 special tapes were transmitted during October 1994. Transmissions were received at five sites spread throughout the UK. The questionnaire distributed for the live programmes included questions on technical quality and others related to the programme content. The students were not informed that the transmission was compressed. The live programme was followed by a specially prepared tape played in four short sections. The bit-rate was varied between sections and students were asked to rate the technical quality. At this stage they were informed that they were watching a special transmission. A detailed report is now with the European Space Agency, but at this stage the results can be summarised as follows.

- There was no comment on technical quality in the free response section of the questionnaire.
- The ratings for picture colour and picture detail were above average for all programmes including computer training which used detailed screen transmissions.
- During the technical trials using the special tape there was no discernible fall-off until below 2 Mbits/sec. This is confirmed by technical measurements taken of reception parameters.

It must be emphasised that these results are from a small number of respondents (368) viewing in normal lecture room conditions on existing television replay equipment. The results, however, are so consistent that the technical threshold is unlikely to change in a larger-scale experiment. Developments of the next standard (MPEG2) will improve quality even further.

The consequence for educational satellite transmission is important. Since transponder costs constitute half the cost of delivery a reduction to probably 10% of current bandwidth requirement will provide significant savings. The number of satellites available is increasing and the new launches include transponders which will be accessible by several users simultaneously. EUTELSAT, a major operator, estimates that even full transponder costs will be halved over the next five years.

Evaluation

The early STARNET series was evaluated by Diana Laurillard of the Open University (Laurillard *et al.*, 1991). Her team identified ten factors that contribute to the viability of satellite transmission for training.

1. Programmes are relevant to students' and trainees' needs.
2. Participants receive briefing and debriefing and integrated study material to follow up the issues raised in the programmes.
3. Participants are able to attend all the group viewings of the programmes at the transmitted times.
4. A local site facilitator is available to supervise technical set-up and to provide

control and encouragement of use of the audio bridge.
5. The local institutions value and give support to the medium.
6. An understanding of the subject is enhanced by detailed and anecdotal discussion and argument, or the subject matter is topical and requires immediate delivery, to ensure that benefits are maximised.
7. Participants are likely to value each others' questions and viewpoints, to ensure that benefits are maximised.
8. Participants are located near to a satellite receiving station to reduce their time costs.
9. Delivery costs can be shared with other projects also requiring satellite reception.
10. Programme production costs are commensurate with audience size.

These results are borne out by the findings of the compressed video research for ESA. Although the main purpose was to determine a suitable level for compression, the answers to the other questions are relevant. Because of delays in delivery of equipment and the availability of suitable transponder time some sites were not able to provide students matched to the programme content. Since many students are used to fast-paced entertainment programmes on broadcast television, unless the programme is directly relevant to their studies they are very critical. The results also emphasised the importance of marketing and briefing. Few students had experience of educational broadcasts and stated that they expected production standards equivalent to BBC or ITV rather than a distributed lecture. They were, however, enthusiastic about the opportunity to ask questions of the studio experts, perhaps best illustrated by the comment, 'you can ring in and get your questions answered by someone who may know more about the topic than your own course tutor'.

Future developments

A group chaired by Martin Bangemann met in Corfu in June 1994 to prepare a report for the European Council. Their recommendations, *Europe and the global information society*, form the basis of European policy and have led to the large-scale Telematics Applications programme 1995–9 for which £650m of funding will be available. The Bangemann group recommended 'urgent and coherent action at both European and Member States levels to promote the provision and widespread use of standard, trans-European basic services, including electronic mail, file transfer and video services'. The group set a number of targets. Of particular relevance to this discussion are:

- **Application 2:** Telematics distance learning in use by 10% of small to medium enterprises and public administrations by 1996. Awareness campaigns among the professional associations and education authorities.
- **Application 3:** 30% of European research centres and universities linked through advanced communications networks by 1997.
- **Application 4:** 40% of firms with more than 50 employees using telematics networks by 1996.

It is important that education and training are an integral part of this information society. The activities described above show that systems and techniques for live delivery at a distance are now proven, but as yet except in the medical field there has been no long-term self-funding delivery of courses using satellite or terrestrial links in Europe. As compression techniques develop, increasing quantities of information can be sent through terrestrial links, while at the same time less bandwidth is required for satellite transmission. What is important at this stage is to establish criteria for effective delivery and to integrate the available telematics systems so that a 'best-fit' scenario can be provided for all users. The opportunity to use telematics to bring the message from the leading expert in the field to the student in the village hall must not be lost.

References

Abbott, L, Dallat, J, Livingston, R and Robinson, A (1994) 'The application of video conferencing to the advancement of independent group learning for professional development', *Educational and Training Technology International*, **31**, 2, 85–93.

Bangemann, M *et al.* (1994) *Europe and the global information society*, European Council Report, Brussels, Belgium.

ESA (1994) *Olympus and Beyond*, European Space Agency, Noordwijk, Netherlands.

Keegan, D (1986) *The Foundations of Distance Learning*, Croom Helm, Beckenham.

Laurillard, D *et al.* (1991) *Starnet Evaluation Report*, Learning Technologies Unit, Manpower Services Commission, Sheffield, UK.

Address for correspondence: **Ray Winders**, Telematics Coordinator, Academic Services, University of Plymouth, Drake Circus, Plymouth PL4 8AA.

24. People Networking: Learning from Past Experience to Develop Effective Networks for the Future

Jane Field, *Consultant Education & Development Services*

SUMMARY

This chapter will briefly consider good practice and pitfalls identified from past and existing networks. In the light of the emphasis on networks in the new European training and development programmes, it is useful to consider the role of transnational partnerships (the favourite EU term for networks) and how effective partnerships can be developed and written into applications. The UK government also has a recent history of pump-priming consortia and 'strategic' partnerships.

It is not only in education that networks have been expanding in numbers; industry too has been involving itself in networks, more often referred to as 'strategic alliances'. It would seem pertinent, therefore, to consider whether the experiences of industrial networks bear any relevance to educational networks. Finally, I would like to encourage further discussion as to how new technology might be exploited to facilitate people networking. This chapter does not intend to provide the definitive answer, rather it is an opportunity to raise some of the issues and encourage positive developments in people networking.

Introduction

The term 'networking' is used here to describe any informal or formal group of individuals or institutions, sharing information, meeting and working together – hopefully with common aims and objectives. Networking is a way of organising, setting about getting the job done, without a hierachial pyramid. The aim is to encourage debate and, ideally, the practice of effective networking.

People networks will identify themselves in different ways (consortium, association, partnership, union, federation, forum, etc), the key being that the network can achieve more together than the individuals or institutions working on their own. 'More' might be more information and knowledge, greater funding, more opportunities, a wider market, increased income. Whatever 'more' is the goal, the effective network will provide new contacts, collaboration and shared experience. Chris Mulvey's descriptive image of networking is 'a net or honeycomb, a collection of equal parts connected up to one another... the flow of power, energy, information, resources is horizontal' (Mulvey, 1994).

From the mid-1980s and into the 1990s, there has been an explosion of networks at all levels, from government-funded initiatives, both education/industry consortia (eg Regional Technology Centres and Language Export Centres), and 'strategic' partnerships (such as City Challenge) regional consortia, where higher and further education have tried to work in collaboration rather than in competition (eg the East

171

Anglian Universities Environment Consortium, the CONTACT consortium in Manchester and the Coventry Consortium), to networks across Europe (such as SATURN and the European Universities Continuing Education Network).

The scope and nature of networks varies from those restricted to a specific geographical basis to thematic networks which could be local, national or international; strategic and policy-based networks to those with a specific function and goal in mind from the outset. Others will have a lobbying mandate, and some networks have developed with the sole intention of running as an effective lobbying group. Adding a note of realism and cynicism, there are also a number of networks that are established predominantly in response to opportunities to bid for funds.

Here I discuss three evaluation research projects I have carried out, which show the scope and variety of networks that exist. The first project, in the summer of 1993, looked at university continuing education departments to identify the extent of, and objectives for, networking across Europe. This was carried out in association with the Universities Association for Continuing Education, using a postal questionnaire to which 55 universities responded – a 60% response rate (Field, 1994).

The second project, funded by the Department of Trade and Industry in 1994, evaluated the role of consortia, giving particular consideration to how they might be further exploited to increase higher education and industry links. The recommendations from this project were circulated to the Committee of Vice Chancellors and Principals and university industrial liaison officers.

The most recent project, with Making Belfast Work (Department of Environment in Northern Ireland) was completed in March 1995, and considered how to facilitate and support the development of effective partnerships in areas of urban deprivation in Belfast; with representation on the partnerships from the community, statutory bodies, councillors, the private sector and other organisations. The project considered how these partnerships might be strategically developed across areas of urban deprivation in Belfast to reduce social exclusion, develop employment opportunities and improve the quality of life – perhaps one of the most ambitious network projects yet. More tangibly, the project also identified good practice, pitfalls, necessary information and communication channels and the role of the central unit in developing these partnerships.

Good practice, procedures and pitfalls

Without doubt there is much to be gained by learning from both good and bad experiences of other networks. From the research projects, case studies and other documentation, I have developed a series of checklists and guidelines for good practice, procedures and potential pitfalls. These are included in the appendix (p.180), while in the main part of this chapter I have identified some of the key issues, supported by case study examples, from the three projects.

It is useful to expand on examples taken from the good practice checklists; the need to identify practical targets and goals, and the network members achieving together what individuals and individual institutions cannot. In order to gain credibility and a belief in the benefits that the network team can derive, it is necessary to achieve success. A local community forum, comprising three estates at the end of the Shankill Road in Belfast, felt much scepticism about the opportunities to be gained from working together. Shortly after they began to establish the forum, a one-day festival was held on the three estates. This event, organised predominantly by a member of the Action Team (part of Making Belfast Work), was seen to be such a success that the following year the forum members organised and ran a week-long festival. Learning from the success of this event, and believing that they could work together as a team, they have now developed a number of working subcommittees on a range of issues, and having achieved previous success together feel that it is both worthwhile and possible to consider 'riskier' ventures where there is a possibility of failure.

Perhaps one of the key issues is that the network needs to be able to achieve together what individuals and individual institutions cannot. This is the 'added value' that the network can provide – whether it is the sharing of knowledge, information and expertise; that a training programme can be developed using the complementary expertise of the members; or that an application for funding has more chance of success coming from a consortium than from an individual organisation.

A lesson to be learnt from the potential pitfalls is that it is far better to bring forward issues of concern at the outset, rather than to hope they will not emerge as problems if no one mentions them. For example, agreement of proposals for (at least) two Regional Technology Centres was dragged out over a period of almost two years due to factors such as distrust between members, hidden agendas, and a general breakdown in communication. Additionally, the need to respect and try to understand different cultures is essential for success, for example the different approaches to solving problems taken by education and industry.

In terms of the procedures and evaluation checklists, one key issue that is often neglected is a regular review of the network. It is possible that the network may need to refocus and revitalise itself in order to continue to operate effectively. In the survey of university continuing education departments it became apparent that building and developing transnational networks is a slow and time-consuming activity, the benefits and outcomes of which can take over two years to identify. From this survey it was also interesting to note that all respondents thought it worthwhile allocating resources to European networking, predominantly with a view to widening potential markets and identifying and developing potential transnational partners.

During the network review it may be necessary to ask whether the network should continue. After five years, in 1993, Norfolk Export and Language Services (NELS) asked themselves this question and decided that, as language training programmes had increased in number and participation locally – two resource centres, offering different services and products had been funded and established in the past two years – and with the demise of the regional Language Export Centre, it was a logical time to cease the activities of NELS.

If a network does decide to fold once it has achieved its original goals, then this should be viewed as a success, not a failure (eg the STRIDE project in Yorkshire, where regional universities are working together with the Regional Technology Network).

Industrial networks

Mitchell Koza (1993) believes that there is a lot to be learned by looking at business networks, more commonly known as alliances. Strategic alliances have been increasing in the commercial world since the mid-1970s. Koza gives three 'essential complementarities' for successful alliances:

* market access and development
* competencies and skills
* technological innovation.

He argues that higher education faces similar challenges to the business world and that the essential complementarities should be seriously taken into account by those involved in HE alliances. Koza further states that many industrial alliances are short-lived, ending once the goal is achieved, which makes commercial sense.

Andrew Fearne (1994) has studied strategic alliances in the food industry and concludes that alliances may be either vertical or horizontal in nature. Vertical alliances, entered into freely by buyers and sellers, 'facilitate a mutually satisfying exchange over a period of time'. Horizontal alliances involve businesses operating in similar market sectors and have two key motives:

* to increase bargaining strength with major buyers or sellers
* to maximise their competitive advantage by accelerating the pace and sharing the costs and technology associated with new product development.

One of the predominant motives for horizontal alliances is the need to coordinate activities in order to meet the needs of the retailer. Such alliances also provide an opportunity for the retailers to maintain their strength and to become directly involved in the development and manufacture of products.

Both Fearne and Koza believe that there will be a steady increase in industrial alliances across Europe. There are some interesting similarities between industrial alliances and HE networks. Perhaps by studying the industrial alliances there might be clues as to how to involve industry in education/industry consortia more successfully and to consider exploiting opportunities for 'strategic alliances' within educational networks.

The European dimension

National interest in networking is in line with developments across the European Union, not least within the Commission's new funding programmes. The employment programmes (Now, Horizon, Youthstart and Adapt) all require eligible projects to be involved with partners representing at least three member states. Other EU programmes, for example Leonardo, Socrates and Community Initiatives, also require evidence of active transnational partnerships.

Presumably reflecting the new status of networks within the 1994–99 programmes, a pilot project, 'Improving Academic Networking', was commissioned in 1994 by the European Commission's Taskforce for Human Resources (now DG XXII), and undertaken by representatives from each member state on behalf of the Committee of European Rectors (in the UK the CVCP). The project had the primary aim to consider the improvement of academic networks, particularly in the context of the proposals within the Socrates programme. Surveys were carried out within each of the then 12 member states, asking universities to evaluate networks in terms of their uses, the added value, opportunities for improvement and limitations; and to consider how the number of networks could be reduced, and the viability of network mergers.

The initial Socrates proposals on networking were to establish durable, well-structured, large transnational networks. The aim was to be one of rationalisation, to gain cost-savings, strengthen cohesion and improve the quality of education. It was proposed that large networks will be convergent, rather than haphazard, looking to institutional rather than individual support. Concern was voiced about this, both in the response to the pilot project and by others, as more often than not successful consortia exist because of the energy and enthusiasm of individual members. The Socrates programme has subsequently made changes to the initial proposals.

It is interesting to note some of the points made in the UK report to the CRE:

- there was no clear definition of what is meant by 'network';
- there is a fear of losing established ICPs;
- few universities have a defined European policy;
- network activities within universities should be recognised and acknowledged;
- it is necessary to have adequate funding and resources to maintain networks;
- further support for networks is needed from UK agencies;
- that language training is deficient in the UK.

The 'Improving Academic Networking' project recommendations (CPU-Corex, 1994) include:

- the need to train administrative personnel for international cooperation;
- to recognise network activities when defining workloads;
- to lighten the administrative burden by making the use of the ECU mandatory and also by simplifying contracts, evaluation forms, etc;
- to undertake support initiatives, such as meetings, debates and conferences to permit the exchange of opinions and experiences;
- to encourage better access to information on other countries;
- to maintain a European register listing networks.

The CVCP has recently issued a shorter version of the final report to Vice-Chancellors and Principals (CVCP, 1995).

Experience to date with the new employment programmes shows that it is no longer the case that one partner is expected to adopt the role of coordinator, developing a bid that all transnational partners agree. In the new employment programme it is required that each transnational partner develop their own project, and submit this bid to their own member state support structure. Each hopeful transnational partner does this, listing the other potential partners and the only overt key to the fact that they are in a partnership is that the same project name is used by each partner. In addition to the application form there is 'transnational partner documentation', which in the UK is completed during the second stage of the application procedure, but in some member states is completed and submitted with the application form. The member state support structures will then (somehow) discuss which applications are merit worthy, and whether this applies to some or all of the partners in any proposed partnership. They may offer alternative partners to some applicants if it is felt that their initial partners do not come up to scratch. Confused? At the time of writing, this system has yet to be developed, tried and tested.

Transnational partners figure very highly in the new Leonardo programme, with almost every project requiring partners from a minimum of three member states (or other approved players). Under the Leonardo programme it should be noted that one partner will take on the role of project coordinator (as in previous programmes, such as COMETT and FORCE) and submit the bid – the partners will submit copies of the bid, but may lobby on the project's behalf if the coordinator's bid is rejected. It is interesting to note that financial allocations have not been made in advance to each country (unlike the European Social Fund, for example, where each country knows in advance what share of the funding they will receive).

What is apparent is that, realistically, it will no longer be possible to leave the development of bids requiring transnational partners to the last minute. These bids, and the selection of partners, will need serious development if the application form and the 'transnational partner documentation' can be meaningfully and competently completed.

Choosing transnational partners perhaps needs more consideration than entering into regional or national networks; certainly there are different considerations to be taken into account. The following list suggests some of the issues:

- a common philosophy and approach to activities;
- written clarification of the purposes of the project;
- agreement of the transnational activities;
- a similar range and level of activities, professional knowledge and experience;
- an interest in learning new skills and meeting challenges;
- an involvement in promoting and encouraging European integration and knowledge of other cultures;
- realistic and innovative attitudes to transnational partnerships and cooperation;
- a common vision of what they can expect from and contribute to possible projects;
- a clear idea of how to put the partnership into practice;
- opportunity and commitment to financially resource projects;
- working language(s), at meetings and in documentation;
- commitment at senior management level;
- roles and responsibilities of the individuals involved.

Kilday (1992) provides a case study of his experiences in managing a transnational network. He warns of the initial problems of dealing with 'an extremely complex regional structure in Europe', that it will take at least a year to establish the network, not least to overcome organisational problems and, as might be expected, language and cultural differences. Reports from the Commission give examples of the Commission's view of good practice across transnational partnerships. For example, the TEMPUS annual report for 1992–93 suggests that factors contributing to the impact of TEMPUS projects include:

* the involvement and cooperation of all project partners on an equal basis;
* strong personal commitment of all partners, with the success of a project often dependent on strong support from individuals;
* realistic project aims understood by all the partners.

The report on COMETT University Enterprise Training Partnerships (European Commission, 1994) provides information on both transnational and university/industry partnerships. The analysis highlighted three basic factors underpinning the launch of all partnerships:

* the project promoters have interests in common;
* there is a combination of incidental factors, including chance and necessity;
* one of two principal types of partnership evolution is followed: short term (serving specific projects) or long term (for structural-type partnerships).

When measuring the success of partnership projects, three major categories are identified in the COMETT report: raising awareness (changing outlook and mentality); introducing strategies for cooperation and action and new concepts and new approaches; new professions and new policies. To gain the most benefit from transnational partnerships in the future the report offers four key words: integration, synergy, partnership and quality. An example of the activities of a transnational partnership is the Parsons Cross College, Sheffield (Nasta, 1993). The network, funded through the PETRA programme achieved:

* a forum for the heads and directors to discuss problems and share ideas on management issues;
* two-way student exchange programmes;
* collaborative cross-network curriculum projects;
* staff development seminar for staff from the partner institutions;
* sharing of practice, information and resources;
* a programme of structured staff visits;
* the potential for joint developments in the future.

For many, the possibility of developing transnational partnerships is exciting and stimulating. There are numerous ways of developing links and identifying potential partners, not least through one of the 57 university Euro-networks, only five of which are over 15 years old, identified by Mitchell and Thomas (1993). They argue that the benefits of European networking include the stimulation of transnational academic activities and broader funding opportunities.

The Euro-networking survey of continuing education departments (Field, 1994) confirmed that collaboration with European partners was widespread among university continuing education departments, showing that most respondents were involved in at least a couple of formal networks, as well as developing more informal, personal links. In the two years since this survey was undertaken, many universities have been involved with transnational projects working with partners, and one of the concerns now is that it may be too late to develop partnerships. Recent experience indicates that this is not the case; there are a lot of opportunities to identify new partners with similar interests. Reports and compendiums, available from European Commission offices, provide examples of transnational projects that have been funded, and usually provide contact names and addresses. Very often those experienced in transnational partnerships are willing and able to coordinate and lead projects, and are willing to include new partners into existing or new networks.

Networks and new technology

Video-conferencing provides the opportunity to have visual contact with partners located at a distance without incurring the costs and time involved with travel. With the use of 'Super Janet', the costs are negligible once the system is set up. Audio-conferencing provides similar opportunities for a number of users at different sites to link up.

At present one of the most exciting challenges is to exploit the use of e-mail. As well as developing personal e-mail lists it is possible to access mailing lists established by others. In the UK, Mailbase offers a range of lists, a number of which are relevant to those in education and development, in particular the continuing education list, consisting mainly of individuals from UK universities. There are a number of European and international lists including a European access list on Mailbase and a list run by the European Society for Research in the Education of Adults.

E-mail is an excellent way of sharing information, requesting information and allowing equality of access. Like all things, some form of motivation is required to get to grips with the technology, but it is arguably a cost-effective and simple method of reaching one or more people at the push of a button.

These are a few initial and perhaps obvious ideas, but it seems likely that if networks are to continue to develop, particularly transnational networks, then exploring the opportunities offered by new technology is a logical way forward.

Conclusion

While there are many inter-university networks, there are few real inter-agency networks, or effective education/industry consortia. Transnational networks are going to increase with the new round of EU programmes, if for no other reason than that proposals will be ineligible without the transnational element. It is essential, if the benefits of networking are valued, that hindsight and lessons learnt are put to good use, developing a generation of positive, active networks. People networking is about social change and developing strategies, relationships and progress. Inter-agency, education/industry and transnational partnerships, if effectively developed, offer a means to influence society on a global scale.

The opportunities are considerable, and it is therefore important that we restrict ourselves to those networks that can really provide added value to our work and our institutions if we are to avoid network fatigue.

To conclude, I believe that recently established networks have replaced the 'old boys network'; that in a society where few professional people will have the roles and responsibilities with which they started off, and where it is possible to influence social change through effective lobbying, networks have an important role to play. With the proliferation of educational networks, the experience of evaluation and case studies and the Commission reports there is an opportunity for education to lead the way.

References

CPU-Corex on behalf of the Liaison Committee and CRE (1994) *Improving Academic Networking,* Report to the Taskforce on Human Resources, Education and Youth, Brussels.

CVCP (1995) Liaison Committee Project Reports N/95/61, Committee of Vice-Chancellors and Principals, London.

European Commission (1994) *Networks and European Training Partnerships*, Office for Official Publications, Luxembourg.

Fearne, A (1994) 'Strategic Alliances in the European Food Industry', European Business Conference, University of Nottingham.

Field, J (1994) European Networking, *Adults Learning*, **5**, 10, 267–8.

Kilday, A (1992) 'Forming and running networks, an overview', *Strategies for European Interregional Partnerships*, European Centre for Regional Development, pp.81–90.

Koza, M (1993) 'Business alliances and what can be learned from them for education', European Association for International Education (EAIE) Conference.

McNay I, Wogan P and Bell M (1994) *Review of European Networking in UK Universities*, Report to the Council of European Rectors.

Mitchell, V and Thomas, E (1993) *European Co-operation in University Continuing Education*, European Universities Continuing Education Network, Barcelona.

Mulvey, C (1994) 'The Importance of Networking', *The Adult Learner*, Dublin, pp.46–51.

Nasta, T (1993) *Change Through Networking in Vocational Education*, Kogan Page, London.

Address for correspondence: **Jane Field**, Education and Development, 18 Caien Road, Carrickfergus, Co Antrim BT38 9AP.

Appendix

Networking – Good Practice

Objectives:
- specific goals (preferable to grand plans)
- the network as a facilitator
- identification of practical targets
- exploit synergy and develop added value activities.

Strategies:
- short- and long-term planning
- serve clearly defined goals, which may generate additional spin-offs
- bring active people on board
- demonstrate seriousness and commitment of purpose
- focus ideas and agree on rationale
- identify practical targets.

Tasks:
- network's image and influence
- information dissemination
- public relations (local press, radio and television coverage)
- action oriented, leading to projects
- staff development opportunities
- working with other networks and partnerships
- evaluation and monitoring of performance
- awareness raising activities for the consortium
- develop links with government departments and other key agencies
- make skills and expertise available to the community
- use of market research data and labour market surveys.

Network publications:
- a general leaflet, outlining aims, objectives, membership, client-group
- regular bulletin (quarterly)
- thematic and conference reports.

Attitudes of the members:
- willing to share information, expertise and experience
- openness about institutional needs
- prepared to accept times when leadership is necessary
- ability to innovate
- commitment and involvement of all members
- collaboration leading to acquiring a common language
- mutual respect and trust
- energy, leading to action
- common purpose
- an agreed spectrum of interest.

Meet the needs of the members:
- flexibility
- identification of members interests
- allow time for discussion of current activities
- ability to innovate
- respect differences
- opportunity for personal contact
- a feeling of ownership by the members.

Infrastructure:
- membership fee
- one contact point within institutions
- develop a database of members' expertise
- agree administrative duties, require a reliable, efficient secretariat
- supportive, influential steering group
- small working and interest groups
- the flow of power, energy, information, resources is horizontal
- recognition of formal, informal or contractual status
- agree open financial transactions and records.

The processes involved in developing networks

Set objectives

⇓

Attract members

⇓

Attract funding

⇓

Survey the market

⇓

Refine the market

⇓

Attract more members

⇓

Agree methods of working

⇓

Attract further funding and
income-generating activities

⇓

Awareness raising/marketing

⇓

Continuing provision of services

⇓

Review

Evaluating networks

As part of the review process evaluation should be one of the logical steps. The checklist below suggests some of the questions that might be asked of networks.

- Their uses – what are they doing, who benefits?
- The added value – ie what does the network offer that individual institutions cannot?
- Are there opportunities for improvement and future development?
- What are the limitations? (Accept what the network can and can't do.)
- Should the viability of network mergers be considered? (Too many networks lead to network fatigue or they may become too large to function effectively.)
- What are the costs of time, money and other resources compared to benefits?
- What is the impact of the network, assessed in terms of the task and the processes?
- How representative is the network?
- Is there participation by and involvement of all members?

Potential pitfalls and issues for consideration

Between network members:
- the need to break down barriers (especially mutual suspicion)
- self-protectionism
- misunderstandings
- hidden agendas
- need for clear understanding on aims
- understand and accept cultural differences
- mobilising resources
- proactive *vs* passive.

Within members' institutions:
- communication practices within institutions
- political issues
- incentives to take out and maintain membership
- protectionist behaviour towards own contacts and links
- awareness that benefits are not always immediate
- gaining support at senior management level.

In order that the network can meet its objectives:
- practical applications are often needed
- it can be difficult to get SMEs involved
- agreement of systems, especially administrative and financial
- monitoring and evaluation
- mechanisms for taking decisions, particularly between meetings.

Miscellaneous:
- geographical size of the region, ie where to meet, where to locate the centre
- how to deal with repeat business, ie the network's role
- how to monitor the progress of the network
- how best to mobilise resources.

25. Instructional Design for Group-Based Learning by Computer Conferencing

Anita Pincas, *University of North London*

SUMMARY

The Internet, or Information Superhighway, has revolutionised contact between people in the past decade. Distance education is being altered beyond recognition by computer-mediated communication (CMC), and traditional on-campus education will certainly also be influenced by the flexibility it offers. CMC may be used in several different ways:

- As a communication support system, it can add a convenient time and place independent means for students and tutors to contact each other, either individually via e-mail or for group discussions by computer conferencing, whether for on-campus or distance courses.
- As a pedagogic system in itself, it can form an adjunct to traditional courses, by enabling seminar discussions that are otherwise inconvenient to timetable, or it can itself be the backbone of a course, particularly a distance course.
- As a delivery system, it transmits text or multimedia materials to onsite or remote students, for self-study or group work.

Computer conferencing for higher education

This chapter looks at computer-mediated communication as a pedagogic medium. It is based on personal experience in using computer conferencing as the backbone of two ongoing courses: an MA for English teachers and a Certificate in Online Education for staff in universities and colleges (both given at London University Institute of Education and available internationally). I believe that if the medium is well handled it is particularly effective in promoting student-centred collaborative learning. I question the presumption that students' mere presence in traditional lectures and face-to-face seminars ensures learning. I would also suggest that as education becomes more and more international, just-in-time, work-related and learner-driven, a flexible medium that allows students to remain in their own environment will more effectively relate to local needs and interests than the traditional, rigidly structured, prepackaged college courses to which students often relocate.

UK higher education is now moving towards a view of education that takes learners' real needs into account and lets teachers and students develop their courses in highly individualised ways. In this scenario, Computer Conference has a crucial role to play because it is ideally suited to busy people who wish to work in their own time, in their own style, on the areas of knowledge that are of most relevance to them in their personal environment. A quick comparison of Computer Conference with other pedagogic modes shows Computer Conference's positive benefits:

	Lecture	Seminar	Workshop	Conference
Stimulates learning activity	No	Maybe	Yes	Yes
Enables learner collaboration	No	Maybe	Yes	Yes
Caters for individual differences	No	Not much	Maybe	Yes
Is time/place independent	No	No	No	Yes
Widens learner access	Maybe	Yes	Yes	Yes
Motivates learning	Maybe	Maybe	Yes	Yes
Diminishes stress	Yes	No	Maybe	Yes

The key points in the chart are that Computer Conference stimulates learning activity and enables learner collaboration. The reason for this lies in the nature of the medium. If you bring people together in a text-based medium with asynchronous communication, they are not truly present to each other unless they are contributing messages to the conference. It is quite different from bringing students together in a classroom, where they are all present even if they remain silent. *In Computer Conference, to be there is to 'say' something.* Not only do Computer Conference students feel free to speak as much as they wish at their leisure, they feel a need to do so in order to register their existence in the course. I have no doubt that it is this peculiarly Computer Conference factor in the courses I have run, that has not only created the opportunity to shift towards learner-centred collaborative activities, but has indeed required it.

There are two further motivational aspects of asynchronous Computer Conference. Stress is much diminished, first, by the fact that students work when they are ready to (contributions can be considered before being put online) and, second, by an environment where personal features are irrelevant. In this sense, Computer Conference can cater for individual differences by freeing students to work at their own pace in their own way. Moreover, students can go back over previous parts of a discussion, rethink the issues, and develop them further. They thus have ready-made equivalents of lecture notes that can be annotated, reorganised, summarised, and used for general learning purposes.

Successful use of Computer Conference for education also involves careful structuring of the interactive discourse, and this depends crucially on the goals of the course. A method has to be found to enable students to glean the knowledge they need either from relevant material or from participation in the conference. Traditional pedagogy starts with input from a teacher, usually followed up by some kind of student activity, in which the knowledge presented by the teacher can be activated, clarified, assimilated and refined.

Initially, there is a temptation to mimic that traditional pattern in Computer Conference courses. One can present students with video copies of lectures or demonstrations, and follow up with exercises. In my courses, this method has actually worked very satisfactorily. But it is extremely expensive and time-consuming in preparation. Fortunately, it is not the only way to organise learning by Computer Conference, and indeed it may not be the most effective.

An alternative student-centred approach has been found equally satisfactory. This turns the teacher-input leading to student-activity pattern around, and starts with tasks that students are asked to do before they have received any teaching. The teacher is then in a reactive position, acting as a commentator on the students' work. I am referring to what might be called 'directed learning by discovery'.

The Computer Conference medium is particularly suited to this because it has the benefits of allowing students to do their tasks at leisure and then communicate conveniently in a group environment. It is quite different from face-to-face workshops where the students are forced to cooperate with each other in the here-and-now situation; they have little time to reflect at their own pace, are often led by faster students (or an impatient teacher who needs to finish the class on time!), and frequently have to stand aside because there is no space for everyone to take part.

The key to my own Computer Conference approach is task-based learning with student collaboration built in. The method is to demarcate a number of small areas of the topic, and to give each student one or two tasks to perform within each small area. The tasks might be based on some necessary reading, or on reflection on past experience, or on a small experiment to be carried out. All the tasks for each small area constitute an overview of that area. So that, when all the students have put their answers online, the area has been covered. The collection of all the small areas together gives a view of the wider topic.

In practice, what occurs online in the conference is not simply a list of answers to the tasks, but a discussion among the students. They comment on each others' answers, or ask for help when they are confused. In order to allow this kind of fruitful collaboration, it is important for the student groups to be quite small, otherwise the number of tasks and messages becomes too difficult to follow. Just as in face-to-face contexts, a discussion among more than about eight or ten people is unlikely to succeed if all want a role in it.

Further, it is necessary to help students to establish a community atmosphere. My courses all start with face-to-face meetings, the purpose of which is as much to help people become friendly with each other as to initiate the courses. However, students who cannot attend these meetings do not feel excluded because everyone receives a sheet of photographs and certain personal details of all course members and tutors.

In Computer Conference, there is unlimited time to 'chat' as well as do the coursework. The 'Café' area of all my courses always has at least double the number of messages of any other area. In time, multimedia packages will connect a picture of message senders, and will allow live video-conferencing. But in the meantime, a text-based system can already achieve group cooperation and personal relationships over a period of time. As can be seen from the extracts at the end of this chapter, the tone of the messages is highly conversational and informal. It reads like a genuine chat between fellow students even though it took about ten days to complete and the students were scattered all over the UK.

Computer Conference uses technology very similar to that used for e-mail , but the software is different. E-mail bombards recipients with an unordered list of message-headings from different people, which then have to be selected, opened and collated. In Computer Conference, users are automatically brought into contact with all other participants, since logging in to a conference opens up the entire discussion and one can see the discussion developing.

For educational purposes one can think of what occurs in any one file of a Computer Conference as the written analogue of a live face-to-face seminar. The computer seminar extends over any period of time that the tutor allows (eg, the duration of the whole course). This enables students to enter and leave the seminar at times convenient to themselves, knowing that they never risk missing anything.

The tutor could edit the conference to make it more coherent, summarise it, remove unacceptable input, add further comments, and so on. It is possible to discover who has been into the conference, and follow through to people who have been absent. A Computer Conference becomes a database in itself, filled with information provided by the members. But it is more flexible than a database, which normally has a preordained format.

Course design

A conference is divided into a number of separate areas for discussion. These are separate files which, in the conferencing system being used on my courses (CoSy) are called 'Topics'. The table below shows the structure of one ten-week term of the Masters degree, which is the computer conference analogue of the well-established full-time course. The five subject areas are covered in five Topics each of which lasts two weeks. The 24 students are allocated to one of two groups for each subject. In addition there is Noticeboard, and a blank area, 000, for general discussion. There is also an online café in which a great deal of personal chat takes place.

Topic	Description
Notices	Noticeboard
000	General discussion
Café	Social chat
Theory 1	group 1 to discuss Nature of Theory
Theory 2	group 2 to discuss Nature of Theory
Aspects 1	group 1 to discuss Aspects of Language
Aspects 2	group 2 to discuss Aspects of Language
Disc 1	group 1 to discuss Discourse Analysis
Disc 2	group 2 to discuss Discourse Analysis
Levels 1	group 1 to discuss Levels and Scope of Linguistics
Levels 2	group 2 to discuss Levels and Scope of Linguistics
Lexis 1	group 1 to discuss Lexis
Lexis 2	group 2 to discuss Lexis

My course design involves the following components:

- A pack of edited videos of parts of the full-time face-to-face sessions for each of the five Topics, made informally during regular classes.

- A timetable setting out the progression from Topic to Topic over the ten weeks of the term.
- A list of readings, including set textbooks and recommended books and articles.
- A set of workshop tasks for each Topic. Students contribute their answers at some time during the two weeks that the Topic runs, and other students comment on them as they see fit. I, as tutor, intervene very little during this period, but at the end of each Topic, I provide a summary with my comments on the students' work. In this way the teacher-input leading to student-activity pattern has been reversed: student-activity leading to teacher-input. It is roughly equivalent to a face-to-face situation in which a number of workshop groups are set up in the room, the tutor moves from one to another, and at the end chairs a plenary session where the work of all groups is brought together.

Skills required

A clear advantage for both distance and on-campus education lies in the opportunity for constant and unlimited interaction among students and tutors. In fact, this interaction has proved so rich that students sometimes complain of 'overload'. One reason for this is that unlike a face-to-face seminar in which only a small number of students manage to say anything, this medium allows everyone to put in as many messages as they wish. But in my view overload only becomes a problem in open discussion. It does not occur in the pattern of task-work I have described because that gives precise guidelines as to what and how much work each student is expected to do, and leaves the group with a sense of closure when the tasks have been completed.

In both of my courses it has been found advantageous for students to be able to type adequately and be able to perform basic word-processing tasks. It is essential to manage a modem and appropriate software. For novices in electronic communications, it is not easy to learn how to use these from the manuals alone. It is expected that in the future many of the problems that our pioneering students have had with the technology will be overcome by more user-friendly software solutions.

Many students do experience difficulty and frustration in the early weeks, and the courses have to make allowances for this. It would, of course, be highly desirable to ensure that all course members were using the same modems and communications software, so that we could offer training to all. But for many institutions such as my own, this is unrealistic at present.

It may also be desirable for a degree course to start with a pre-sessional skills period. But experience has shown that students do not take advantage of these, and it might be necessary to make such a period compulsory. For both of my courses, the computing facilities have been made available more than a month before the start date. But very few students have taken advantage of this opportunity. Some have not even set up their system by the time the course starts! This is no doubt partly due to the optimism of inexperience.

It is also essential to transfer the communication and interaction skills familiar to face-to-face environments into a totally written mode, at a distance in space and time from the interlocutors. Learning to handle this new mode of communication takes a little time, both for tutors and students. Human communication seems very adaptable to new media.

The interface of a text-based Computer Conference system like CoSy which my courses use, has an unexpected effect on users that one might not believe unless one has experienced Computer Conference. Sitting at the screen, reading and then responding to a message, one feels an immediacy of communication, even though one knows perfectly well that one is alone with the computer. This is because the transcript of a Computer Conference looks like the transcript of a long discussion (see extract). *The very appearance of a real discussion influences the participants to behave as if it is.* And this is crucial for collaborative learning (currently popular Windows-based systems like First Class lack discussion-like interfaces, a serious shortcoming in my view).

Evaluation

Comments from one of my recent evaluation sheets for the Masters courses include:

> 'Fun as well as instructive.'
> 'Feel part of the course as soon as you switch on the computer.'
> 'More time to mull over new ideas, concepts.'
> 'Experience of group is high.'
> 'I feel very fortunate to be part of this pioneer work.'
> 'I'm very positive – it's an interesting medium of exchange and I think it has some significant advantages over traditional distance learning. The quality of discussion is I think often well above that generated in (traditional) face-to-face.'

Of the 22 students on the Masters course:

- all reported that they enjoyed the course itself;
- only two claimed to have had any difficulty learning the conferencing system;
- only one found the medium dissatisfying because they had not overcome technical problems;
- half found it as satisfying as a face-to-face course;
- 16 found that they were getting as much or more help from fellow students as from tutors;
- 14 consider it less time-consuming than an equivalent part-time face-to-face course would be;
- 18 listed flexibility (of time, workplace, methods) as the main reason for satisfaction.

The future

There are many educational issues that arise out of this mode of delivery. What seems evident to us already is that Computer Conference is a suitable mode of course delivery for the two types of course we have attempted (ie, for a higher degree in a humanities subject – in this case post-initial training of English teachers – and for educators to learn the mode itself). Its great advantage for distance education – and possibly also for on-campus courses – lies in the opportunity for constant and unlimited interaction among students and tutors. Issues to be explored include:

- ways of training tutors and students in the new technology;
- developing useful interaction skills in the medium of writing;
- integrating Computer Conference with other media in course delivery;
- integrating Computer Conference with face-to-face teaching;
- keeping special materials to a minimum;
- the new language skills required;
- the most cost-effective way of using the medium.

Conference extract

The extract shows only those parts of the messages that indicate students' collaboration. For the sake of brevity, actual subject content is omitted, as indicated by [...]

Tara: 23.2.94   20.50
No one seems to have started discussion of the texts in session 4 yet. I don't think I was 'down' to answer one of the questions but I'd like to ask if anyone has done question b) i) yet (what knowledge and theory do you need before you interpret the data?) My question is what is meant by theory and knowledge here? I've done the rest of the questions but I got stuck on that one.

Bob   23.2.94   21.39
i. Title: 3b i Knowledge and theory to interpret the data. I really do agree with Tara. I find these questions vague in the extreme. So I'm only guessing at what is meant. I think [...]

Paul   27.2.94   13.25
Title: Session 4 3(b) GULP!!! 'Goosie Goosie' to quote Bob. [...] you need the following knowledge [...]. Like Tara and Bob, I'm rather stumped as to the 'theory' question [...] but [...] I'm not going any further cos I don't want to be the one who looks like a real twit!
3 (b) ii   I feel that [...]
3 (b) iii   I feel that [...]. I remember reading in [...]
HELP, has anyone else read it? Ch. 6.
3 (b) iv.   Sorry, can't understand what this question wants

Laura   28.2.94   19.04
Title: Comment on message 3.
Session 4 Tasks b(i) Paul I agree with what you say about the knowledge [...]

Mary   28.2.94   21.49
Session 4 Tasks b Knowledge and Theory needed to interpret data might be [...]

Paul   4.3.94   18.28
   Hi, Laura Thanks for the comment I'm not clear what you mean
by [...] A bit more?? A further comment on input from Laura, Mary
and Tara on [...]?

Address for correspondence: **Anita Pincas**, Lecturer in Education, Institute of
Education, London University, 20 Bedford Way, London WC1H OAL.

26. Support Implications for Hypermedia Flexible Learning Resources

Clive R Betts, *IT Services, University of Exeter*

SUMMARY
Recent advances in information technology have dramatically enhanced the quality and value of computer-based hypermedia learning resources. Access to such resources is also rapidly improving with the use of local networking and Internet facilities, giving rise to genuinely flexible materials.

However, successfully developing and exploiting such resources requires a very special support environment. Advice and help need to be available on a host of different topics ranging from highly technical hardware problems, through how to use different software packages, to the essentials of screen design.

Using experiences from Exeter University's IT Services, this chapter explores what sorts of facility are needed and how these may be developed and maintained effectively, while addressing the traditional problems of cost, time and staffing.

Although aimed at offering practical solutions to support problems, this chapter also raises fundamental questions about how and why we exploit IT resources for teaching and learning and, indeed, whether we should exploit them in the first place! It is a 'flattened' version of a hypermedia presentation: some elements of the original have therefore been lost in the squashing process (in particular the images and cross-referencing). The hypermedia version can be obtained by file transfer protocol (ftp) from ftp.ex.ac.uk. in the BETTS directory.

The flexible learning environment

Different people give different definitions but a reasonable consensus might include:

- resources that are not restricted to a specific room or laboratory;
- adequate provision for associated activities (eg, reading, writing, computing, viewing videos, listening to tapes);
- available help and support for these activities (eg, people, books, videos, tapes, computers);
- unconditional access (eg, not available on a departmental basis);
- wide access to all available resources;
- resources, including rooms, not bookable for certain people (eg, classes).

At Exeter, some facilities are already available and there is pressure on support services to provide more and better facilities, although it is a little unclear in some cases who should be responsible for funding, establishing, and maintaining, such resources.

Are computer applications flexible?
The flexiblity of computer applications is dependent on their mode of access. They are not very flexible in the sense that most of us cannot carry them around in a bag or pocket or have access to them in a study bedroom or at home, although this is rapidly changing as Halls of Residence are networked and better modem communications are implemented.

Access is greatly improved in a network environment: all you need here (in theory) is to actually find a vacant computer. This, of course, raises the question of who provides the vacant computer – to be truly flexible the resources provided must be freely available to all members of the institution, not tied to a department or faculty. In addition, the computer must be capable of running desired applications effectively, and support for these applications must be provided.

Why get involved with hypermedia work?

Keeping up with the Joneses
There has been a rapidly rising tide of interest in the range and accessibility of hypermedia products for teaching, learning and 'kiosk-type' information delivery (ie, like an interactive map of a library; see Aidie, 1993a; Hall *et al.*, 1990; Mapp, 1992; TLTP, 1995). From the point of view of a support department, it is the user community that has driven this interest.

- Users have seen the slick commercial products (eg, see Begg, 1993; Cooke, 1992) like Microsoft's *Encarta* or the Multimedia *Encyclopaedia of Mammalian Biology* (see Brake, 1994).
- Lecturers, tutors and trainers have more students to teach with less contact time – they perceive hypermedia might offer a solution.
- There is a desire, among many, to respond to current trends and not be left behind.
- Some see hypermedia as a way to finally update and revitalise old course material.

Users wishing to exploit hypermedia technology need support in the form of advice and help. IT services have to address these issues.

Industry pressure
Magazines, books, media coverage, equipment manufacturers and software vendors have provided a significant momentum for the uptake of hypermedia products by consumers. These consumers can be identified as business users, users from the home-entertainment market and, by far the largest group, the educational institutions and authorities (Commission of European Communities, 1993).

The 'multimedia industry' as a whole has also focused heavily on the CD-ROM delivery medium and especially, in Europe, CD-ROMs for the PC. We should not ignore the strength of push from such sources, which may be directed less at providing valuable learning resources and more at exploiting good-looking products that can be sold to eager, but naive consumers.

Functionality

Hypermedia resources appear to be attractive (at least at first) because they permit:

- dynamic presentation, which makes good use of graphic material;
- the combination of diverse media (eg, video, animation, still images, sound and text);
- full, partial or interactive automation of tasks (eg, modelling, searching, database querying, questioning);
- easy and effective navigation through large quantities of information.

Pedagogy or toy?

From the pedagogical point of view many subscribe to opinions like that of Laurillard (1993) who states that hyper*text* (a major component of hyper*media*) 'as an educational medium, enabling the student to develop their academic understanding, has little to offer.'

Precisely why this is the case is beyond the remit of this chapter. Laurillard's synthesis offers some insight, but the text skims over the potential for improving students' understanding of complex subject areas which current methods leave to massive, expensive textbooks, inaccessible journals and seldom-seen films or slides. Hypermedia does, nevertheless earn some recognition even from Laurillard by providing dynamic interactivity ('pedagogically very valuable') and the ability for students themselves to develop their own hyperdocuments ('a good thing to do'). The latter offers some promise, providing that sufficient feedback can be gained from the tutors involved to assess the students' work, and is an area where the World Wide Web (WWW) could have an important role.

Educationalists will continue to argue over the efficacy of technologies like hypermedia. Support departments, in the meantime, must be able to provide expertise and advice to those who choose to exploit these technologies. In this sense support departments cannot sit on the fence – we must aim to help distil useful products given the resources on offer.

Consequences of getting involved

Interest from users has led to a demand for appropriate resources:

- available space and facilities (machines, desks, books, etc) – somewhere for students to use flexible learning materials and somewhere for staff to develop them;
- adequate hardware and software for development and delivery of products;
- state-of-the-art support from skilled and well-informed support personnel;
- training covering use of available resources (including books, machines, etc).

Exactly what resources are needed, with what kind of support and what sort of training are issues to be resolved at an early stage.

All this implies considerable change for support staff and the user community (see Laurillard, 1993; Draper *et al.*, 1994). Addressing these issues and trying to keep track of new developments means support staff need constant skills and

knowledge updating. Exploitation of hypermedia resources for teaching and learning means changes in working practice for the tutors, trainers, lecturers and
demonstrators and consequently a change in the students' learning experiences.

Questions and answers

Those who seriously want to exploit hypermedia resources in their work often need
answers to the same sort of generic questions:

- For what can I exploit hypermedia flexible learning?
- What facilities do I need to do this; what is the best computing environment?
- What are the required components; where can I get them and how do I use them?
- Where do I start; what are the steps involved?
- How much time will it take to complete; who is going to do the work; how much
  is it going to cost?
- How do I get my soundcard to work?

Finding help
Answers to these and many other related queries, especially technical ones, have
been given many times before. The sources below can also yield some excellent
examples of working hypermedia applications, software tools and hardware and
software evaluations (fuller details are given in the reading list at the end of this
chapter).

- The Internet (Usenet News, Listservers, Bulletin Boards, ftp sites, WWW).
- Books and magazines (eg Arnold *et al.*, 1994; Badgett and Sandler, 1994; Kelly,
  1994; Mapp, 1992; Multimedia White Paper, 1994), OEM material.
- Workshops, conferences, seminars (watch especially for ALT workshops, BSC
  seminars, and CAL conferences).

If you are researching particular areas, such as how to record onto video tape from
a PC, the best advice is always from someone who has already done it (usually via
the above sources).

Likely candidates for hypermedia, flexible learning material
It is generally agreed that the use of hypermedia flexible learning resources still
requires more traditional teaching and learning methods to be in place. These
resources should never be intended to replace conventional lectures, seminars and
tutorials. Flexible learning implies that any information normally only available for
restricted periods (eg, lectures, practicals) is a good candidate for a move over to a
more open system, but I suggest there are a few generic areas where the use of
hypermedia might have a particularly useful role.

- Rare or fragile material not easily accessed by students: this could include
  artefacts (eg, stuffed animals, pottery, cloth, maps, gem stones), rare or valuable
  books and manuscripts (British Library Newsletter, 1994), models and so forth.

- Information only accessible on several different media: including cinefilm, video footage, animations, laser-disk archives, audio recordings.
- Complex information that is difficult, or impossible, to scan, search and annotate (eg, large poster displays or heavily cross-referenced information).
- Very large quantities of information usually 'potted' for delivery over long periods: this could include indepth technical accounts, details of experimental work or original research.
- Information usually impossible to provide unrestricted to students: in particular the personal property of lecturers/tutors like 35mm slides, OHP transparencies, and their associated anecdotal information.

Existing resources
Useful material may be already in existence, which could be used either freely or at a price. The methods advocated above may help find some of this material. A plea for help by e-mail to friends and colleagues can also bring pleasant surprises. I have found the Internet Listservers to be invaluable for my work, in particular the staff-development list (staff_development@mailbase.ac.uk) and library and information services list (LIS-LINK@mailbase.ac.uk).

Roll up your sleeves!
The best understanding of the above issues can only be gained by practical experience – it has the benefit of being more flexible and longer lasting. The only way to gain practical experience is to get your hands dirty and work with a real application. A good place to start is with an existing hypermedia application, be it a Microsoft 'toy' or something from, for instance, a TILT project. This will give a novice user a feel for how hypermedia can be exploited with a variety of resources and end results.

To really get to grips with the processes involved there is no substitute for building your own application. See Betts and Burgess (1995) for an indepth account of how you might approach this. (*Note*: Betts and Burgess (1995) is included in the hypermedia version of this chapter.)

Developing resources: choice of computing environment

The WWW
The World Wide Web is seen by some as the answer to many problems with hypermedia resources (see the Proceedings of New Directions in Software Development Conference, 1995). The WWW is the collective information space provided by computers around the world which operate as information (or web) 'servers', linked via the Internet. Your own computer, called a client, needs an Internet connection and software to request and display data from the information server. This software comprises browsers (or viewers) which interpret the way information is stored and display it in a set format.

The WWW has some very clear strengths over stand-alone applications from commercial software vendors.

- *Accessibility*: as it is a network resource the problem of access is reduced to finding a computer with a network connection and appropriate software.
- *Standards*: WWW operates using a *de facto* standard for communication, hypertext transfer protocol (http).
- *Openness*: WWW is a classic 'open' computer system – its description and standards for use are widely and freely available and it has common usage internationally.
- *Ease of use*: staff and students alike can create attractively presented, informative screens with only a limited amount of experience.

Other platform-based systems cannot boast the same range of attributes, but there are some drawbacks with WWW resources.

- *Speed of access*: even local WWW pages can be very slow to view – the use of graphics and video slows the whole system even further.
- *Changing sources*: because of the distributed nature of WWW sites the sources of the information sometimes disappear, or change unexpectedly, without users being told.
- *Navigation*: it is easy to get lost in Web-space and difficult to trace where you have been or find out where you want to go – the tools available to implement navigational aids are limited.
- *Linking*: all hard-wired internally – there is no flexibility and documents are not easy, at present, to repurpose.
- *Appearance*: you are restricted (understandably) to a plain format with little room for design or variety.

Stand-alone environment
Working in a stand-alone environment, resource developers are restricted to packages which fall loosely into the two categories, open and closed. The former has only one real contender, Southampton's widely respected Microcosm (Adie, 1993b; Microcosm Team, 1994). The latter comprise 'true' hypertext authoring software in the shape of guide and development assistants like Multimedia ToolBook and Authorware Professional (see the Computing Product Focus, 1992).

All these packages require considerable learning prior to use and require some programming to take full advantage of all their features. They are also relatively expensive and, with the exception of Microcosm, do not produce easily repurposed products.

Platform and configuration
The software chosen for authoring has an affect on the platform being employed for delivery, although users are usually driven much more by the installed computer base.

The configuration of hardware for development and delivery is also a consideration. Problems arise where applications need to make use of video and sound which are not easily handled by less powerful PCs and only perform marginally better on Macs and basic UNIX machines.

Using hypermedia flexible learning resources can impose a considerable strain on existing computing facilities as they require well-specified computer hardware. Poorly specified hardware can be a major problem at the delivery end and considerable funding for 'multimedia' PCs, for example, may be required to make the use of such resources worthwhile. Without such investment there is a real danger of the whole system collapsing, leading to disillusionment and even aggressive opposition from staff who feel they have been put in an untenable position.

Availability of adequate hardware, and indeed the hypermedia software itself, is the most persistent problem without dedicated facilities.

Developing resources: production processes

The buck stops... where?

Whether you choose the WWW or stand-alone environments, the same processes are involved in making the end-product, from finding the data you want to use right up to testing the screen displays on end-users for integrity and functionality.

It is debatable who, if any one department, should provide the facilities required to perform the tasks discussed below. At Exeter a range of facilities are provided centrally by IT Services while others are begged from academics, technicians and other support services. Clearly a coordinated service would be much more effective and would encourage more and better use of the facilities we already provide somewhat haphazardly.

There is, however, the question of funding and maintenance and of property (eg, the academic who stands to lose the resource located in his or her office but funded by the department). Making sure all parties are satisfied is a long-term process.

Gathering information

Facilities need to be available for the following:

- Video and still photography: hire or loan of camcorders, 35mm cameras (maybe even use of a darkroom), or services of someone to do this for you.
- Sound recording: sound studio facilities or even a simple condenser microphone and a decent tape recorder.
- Text processing: wordprocessing facilities.
- Internet access: a number of items might be available over the Internet or stored at other sites – particularly for things like rare manuscripts.

Storing information

Facilities need to be available for:

- Hire/purchase of blank video and audio tapes, computer diskettes.
- Hard disk storage or an alternative, like magneto-optical technology (which is more portable), or network storage (which is less easy to administer).
- CD-ROM access (eg, Photo-CD, see Barker, 1992; Bonime, 1994; Laing, 1993).
- Back-up for user files (eg, tape-streamer).

Editing

Facilities need to be available for:

- Video and sound capture: soundcard, video capture card, MAC A/V hardware.
- Video and sound editing: software for above.
- Text scanning and editing: a scanner with software capable of Optical Character Recognition (OCR).
- Image scanning and editing (colour scanner with photoretouching and manipulation software).
- Image capture from Photo-CD: Photo-CD Access or similar.

Information presentation: design

When they use computers many people suddenly become designers. DTP users are particularly prone to this and hypermedia developers are no exception. The problem is that a large proportion of these users do not have a clue about design. Matters are improving with the use of professionally designed templates which help to constrain users to less outlandish layouts and colour combinations; similarly there are some good books available (eg, Arnold *et al.*, 1994; Badgett and Sandler, 1994; Clarke, 1992).

Information presentation: points to consider

Here are some issues that do require some fore-thought, but which tend to get addressed on-the-fly:

- What do you put on a single screen?
    Titles, identifiers: what position, size, colour?
    Images: what size, resolution, colour depth, position?
    Text: what typeface, size, colour, format, wrap, position?
    Hyperdata: what, where, how (eg, pop-up text boxes or links to another screen)?
- How much of each media goes on each screen?
- What colour/texture background do you want? Is this going to work with all screens or do you change it throughout the application?
- How are you going to let the user navigate through your information?
    Avoid 'the tyranny of the button' by employing link databases as in Microcosm?
    Or hard-wire all your links and connections?
    Have 'hot' links hard-wired to pop-up boxes, etc?
    Create an index of all screens or nodes, or just certain information?

Prototyping

As with most products of this nature by the far the most cost-effective way of establishing working solutions is to create a prototype and test this with real end-users. This prototype is then modified and retested until the prototype is refined into the desired end-product or set of final templates on which your 'real' data can be placed.

Training provision

For resource developers

There are many different skills and techniques involved in the production of hypermedia flexible learning resources. The majority are concerned with how computer software and hardware works and how best to make use of these tools to arrive at a desired end-point. Other training needs tend to cover more nebulous skills like design and planning. Training to address these needs can be divided loosely into two categories.

1. Core training provision which gives a large number of users the necessary skills and knowledge to start producing material.
2. Special training which focuses on individual needs and is demand-led and easily customised.

Training can be delivered in one, or a combination, of ways:

- Short courses – suited to tutoring small groups of people, and subject to all the points listed above about being flexible.
- One-to-one tuition – expensive but useful for high-level, individual tasks like specialised template production or manipulation of digital video.
- Training videos – for low-level tasks and use by small groups or on a one-to-one basis where short courses would not be cost-effective (eg, 'How to set-up the scanner') and where the training is required repeatedly but not necessarily regularly.

For resource users

Training for end-users is aimed at two separate needs: use of the hardware and software environment in which the product works; and use of the product itself. The first need can often be met with existing short courses or by one-off classes. The second need should be considered carefully by the designer and creator of the product. Many products now have their own introductory screens which guide users through the product and highlight areas where there may be problems and what to do about them.

Additional services

There are bound to be gaps in training provision whether from users who could not make a course or from providers who could not cover a particular topic. This gap can really only be filled effectively by provision of an adequate help desk or advisory service skilled in the appropriate areas. Most advice for product developers will be directed towards solving technical and logistical problems. With product end-users the advice tends to be bug-solving, troubleshooting and misunderstandings, often as a result of poor product design and implementation.

A good range of third-party books (eg, Badgett and Sandler, 1994; Arnold *et al.*, 1994) and technical manuals are essential for the serious developer. It will certainly help the more technically minded but most users, especially novices, will tend to ask the help desk first.

Computer-based training programs can also be employed on the hardware being used to develop the resources – these can be effective but are thin on the ground at present and highly subject specific. A good example might be the ITTI *Authorware Tutorial Toolkit* (IBiS, University of Nottingham) which can be used to learn about Authorware and to produce basic presentations.

Lessons learned at Exeter

The work carried out over the last two years at Exeter has revealed some interesting and valuable insights into how we can exploit hypermedia flexible learning resources and what we, as a service department, have to commit ourselves to supporting.

A lot of time and effort has to be committed from product developers to get things right – considerable knowledge and skills are called upon during the production process. It is debatable whether the end-products are worth the investment in time and money if their educational value is not yet fully appreciated or understood.

However, our experiences at Exeter have shown that a well-produced hypermedia learning resource can be effective as a supplement to traditional teaching methods, can improve the quality of teaching, and can help conserve fragile artefacts – all this cheaply and quickly too!

References

Adie, C (1993a) *A Survey of Distributed Multimedia*, RARE Technical Report 5, 84, 87–8.
Adie, C (1993b) *Network Information to Multimedia Information*, RARE Project OBR(93) 015, 30–31.
Arnold, S, Barr, N, Donnely, P J *et al.* (1994) *Constructing and Implementing Multimedia Teaching Packages*, University of Glasgow, TLTP.
Atkins, S (1992) 'Authoring on the Mac', *The European Multimedia Yearbook*, Interactive Media International, pp.65–8.
Badgett, T and Sandler, C (1994) *Creating Multimedia on Your PC*, Wiley, Chichester.
Barker, A (1992) 'Photo-CD', *The European Multimedia Yearbook*, Interactive Media International, pp.60–62.
Begg, P (1993) 'Dinomania!' *Personal Computer World*, **16**, 11, 300–302.
Bervenson, A (1992) 'DVI, Video, Compression', *The European Multimedia Yearbook*, Interactive Media International, pp.81–3.
Betts, C R and Burgess, P (1995) *Cheap and Cheerful? Developing and supporting hypermedia resources at Exeter*, Proceedings of Hypermedia at Work Conference, University of Kent.
Bonime, A (1994) 'Kodak's New Photo-CD portfolio: Multimedia for the rest of us', *CD-ROM Professional*, July/August.
Brake, D (1994) 'Multimedia Encyclopaedias', *Personal Computer World*, **17**, 6, 502–4.
British Library Newsletter (1994) *Initiatives for Access,* Issue 2.
Cain, C (1993) 'Multimedia moves ahead: motion video', *Personal Computer World*, **16**, 6, 376–80.
Clarke, A (1992) 'The principles of screen design for computer based learning materials', Learning Methods Project Report, Learning Methods Branch, Employment Department, Sheffield.

Commission of the European Communities (1993) *European Multimedia Industry Survey: Perceptions and Needs*, Analysis of Response, Electronic Publishing Services Ltd, London.

Computing Product Focus (1992) 'Multimedia Authoring Software', *Computing*, June, 25–7, VNU Business Publications.

Cooke, S (1992) 'Multimedia Entertainment', *The European Multimedia Yearbook*, Interactive Media International, pp.106–8.

Draper, S W, Brown, M I, Edgerton, E *et al*. (1994) *Observing and Measuring the Performance of Educational Technology*, University of Glasgow, TLTP.

Finney, A (1992) 'Audio techniques', *The European Multimedia Yearbook*, Interactive Media International, pp.72–4.

Fletcher, P (1992) 'Multimedia platforms', *The European Multimedia Yearbook*, Interactive Media International, pp.2–4.

Fox, E (1992) *Multimedia: Applications and Practice*, Eurographics '92, Cambridge, England.

Hall, W, Thorogood, P, Hutchings, G and Carr, L (1990) 'Using Hypercard and interactive video in education. An application in cell biology', *ETTI*, **26**, 3, 207–14.

Kelly, P (1994) 'Book into CD-ROM', *PC Magazine*, September, 269–70.

Laing, G (1993) 'Picture this: Kodak Photo-CD', *Personal Computer World*, **16**, 9, 300–304.

Laurillard, D (1993) *Rethinking University Teaching*, Routledge, London.

Mapp, L (1992) 'Multimedia in UK schools', *The European Multimedia Yearbook*, Interactive Media International, pp.101–3.

Microcosm Team (1994) *Microcosm: A technical overview*, University of Southampton.

Multimedia Whitepaper (1994) *Understanding Multimedia*, 17 June.

Nott, T (1993) 'Microsoft Encarta', *Personal Computer World*, **16**, 8, 380–85.

Proceedings of New Directions in Software Development Conference (1995) *The World Wide Web*, University of Wolverhampton and BCS.

Teaching and Learning Technology Programme (TLTP) (1995) *Science Case Studies*, TLTP, Bristol.

Williams, J (1994) *The Use and Capture of Images for Computer Based Learning*, Educational Technology Service, University of Bristol, ITTI.

Clive Betts has worked with Information Technology for 15 years in scientific research, the Civil Service, international business and, since 1989, higher education. He is currently an Honorary Research Fellow in the Department of Computer Science and works in IT Services at the University of Exeter where he has an interest in staff development and training, and multimedia technologies. He is particularly concerned with the utilisation of computer-based technologies for teaching and learning.

Address for correspondence: IT Services, University of Exeter, Laver Building, North Park Road, Exeter EX4 4QE.

27. A Systemic Approach to the Development of Open and Flexible Learning Environments: Studies of Implementation in the UK

Robert Adams and **Tom Hopkins,** *The Open Learning Foundation Group*

SUMMARY

Frequently, open and flexible learning are discussed as though their incidental benefits – better learning support using new technologies and quality assurance through standardising learning materials – are more important than their systemic purpose, which, in the case of higher education, should be to enable institutions and their employer partners to redesign their learning environments in order to meet the flexible learning requirements of future generations of learners.

The fact that the development and production of open and flexible learning materials in the UK is a flourishing cottage industry has not helped to move to this position. This chapter develops some of the major implications of this argument, in the light of research into the implementation of open learning initiatives in social work in the UK, carried out by the Open Learning Foundation (OLF), a consortium of universities and colleges based mainly in the UK.

This chapter deals with the following:

- concepts of open, flexible and distance learning;
- the context of professional social work education in the UK;
- relevant developments in open and flexible learning;
- mobilising factors, drawn from case studies of successful initiatives;
- barriers to open and flexible learning initiatives;
- wider relevance of findings;
- implications for other professional/vocational areas of higher education;
- the case for a systemic approach to the development of open and flexible learning environments in higher education.

Concepts of open, flexible and distance learning

Many different definitions of the terms open, flexible and distance learning exist. Invariably, distance learning is conceived as though it simply involves conventional learning, at a distance from the educational provider, perhaps with the novelty of using new technologies (Garrison, 1989). Again, open learning is sometimes presented as if it is another way of describing part-time courses. On the contrary, the major benefits from the adoption by educational institutions and employers of open learning approaches derive from regarding them as fundamentally different from conventional learning approaches. All too often, the implicit assumption, even in discussions about using open learning to enhance student-led learning, is that the learning is provided *for* rather than *with* the students (Thorpe and Grugeon, 1987);

that is, the student is a consumer rather than a co-owner of the learning process (Bosworth, 1991, p. 54).

In this chapter, we use the term open learning to describe any one of a variety of flexible approaches by which teachers and learners are empowered, by having maximum choice over what, how, where, when and at what speed, they learn. We make the assumption that distance learning would also be one alternative to conventional learning which could be developed in a new learning environment.

Context of professional social work education in the UK

Professional social work education in the UK in the 1990s is developing in a somewhat constrained and uncertain context. Four main factors contribute to this:

1. The lack of available government funding for both open and flexible learning initiatives and students. Neither non-full-time students nor open learning provision attract government funding as of right.
2. The uncertain location and future of social work as a profession. Many social workers, apart from senior practitioners working in specialist settings, feel deskilled by the trends towards fire-fighting roles (eg, child protection, rather than long-term therapeutic work with children who have been abused) and social control roles (eg, the trend in the probation service towards custodial and community-based punishment of offenders rather than rehabilitation).
3. The stressed circumstances of teachers in educational institutions, which leave many of them demoralised. Many staff fear that employers will use the spread of vocational qualifications as a means of reducing the proportion of the professions qualified through higher education.
4. The fact that practitioners in the workplace feel increasingly vulnerable to the spread of new ways of judging their effectiveness. Major 'innovations' in this area include performance criteria, based on the analysis of key roles of staff, and producing new occupational standards being introduced across the health and social care sector by the National Council for Vocational Qualifications (NCVQ) and in social work by the Central Council for Education and Training in Social Work (CCETSW).

Criticisms of competence-based approaches to professional education and training are that they focus selectively on skills, neglect personal qualities which are difficult to measure and tend not to reflect readily the conceptual basis of critical reflection and action (Adams, 1994a, pp 86–7; Cockerill, 1989; Mangham and Silver, 1988; Sparrow and Bognano, 1993; Tichy, 1983). National Vocational Qualifications (NVQs) and Scottish Vocational Qualifications (SVQs), have led some employers and educators to be hesitant about adopting them in their programmes. Nevertheless, in the UK, competence-based approaches, in the joint OLF/OU management development programme in health and social services, for instance, have addressed these criticisms with significant success (OLF and OU, 1994; Health and Social Services Management Programme: management education scheme by open learning, 1994, OU).

These factors, combined with a government-driven shift to deregulated and privatised welfare services, have created a climate of uncertainty as to the future shape, identity and function of social work services in the UK.

Relevant developments in open and flexible learning

The Open Learning Foundation (OLF) is a consortium comprising 23 member universities plus a number of associated colleges and professional organisations. It provides a means by which its members can engage with each other, at senior management level, and work at the development and implementation of institutional teaching and learning strategies. It also operates as a collective means by which subject-based materials development, staff development and open learning initiatives within specific education and training programmes can be resourced and progressed.

Most members of the OLF are located in the UK. However, the OLF increasingly acts as a bridge between open learning developments in Britain and other parts of the world. The OLF provides educational development in higher education by employing a small team of staff in its central office, who have responsibility for formulating policy and working with senior managers; it also employs subject experts, based in member institutions, who undertake development work with contracted staff, writing open learning materials against targets agreed between the OLF and its members.

While providers of professional educational programmes have for many years been sympathetic towards open and distance education as a means of improving the access of students to courses (Kirkup, 1988, pp.287–8), there is a dearth of material concerning improving the participation of students in developing learning strategies, shaping the curriculum and determining the content of courses. Yet the evidence is that if the learning environment were significantly reshaped, learners would reward it with their increased take-up of courses.

Traditionally, significant numbers of employees, for example in the field of health and social care, have sought personal and professional advancement not just as full-time students under 21 years of age, but as mature part-time students and through in-service training. Enquiries to the OLF about the availability of qualifications by open learning provide growing evidence of a significant demand for such education and training to be delivered flexibly, with a particular emphasis on open learning in the workplace.

The growth of more flexible professional and vocational programmes is justified on the grounds that they increase access to learning for those who otherwise would not have such opportunities. Many practitioners and students attach high value not just to professional development in the workplace, but also to its academic certification, through the contribution it makes towards a degree qualification, for example.

Mobilising and inhibiting factors drawn from case studies of initiatives

Research carried out by the OLF on the implementation of open learning initiatives in social work programmes illustrates the slow progress made in some institutions. But it is noteworthy that change can occur relatively speedily where the alternative to innovation would be the termination of an existing programme. This research has identified a number of key factors, both helping to mobilise towards change and acting as barriers to change.

It is possible to identify the coalescence of factors into significant clusters which impact positively or negatively on the introduction of open learning. For example, it is clear from the research that a critical mass of motivation among teaching staff, combined with even limited interest by senior management, is a potent force for change.

Mobilising factors include:

- the demand for the initiative, particularly from employer partners and potential students;
- the level of support from senior management;
- the extent to which resources are available from external grants;
- the priority and significance given to the initiatives;
- complex and difficult processes of approving open learning in parts of programmes, or entire programmes;
- a lack of commitment by institutional key managerial and practitioner staff;
- a lack of resources within the institution.

Wider relevance of findings

We look now at the implications of this research for the further development of open and flexible learning in higher education with regard to what can be learned and applied in social work and in other subject areas.

Open learning is fundamentally different from conventional learning (Adams, 1993), in that while in some circumstances it may limit the freedom of the learner to question the assumptions on which it is based, it also is potentially capable of empowering the learner, and may require a reconsideration of the assumptions made about the environment within which teaching and learning takes place (Adams, 1994). It also necessitates a systemic rather than a piecemeal approach, in which the development of new learning materials and the technology and other resources to support them, should be regarded as means to the end and not the end in itself.

There is increasing recognition by OLF member institutions of the importance of developing more flexible learning environments, invariably linked with the adoption of strategies based on systemic approaches to open learning initiatives (Lewis, 1994). One of the roles of the OLF includes feeding back to institutional managers the findings of such research, indicating where the structural and procedural barriers to implementation actually lie (Adams and Hopkins, 1994) as well as how uncertainties and fears among programme staff may impede open learning initiatives (Adams et al., 1994).

It has become apparent that institutions and their employer partners have benefited in some circumstances from consultation which the OLF is also well placed to provide, with the four main phases of implementation, each of which involves characteristic challenges to those involved. These phases include engendering commitment, developing proposals, launching initiatives and embedding them in practice.

Implications for other professional and vocational areas of higher education

Specific initiatives have both enabled teaching staff to diversify teaching and learning opportunities within modules (components of programmes) and also to adopt flexible learning across whole programmes. The spin-offs from this have wider application beyond the area of professional social work education. They include:

- the opening up of access to more students, especially where employment-based programmes can be developed using open and flexible learning approaches;
- the increased likelihood of a levelling-up of the quality of teaching and learning in different settings as standard support materials become available across the sector.

Analysis of the total system in which learning opportunities are provided should include not only the educators and employers but also the interests of the learners, whether students or employees. The problem here is that employing organisations and educational institutions are a concentrated, permanent feature of the total system in which teaching and learning takes place, whereas existing and potential students and other learners are a relatively dispersed and transient group. There is a need to address the problem of maximising the participation in the development of flexible learning strategies of the users of the products of education.

There may be tensions between the goal of empowering the learner and the styles of institutional, goal-driven management which predominate in resource-constrained educational institutions and employing organisations in the human services. Following research by Badaracco and Ellsworth (1989), Paul advocates an open management style as the most effective approach to managing higher education, combining a directive approach in some circumstances with an uncompromising commitment to maintaining the fundamental values embedded in the mission and goals of the institution (Paul, 1990, p. 69). This suggests the need to address any consequent tensions between meeting the requirements of educational providers and satisfying the individual learners.

Conclusions

We have used the findings from research into the implementation of open and flexible learning initiatives in social work higher education in the UK to demonstrate the necessity for the adoption of a systemic approach involving all the stakeholders in teaching and learning. There is evidence of significant progress, from the standpoint of educational institutions, towards the development of teaching and learning strategies.

It is important to acknowledge the urgent need for further research focusing on the introduction and implementation of open learning. This research has highlighted the need to address the complex, and to some extent differing interests and requirements of providers, employers, managers, teachers and learners in higher education. It points to the variety of local conditions which shape the nature of initiatives and the factors which operate as inhibitors of change, as well as those which predispose towards change. It implies that open learning will tend to make rapid progress only when it is included in the mainstream of developments in a university or large organisation, rather than being marginalised by being treated as an interesting, but segregated, innovation.

The OLF is well placed to enable member universities to carry out further developmental work to meet the requirements of the various other bodies having a stake in social work education. Employers in future will have an increasing part to play in the development of more flexible routes to professional social work qualification. Open learning offers them enhanced opportunities to meet the training and professional development needs of individuals and organisations, through making available to employees increasingly flexible education and training programmes.

Learners also will need to be enabled to participate more actively and system-atically than hitherto in the process of educational development, and not simply to be regarded as consumers of its products. Open learning offers the potential of empowering learners by enhancing their choice over the circumstances in which they gain their qualifications – the timing, pace and curriculum of their studies – and not just in the content of what they learn.

References

Adams, R (1993) 'Using the law in social work: a flexible learning initiative', *Social Work Education*, Autumn, 20–27.

Adams, R (1994a) *Skilled Work with People*, Collins Educational, London.

Adams, R (1994b) 'Making open learning an open book', *Professional Social Work*, July, 10–11.

Adams, R and Hopkins, T (1994) 'Issues encountered in implementing open and flexible learning in social work education in Britain', paper presented at the International Conference on Educational and Cultural Barriers to Open and Distance Learning, University of Sheffield.

Adams, R, Deakin, B and Nyland, J (1994) 'Implementing an international modular Masters in Management programme', paper presented at the International Conference on Educational and Cultural Barriers to Open and Distance Learning, University of Sheffield.

Badaracco, J L and Ellsworth, R R (1989) *Leadership and the Quest for Integrity*, Harvard School of Business, Boston, MA.

Bosworth, D P (1991) *Open Learning*, Cassell, London.

Cockerill, T (1989) 'The kind of competence for rapid change', *Personnel Management*, **21**, 9, 52–6.

Garrison, D R (1989) *Understanding Distance Education*, Routledge, London.

Kirkup, G (1988) 'Sowing seeds: initiatives for improving the representation of women', in K Faith (ed.), *Towards New Horizons for Women in Distance Education*, Routledge, London.

Lewis, R (1994) 'Current uses of open learning in higher education', in E Grugeon and M Thorp (eds) *Open Learning at the Centre*, Longman, Harlow.

MacFarlane, A G J (1992) *Teaching and Learning in an Expanding Higher Education System: Report of a Working Party of the Committee of Scottish University Principals*, (MacFarlane Report), CSUP, Edinburgh.

Mangham, I L and Silver, M S (1988) *Management Training: Context and Practice*, Economic and Social Research Council and Department of Trade and Industry, London.

Paul, R H (1990) *Open Learning and Open Management*, Kogan Page, London.

Sparrow, P R and Bognanno, M (1993) 'Competency requirement forecasting: issues for international selection and assessment', *International Journal of Selection and Assessment*, **1**, 1, 50–58.

Thorpe, M and Grugeon, D (1987) *Open Learning for Adults*, Longman, Harlow.

Tichy, N M (1983) *Managing Strategic Change: Technical, Political and Cultural Dynamics*, John Wiley, New York.

The authors would like to acknowledge the comments of Leslie Mapp on an earlier draft of this paper.

Robert Adams is Professor of Human Services Development at the University of Humberside and works as Head of Health and Social Services Educational Development for the Open Learning Foundation UK.

Tom Hopkins is Social Work Associate for the Open Learning Foundation, UK and Principal, Tom Hopkins and Associates, Education and Training Consultants.

28. Models of Knowledge, Learning and Representation for Multimedia Learning Environments

Peter Jagodzinski, Mike Phillips, Tom Rogers and **Chris Smith**, *University of Plymouth*

SUMMARY

The design of multimedia learning environments naturally inherits a great deal from earlier technologies of computer-based learning. However, multimedia can be distinguished from earlier technologies by its much greater facility in bringing to the learner high levels of interaction with and control over still and moving video, animation, sound and graphics. Our intuition tells us that multimedia may be wasted in merely delivering conventional learning material more conveniently. It may be capable of delivering learning experiences which previously have only been available through hands-on experience in the workshop, laboratory, field work, or life in the real world.

Introduction

If multimedia is to realise this potential, its design needs to be based on a re-examination of models of human knowledge and learning. The models need to be reinterpreted to see how they can be applied in what is effectively a new medium. Similarly, models and paradigms from related disciplines, particularly media design, need also to be re-examined to see how they can contribute to the realisation of the potential of multimedia.

The following models of learning were discussed:

- *symbolism*: the formal articulation of knowledge;
- *connectionism*: the idea that all human learning originates as a process of pattern-classification;
- *intuitive learning*: informal (and often inaccurate) models of the world formed from direct experience;
- *experiential learning*: learning that can only be acquired by experience;
- *situated learning*: learning in the social and practical context of the real world;
- *metaknowledge*: how and when to apply learning;
- *social/communicative*: learning about societies' norms and cultures by learning social interaction;
- *emancipatory/self*: perspective transformation arising from reflective learning questioning of norms and cultures.

Symbolicism and connectionism

These two models of the way in which humans represent knowledge and process information underlie most of the psychology of the past 30 years. The symbolic paradigm held sway for most of this period and can be seen to have shaped the way in which much of our teaching is done. Dinsmore (1992) summarises the paradigm as follows:

'There are such things as symbols, which can be combined into larger symbolic structures (or expressions). These symbolic structures have a combinatorial semantics whereby what a symbolic structure represents is a function of what the parts represent, and at the same time all cognitive processes (reasoning) are manipulations of these symbolic structures.'

Symbolicism provides a convincing basis for disciplines such as logic, mathematics and computing, and its recent predominance probably arises from attempts in the 1970s and 1980s to implement psychological models of brain behaviour using symbolic computing. However, this work in psychology also demonstrated that there are many aspects of human knowledge and learning that cannot be modelled in symbolic terms.

Bereiter lists several important ways in which psychology has found the symbolic paradigm to be inadequate:

'Instead of being guided by rules of logic people use mental models of situations (Johnson-Laird, 1983). In dealing with probability and statistical inference people rely on untrustworthy heuristics based on experience rather than using formal rules. (Tversky and Khaneman, 1974) Scientists fully conversant with formal laws of their domains instead use information models when considering actual cases (Bobrow, 1985). People's concepts are based on family resemblance's rather than classification rules (Rosch, 1978). Self-reports of rule-use are often unreliable, people often did not fully understand the rules they were using (Nisbett and Rosch, 1980).' (Bereiter, 1991, p11)

These processes all point to a mechanism other than the symbolic shaping some aspects of human thought. This mechanism must account for the best-fit, experience-based heuristics that seem to mould many aspects of the human thought process.

Bereiter (1991) and Dinsmore (1992) both proposed a sub-symbolic connectionist model which is to be taken in conjunction with the symbolic and accounts for the pattern-matching, experienced-based elements to human cognition and learning. The connectionist model is based on the structure of neurons and synapses in the brain and postulates a set of interconnected nodes and links. Each node has a variable output and affects the other nodes though the connections. The computational properties of a connectionist model result not from the particular activities of each node but from the ways the units are interconnected and work together.

In connectionist models, prototypes of concepts and symbols are stored as a combination of connection strengths between many units. As an object is perceived so the nodes through which it is recognised become activated. The connectionist understanding of cognition is based on this process of pattern recognition. Learning is seen as a process of forming mental prototypes to represent different aspects of the world. Received information is then processed by classifying it in term of existing prototypes, which can be modified as necessary. Connectionism is explained in detail, for example, by Fodor and Pylyshyn (1988).

Thus it seems that the connectionist model accounts for the way in which people acquire new concepts and classify information at an unconscious level, and the symbolic paradigm accounts for the way in which people consciously articulate their knowledge, both for their own benefit and for the purposes of communication with others.

Clearly both models are essential. However, in recent times the symbolic model has been predominant in formal teaching and learning, leading to a culture in which mathematical and rule-based approaches have been seen as more rigorous and respectable than approaches based on direct sensory experiences, such as films and illustrations. This has probably led to a degree of alienation from formal education in large sections of the population.

Multimedia has the potential to return us to more sympathetic culture in which many aspects of learning are recognised as requiring first-hand, or at least simulated, experiences of the real world. The following sections outline approaches which we have developed in order to see how multimedia can bring experience of the real world into learning.

Intuitive learning

The essence of the connectionist/symbolic dilemma is expressed by Diana Laurillard. She argues that 'intuitive' understanding of scientific concepts is qualitatively different from 'analytical' understanding.

'Students make use of a variety of aspects of their experience as they struggle to make sense of the language of an academic discipline: physical experiences, social experiences, emotions, intentional goals, irrelevant experiences – and these are important because they enrich the concepts they develop, and not always in beneficial ways. Against those powerful sensual experiences, academics put up the rather less compelling experiences of language, symbolism and analytical reasoning to develop students' conceptions of such concepts as "velocity", "power", "structuralism", etc. Small wonder that for many students the sensual or emotional experiences hold sway, and the concept remains known "intuitively" rather than "analytically" as the academic would prefer.' (Laurillard, 1991)

The value of multimedia is that it can harness the power of sensual experience in the form of videos, animations and simulations. Furthermore, it can be selected to show material which is typical of the phenomenon being taught to encourage the learner to form prototypes that correspond with analytical knowledge. Multimedia enables such simulations to be shown juxtaposed with symbolic accounts of the phenomena, such as graphs and equations, which articulate and analyse the meaning of what is being experienced.

Finally, multimedia is able to create sensory experience of phenomena which cannot be seen directly, by means of animation, time-lapse photography and slow-motion photography. Examples might include microworlds of the behaviour of gas molecules (too small and too fast) at one extreme and geological plate tectonics (too large and too slow) at the other.

Experiential learning

In some situations there is no symbolic explanation of the phenomena that need to be learnt. For example, when civil engineers dam rivers they have to predict the behaviour of the old river bed, downstream of the dam, when it is exposed to sudden flood flows. If they get this wrong the river bed erodes and the dam is undermined, leading to its collapse.

However, the mathematical models for the behaviour of the stream beds are either inaccurate or impractically over-complex. In real life the engineer models the problem physically using sand and clay in a laboratory. We have called such learning, acquired by physical modelling (or trial and error), 'experiential learning' when it can *only* be acquired through sensory experience.

Again, multimedia can overcome the limitations of conventional classrooms and textbooks by providing direct access to simulations of the sensory experience. The advantages over sequential video and laboratory simulation are the ease of access and possibilities for interactive control offered by multimedia.

Situated learning

Situated learning can be seen as a form of experiential learning. It is described by Collins (1991) as an element of the sociology of learning, exemplified by traditional apprenticeship, in which the learner is situated in an appropriate social and cultural context:

> 'apprentices learn skills in the context of their application to realistic problems, within a culture focused on and defined by expert practice. They continually see the skills they are learning being used in a way that clearly conveys how they are integrated into patterns of expertise and their efficacy and value with the subculture.'

Although it must be a pale substitute for the real experiences, multimedia can help to provide some of these learning benefits, by means of simulation, to learners who do not have access to real apprenticeship. This approach has been used by us recently in the design of a multimedia learning package in software engineering aimed particularly at learners isolated by disability but also relevant to classroom-based learners.

Video elements of the package introduce software engineering in a typical industrial context. The package shows the commercial and industrial functions that are supported by software systems, and traces the development lifecycle through the eyes and roles of the software engineering project team, including their typical working interactions with each other. In this way students are led to understand the relevance of software engineering and the rich mixture of roles, responsibilities, authority and support inherent in development teams.

Metaknowledge

Metaknowledge is briefly defined by Jackson (1990) as 'Knowing what one know's, and knowing when and how to use it'. Essentially it facilitates the matching of knowledge to the contexts in which it is applied, and can be seen to be one important element of situated learning. Again, multimedia can contribute to the learning of metaknowledge by simulating appropriate contexts such as those in the last examples. Software engineering provides a particularly apt example because of its requirement for the application of specific techniques in a specific sequence over a long period.

Social and communicative learning

Many educationalists have emphasised the advantages and importance of social interaction and communication in the learning process (Somekh, 1994). It spurs the motivation to learn, sustains engagement with the materials, and engenders curiosity. Indeed, some (eg, Berger and Luckmann, 1985) argue that our concepts of reality are socially constructed, and that it is through communication and social interaction that we give meaning to our perceptions and understanding of the world.

For Harre *et al.* (1985) social interaction 'creates the core structures and rationalities of our consciousness'. This occurs on an individual basis, within social groups and organisations, and between people representing organisations or institutions. Our perceptions of individuals and of institutions are based on a compendium of visual, auditory and intuitive cues or triggers (Bransford *et al.*, 1990) – and they form into expectations or models upon which we judge our encounters and communications. These models are formed from experience and the social, moral and cultural standards that become instilled within us.

For example, Harre *et al.* cite evidence that rather than dealing with the individual, doctors deal with models or stereotypes of a patient relative to all sorts of social and cultural conventions. Similarly the patient expects of a doctor what they think a doctor should be. Each adopts a personal mode of behaviour which they understand as being appropriate to their roles with respect to the other party. Acquiring appropriate and acceptable models can be an important part of the learning process and, to an extent, this was part of the message of situated learning described above.

However, the qualities of social and communicative learning can also be seen to be present in a much broader range of human experiences, including those outside of formal learning such as personal and family situations. Another of our research projects is piloting an interactive video which aims to help expectant mothers and their families to rehearse the events of pregnancy and, in particular, the decision on where and how the birth should take place. The goal is to provide the parents with experience and information about the roles and points of view of midwives, obstetricians, doctors and other key players, well before they actually have to meet these people. By this rehearsal the parents will be informed about the range of options open to them and thus empowered to make their own decisions. Interactivity enables the mother to select the particular circumstances of medical history, level of detail, family situation, and so on, which are most relevant to her own needs.

Self-reflective and emancipatory learning

> 'Perspective transformation by its very nature entails struggle, as individuals reassess former meaning perspectives and try to evolve new ones.' (Meizrow, 1978)

The experience of learning, particularly social and communicative learning, may have consequences far beyond the mere acquisition of knowledge. Understanding of major life events, such as parenting and childbirth, is likely to lead to substantial and significant transformations in the perspectives of the learner with regard to their own core values, family roles, social and emotional relationships.

People reflect upon prior experience to assimilate knowledge into their own framework of understanding, to resolve specific problems, and/or to generate new ideas. This they do through a process of personal discourse, which adds to their development as 'complex mental beings with individual inner worlds' (Harre *et al.*, 1985). This discourse is not purely verbal, but occurs through the creation of inner mental models (Johnson-Laird, 1983), that transform perception and memory into inner realities. We learn to see underlying patterns and connections, and powerful central themes within larger wholes – making sense of ourselves in relation to the world (Salmon, 1989).

Reflective learning involves:

- assimilation of intellectual or theoretical knowledge into a personal viewpoint;
- reflection upon and consideration of tasks and learning goals from different vantage points;
- awareness of personal, cultural and social influences upon personal plans, decisions and actions;
- confrontation of personal dichotomies or more general paradoxes of knowledge;
- inner rehearsal of expected events or responses to episodes or situations.

This very personal facet of the learning process can 'empower people, and change their role as learners from one of being recipients in a learning situation to one in which they take control of the process' (Weil and McGill, 1989). In seeking actively to engineer perspective transformation for particular ends, self-reflective and emancipatory learning can be seen to be closer to drama, film or literature than conventional learning. Interactive multimedia, particularly interactive video, can address the whole range of possibilities for learning of this type. It should also be recognised as a new medium which grafts additional powers for focusing on and engaging with the interests of the learner, to those of traditional time-based media. Our research with the domain of childbirth is making a start on setting out the ground rules, particularly for the use of film techniques and drama, for this new medium. (Further details are given in Rogers *et al.*, 1995.)

Conclusions

Work towards our original aim of re-examining models of learning and media design has, we believe, started to deliver results in several forms. First, we have a theoretical basis for understanding the contributions that multimedia can make to learning. This provides a rationale for deciding if, how and when to apply multimedia in a learning environment. Much currently available multimedia material consists largely of electronic page turning; that is to say the technology is being used for its gimmick value rather than for any clear learning advantage. The rush to produce multimedia material which does not contribute to the learning experience of its customers may, in the short term, lead to popular disenchantment with the medium. Our design rationale can help to avoid counterproductive and expensive misuse of technology.

Secondly, we have found many ways in which the study of the underlying models has produced innovative ideas and approaches which would not otherwise have occurred to us. For example, the use of multimedia to achieve social/communicative learning or emancipatory learning emerged directly from the recognition in psychology that such forms of learning are an important part of the spectrum of human experience.

Thirdly, in considering how multimedia can be used to support learning we have encountered a number of practical problems and benefits, leading to the following views.

- Multimedia can be extremely expensive to produce and should only be used when it can offer some clear learning advantage.
- Multimedia is rarely as vivid as real experience. On the other hand, it can be viewed conveniently and repeatedly to suit the learner's needs, and can express phenomena which are normally invisible.
- However seductive its message, one multimedia representation can normally only show a restricted viewpoint. Design of the learning material needs to take care to avoid being simplistic, for example by including a range of different opinions or views of a topic.

There is still a long way to go in this research with many facets of the theoretical models left to explore. For example, we have just started to look at the theory of games to see how it might inform design work. We are also starting research involving the combination of multimedia and virtual reality, which demands further rethinking about the design of learning environments and the underlying models of human learning and interaction with computers.

References

Berger, P and Luckmann, T (1985) *The Social Construction of Reality*, Penguin, Harmondsworth.

Berieter, C (1991) 'Implications of connectionism for thinking about rules', *Educational Researcher*, April.

Bransford, J D, Sherwood, R D, Hasselbring, T S, Kinzer, C K and Williams, S M (1990) 'Why we need it and how technology can help', in D Nix and R Spiro (eds), *Cognition, Education, and Multimedia: Exploring Ideas in High Technology*, Lawrence Erlbaum, Hillsdale, NJ.

Collins, A (1991) 'Cognitive apprenticeship and instructional technology' in L Idol and B F Jones (eds), *Educational Values and Cognitive Instruction: Implications for Reform*, Lawrence Erlbaum, Hillsdale, NJ.

Dinsmore, J (1992) *Closing the Gap: Symbolism v Connectionism*, Lawrence Erlbaum, Hillsdale, NJ.

Elvatorski, E A (1959) *Hydraulic Energy Dissipators*, McGraw Hill, New York.

Fodor, J A and Pylyshyn, N W (1988) 'Connectionism and cognitive architecture: a critical analysis', *Cognition*, **28**, 3–71.

Harre, R, Clarke, D and De Carlo, N (1985) *Motives and Mechanisms: An Introduction to the Psychology of Action*, Methuen, London.

Jackson, P (1990) *Introduction to Expert Systems*, Addison Wesley, Wokingham.

Jagodzinski, A P, Parmee, I and Smith, C (1994) 'A knowledge engineering approach to the design of a multimedia learning environment', Hypermeida in Vaasa '94 Conference, Vaasa Institute of Technology, Finland, June.

Jagodzinski, A P, Phillips M and Roger, T (1994) 'A visual paradigm for multimedia design', Association of Learning Technology Conference, 19–21 September, University of Hull.

Johnson-Laird, P N (1983) *Mental Models*, Cambridge University Press, Cambridge.

Laurillard, D (1991) *Learning Through Collaborative Computer Simulations*, Centre for IT in Education Report No 18, 131291, Open University.

Meizrow, J (1978) 'Perspective transformation', *Adult Education*, **28**, 2, 100–110.

Rogers, T, Jagodzinski, A P and Phillips, M (1995) 'Design models for multimedia', Paper presented at AETT 1995 Conference, University of Plymouth, June.

Salmon, P (1989) 'Personal stances in learning', in W Weil, and I McGill (eds), *Making Sense of Experiential Learning: Diversity in theory and practice*, Open University Press, Buckingham.

Somekh, B (1994) 'Designing software to maximise learning: what can we learn from the literature?' Association of Learning Technology Conference (ALT94), Hull.

Weil, W and McGill, I (1989) *Making Sense of Experiential Learning: Diversity in theory and practice*, Open University Press, Buckingham.

Addresses for correspondence: **Peter Jagodzinski**, **Mike Phillips** and **Tom Rogers**, School of Computing, University of Plymouth, Drake Circus, PL4 8AA; **Chris Smith**, Mathematics and Statistics, University of Plymouth, Drake Circus, PL4 8AA.

29. Screen Design of Computer-Based Learning Materials

Alan Clarke, *University of Sheffield*

SUMMARY

Although the value of illustrations and colour in learning materials is widely accepted, the guidelines available to designers are frequently based on personal opinions. The guidelines for illustrations are often the result of investigations into the use of images to support text in books or other paper-based products. Colour guidelines are obtained from work into colour television, 35mm slides and cockpit displays. This chapter reports on research undertaken by Sheffield University into the use of graphics, colour and text in the screen design of computer-based learning materials.

Introduction

Great Britain faces many challenges due to increased economic competition. The success of many of its competitors has been underpinned by major investments in vocational education and training (Employment Department, 1990). New techniques in learning are increasingly contributing to the development of people by allowing them to acquire skills in ways which suit their individual needs (Employment Department, 1991). Computer-based learning has been identified as a key strategic weapon in the competition between corporate rivals (Stefanko *et al.*, 1990). In schools, information technology is already a major factor in education with 28% of primary and 38% of secondary schools reporting that it made a substantial contribution to learning (DES, 1991).

The screen provides the critical interface between the learner and the learning material. If the display is not effective, learning will be hindered. Screen design is therefore a vital factor in computer-based learning. Although the value of illustrations and colour in learning materials is widely accepted, the guidelines available to designers are frequently based on personal opinions or research evidence derived from other media. The guidelines for illustrations often result from investigations into the use of images to support text in books or other paper-based products. Colour guidelines are obtained from work into colour television, 35mm slides and cockpit displays.

Analysis of research evidence

Research evidence related to screen design is limited in a number of ways. The balance of material is skewed, with only text having an extensive well-supported body of research findings. Research into the use of colour and graphics is often in relation to media other than the computer screen. The research results are frequently based on experiments that did not have a learning focus – that is, the content of the displays was not designed to support learning and the subjects were not learners. The research subjects were often undergraduate students who were not representative of the whole population. Computer-based learning consists of multiple screens of tutorial with features such as glossaries of terms, tests and additional information or help systems. It is thus an integrated environment of different types of displays through which the learner moves and interacts. The key question concerning all this research is how much of it can be transferred to the screen design of computer-based learning materials.

A survey of 41 screen design research projects was carried out to consider the nature of experiments undertaken in relation to experimental subjects, media, learning focus and integrated materials. The analysis revealed that:

- 51% of the research projects used students as the research subjects;
- 43% of the research projects were based on media other than a computer screen;
- 41% of the research projects had a learning focus;
- 19% of the research projects employed an integrated display.

Only 15% of the projects used representative subjects, based the research on a computer screen, had a learning focus and employed an integrated system.

Experiments

The research was centred on two experiments. The first focused on the use of colour in computer-based learning materials and testing the experimental approach. The second concentrated on the use of graphics and colour. The research literature provided a number of screen design guidelines relating to the use of text which were used in both experiments.

The basic approach to this research was to create a learning environment for the subjects based on the four criteria used to analyse research projects – that is, representative subjects using a computer-based system with a learning focus employing an integrated environment. The learning materials were essentially tutorials on study skills (colour experiment) and computer science (graphics experiment).

During the two experiments a number of hypotheses were investigated. These were concerned with the use of colour and graphics. All versions of the experimental tutorials were designed to be effective learning material. The overall structure of the material was not altered except in the design of the display.

The subjects for the research were drawn from a wider group than the normal focus on undergraduate students, but they still had a number of differences from the entire population. They were, however, more representative than the typical subjects of the surveyed projects and tended to be broadly similar to those individuals who used open learning materials (Force 9, 1993).

The colour experiment was focused on testing the research methods and the use of colour in computer-based learning. The approach adopted during the colour experiment was to compare learners' use of multiple versions of the same tutorial differing only in the use of colour in each version. The colour experiment provided five versions of the learning material using 3, 5, 7, 9 and 11 colours respectively. The graphics experiment was focused on range of factors:

- complexity of the tutorial displays;
- effects of the learners' prior knowledge of the subject;
- use of graphics in computer-based learning;
- comparison of different types of graphic images in computer-based learning;
- use of different sizes of graphic images;
- learners' use of additional modules not directly in the body of the main tutorial.

The design of the graphics experiment used three types of graphics.

- *Representational graphics*: illustrations which share a physical resemblance to the object or concept they are portraying.
- *Analogical graphics*: these images aim to illustrate a topic or a concept by showing something similar and implying a similarity. In order for an analogical graphic to be useful the learner must recognise or be able to comprehend the object used in the analogy.
- *Logical graphics*: these images do not resemble the physical things they represent but are a logical representation of them. Examples of this type of graphic are flow charts, graphs and charts.

The major difference between the two experiments was that whereas the colour experiment employed a range of different versions, the graphics experiment only used a single system. Within this single system, the different types of graphic images and other features were present and the subjects were free to access each component as they worked through the material. The comparison is thus between the same subjects using different elements of the material rather than different subjects using different versions of the material as in the colour experiment.

Subjects in the graphics experiment were classified into three groups: beginners, intermediates and experts, depending on an assessment of their understanding of the tutorial subject; 60 and 73 subjects took part in the colour and graphics experiment respectively. They were all regular computer users.

The two experiments were interrelated in a number of ways. The colour experiment tested the underlying approach to the research (ie, structure, software and design).

Colour experiment

The results show that colour increases interest and motivation so that users are encouraged to spend more time studying individual frames. The total number of frames accessed by the users did not change significantly up to the version of the tutorial using seven colours. However, as the number of colours is increased beyond seven, users find the colour more distracting and so they have to spend more time on each frame to understand it. This change in behaviour caused by the marginal use of colour indicates the power of colour to motivate learners.

The post-test questionnaire asked the users' opinion of the amount of colour in the version they had used. For versions using seven or less colours they responded positively to the view that 'too little colour' was used, while for versions using more than seven colours their reaction was that 'too much colour' was used.

Graphics experiment

Complexity

In order to provide a means of objectively comparing screen displays using text and different numbers and sizes of graphic illustrations, the complexity of the displays was calculated. The calculation was based on a number of the research findings (Tullis, 1983; Bonsiepe, 1968) as well as a consideration of visual acuity, information theory and the research evidence on grouping information (Tullis, 1981; Dobson and Shields, 1978; Triesman, 1982).

The results of the graphics experiment indicated an overall positive correlation between the measure of complexity and the time spent on each screen displaying text only or both graphics and text. There are, however, differences between the three different groups of learners. Beginners and experts tended to spend less time on a display than the complexity measure would predict, while it is an accurate predictor of the time the intermediates will spend on a display.

Route

All three groups of learners showed a clear preference to follow a sequential route through the tutorial. This sequential behaviour of users of menu-driven computer systems has been reported by a number of researchers (Elliot, 1975; Sasser and Moore, 1984; Bolton and Peck, 1991; Schuerman and Peck, 1991a, 1991b). The expert group participants demonstrated more complex behaviour with only the initial modules of the tutorial being accessed by the majority of learners sequentially.

The behaviour of the three groups seemed to be governed by the following guidelines.

- Learners will tend to follow the sequence of the tutorial as shown by the main menu.
- Learners with expert knowledge of the subject will only initially follow the sequence of the tutorial.
- The best predictor of the numbers of learners who will access a given module is the order the module appears on the main menu (ie, more people will use module 1 than module 2).

There was a considerable difference between the three groups of users. The experts tended to browse the material to a far greater degree than the other two groups of learners. In contrast, the beginner and intermediate groups tended to complete a module before moving on to the next part of the tutorial.

Preferences

The three groups of learners expressed preferences for both the size and type of illustrations used in learning material. However, the strength of these preferences does remain in doubt. The beginners group appeared to be indifferent to the size of illustrations, the experts ranked 'Do not care' as their third choice and only the intermediates seemed to have a firm preference for particular sizes of illustrations.

The overall preferences were for illustrations that occupy a quarter or half of the screen.

The three groups of learners showed preferences for different types of illustrations. All three groups did not like the use of analogical illustrations. In direct contrast to this negative reaction was a preference for realistic images expressed by all three groups. The overall preferences were:

First choice: Realistic illustrations
Second choice   Cartoon
Third choice: Line drawings
Fourth choice: Diagrams
Fifth choice: Charts and tables
Sixth choice: Analogies

Graphic illustrations

The learners' behaviour towards different types of graphic display varied. A comparison between the time actually spent and a prediction based on the complexity of the display shows that overall learners spend less time on displays containing graphic illustrations than would be expected. This could be explained in two main ways. Firstly, learners may find it easier to extract the information contained in an image rather than a text-only display. Secondly, learners may not be willing to invest the effort in extracting all the information contained in an illustration.

Learners generally spent less time than predicted on graphic images of all types with the following exceptions.

- Beginners spent more time on full-screen (ie, illustration occupies the whole screen) representative images (although not statistically significant).
- All learners spent more time than predicted on displays containing two part-screen (ie, display contains two illustrations which occupy only a part of the screen) representative images.
- All learners spent more time than predicted on displays containing three part-screen representative images.

These exceptions are all linked to representative displays which, combined with the learner's preference for this type of graphic image, would suggest that these are the most effective type of graphic to use in learning material. Displays containing four part-screen representative images were studied for less time than predicted. This may indicate that four images provides the limit to the learners' motivation to study multiple representative images.

Learners interacting with logical graphics spend significantly less time than predicted. This would seem to indicate that learners are unwilling to make the effort to understand the structure of the graphic in order to obtain the information it contains. This is in contrast to the learners' behaviour with displays of structured text. Structured text serves a similar purpose to logical graphics. Learners spend more time on structured text than predicted, which would indicate that either they are willing to make the required effort to understand the structure or that the structure is a lesser barrier.

Learners appear to treat analogical images (at least part-screen analogical graphics) in a similar way to representative images. They are clearly not making the potentially powerful links to other experiences which would aid their learning.

Conclusions

Colour
Colour has two different effects on the behaviour of learners. Initially it motivates and encourages them to spend longer on each display. It engages learners to interact with the information displayed. However, as the use of colour increases it begins to interfere and distract them, so that although they are spending longer on each screen it is for negative reasons. The turnover point for the use of colour has been shown to be seven colours. It is likely that other factors not considered in this research may influence this point, such as colour preference, colour combinations and tutorial subject.

Complexity
Complexity was found to be a useful means of predicting and comparing the users' behaviour while interacting with different screen displays. Overall the complexity measures accurately predicted the time spent on the tutorial; however, there were considerable differences between the three groups.

Learners
The behaviour of the three groups frequently followed the pattern of the users' prior knowledge. The behaviour of the experts was frequently different to the other two groups of users. It differed particularly in the reaction to graphic displays, choices of routes through the material, accessing the additional modules and in the operation of the tutorial. This is critical for designers who must have a clear understanding of the nature of their learners.

Graphics
The users' preferences are for representational graphics occupying a quarter to half of the screen. Additionally, the learners do not like analogical graphics and they do not appear to use them to make links with their prior experience. At best the analogical images are considered by the learners as representational images which may well hinder learning rather than assist it.

All types of graphics were studied for less time than complexity predictions would expect. However, representative images motivated learners to study them more unless too many illustrations were employed. On the other hand, logical and analogical graphics did not motivate learners to make the effort necessary to extract the information they contained.

Route
The route chosen by the users was clearly sequential with the best predictor of the learners' route being the order in which modules appeared in the main menu. Only the expert group revealed more complex behaviour and even this group initially

followed a sequential pattern. The experts, however, did operate to a far greater extent in a browsing mode than the other two groups, who were more likely to complete a module before moving on.

References

Bolton, J W and Peck, K L (1991) 'Menu sequence, learner control and achievement in CAI', *Interactive Learning International*, **7**, 95–100.

Bonsiepe, G (1968) 'A method of quantifying order in typographical design', *Journal of Typographic Research*, **2**, 203–20

Department of Education and Science (DES) (1991) 'Survey of information technology in schools', *Statistical Bulletin.*

Dodson, D W and Shields, N J (1978) 'Development of user guidelines for ECAS display design', Report No NASA-CR-150877, Volume 1, Essex Corporation, Huntsville, Alabama.

Elliot, P H (1975) 'An exploratory study of adult learning styles', Doctoral Dissertation, University of Illinois at Urbana-Champaign, University Microfilms, DAH 76-06757.

Employment Department (1990) *Labour market and skills trends 1991/92*, HMSO, London.

Employment and Education Departments and the Welsh Office (1991) *Education and Training for the 21st Century*, HMSO, London.

Force 9 (1993) 'Open for learning marketing proposals', unpublished report for Learning Methods Branch Employment Department, Moorfoot, Sheffield.

Sasser, M F and Moore, D M (1984) 'A study of the relationship between learner control patterns and course completion in CAI', *Programme Learning and Educational Technology*, **21**, 1, 28–33.

Schuerman, R and Peck, K (1991a) 'Menus as lesson structuring devices: The effects of on-menu cueing on sequentiality', *Interactive Learning International*, **7**, 293–304.

Schuerman, R and Peck, K (1991b) 'Pull down menus, menus design and usage patterns in CAI', *Journal of Computer-Based Instruction*, **18**, 3, 93–8.

Stefanko, D, Tonkin, D, Silver, M and Whitman, G (1990) *Education Technology: A Corporate Weapon in the 1990s Marketplace*, Unisys Corporation, New Jersey.

Tullis, T S (1981) 'An evaluation of alphanumeric, graphic and color information displays', *Human Factors*, **23**, 541–50.

Triesman, A (1982) 'Perception of groupings and attention in visual search for features and objects', *Journal of Experimental Psychology*, Human Perception and Performance, **8**, 2, 194–14.

Tullis, T S (1983) 'Predicting the usability of alphanumeric displays', PhD dissertation, Rice University.

Address for correspondence: **Alan Clarke**, University of Sheffield, 11 Newbold Way, Kinoulton, Nottingham NG12 3RF.

30. Multimedia Courseware Engineering – Lessons Learned from the Failure of Technology-Based Learning

I M Marshall, W B Samson, P I Dugard and **J N Sutherland**, *Software Quality Group, University of Abertay Dundee*

SUMMARY

Technologies come and go, leaving very little except store cupboards full of obsolete hardware, and a small selection of inadequate and non-transferable courseware. To develop sustainable interactive learning based on multimedia courseware requires that it be designed to be reusable and transferable to other hardware platforms. Courseware engineering is leading to the development of management tools and metrics to support the development of reusable and transferable courseware. This chapter outlines research to investigate the cost of designing reusable and transferable multimedia courseware and the development of multimedia courseware metrics for cost estimation.

Introduction

Cates (1992) suggested that a 'review of the predicted or promised impact of educational films, instructional television, programmed instruction and computerised instruction in general suggests that when all is said and done, much more is usually said than done'. It would appear from this statement that in technology-based learning each new cohort of innovators seems doomed to repeat the failures of the previous generation. The pattern of exaggerating what the technology can do and under-implementing the solutions before moving on to the next 'great hope' is apparent from the development of programmed learning in the 1960s, to a billion dollar misadventure with PLATO in the 1970s to interactive video in the 1980s (Baker, 1994). These technologies have come and gone, leaving very little except store cupboards full of obsolete hardware, and a small selection of inadequate and non-transferable courseware. Now it is the turn of multimedia to try to build the individualised interactive learning revolution in schools, colleges and universities.

So what lessons can be learned from the failure of previous attempts to use technology-based learning? Perhaps the most important lesson is that if the under-pinning technology is changing rapidly, educational style and learners' expectations and experience of the technology changes almost as quickly. In some disciplines, while the educational content of courseware developed ten years ago may still be valid, the hardware and software environment required to use it may not exist. Even if the hardware is still in working order it is doubtful if most teachers will want to use it. Students' experience and expectations of software have matured. To a generation brought up on fast moving photo-realistic computer games, using a piece of antique courseware is likely to fail to deliver the interaction, visual experience and excitement they have come to expect from software.

McDonough *et al.* (1994) stated that the 'development of CBT is often expensive in terms of both time and money and all researchers agree that to be viable it must achieve high student usage.... High student usage should still be possible if the courseware is easy to customise and re-use elsewhere'. This suggests that to develop a sustainable individualised interactive learning revolution, multimedia courseware has to be designed to be transferable to other hardware platforms. Without this ability, developers are doomed to continuously redevelop courseware with each change in hardware platform or consumer or educational taste. However, re-useable multimedia courseware design techniques are not well documented, nor are the effects on development effort. This chapter presents an overview of current research into re-use and outlines the need to develop courseware metrics for accurate measurement so that costs and benefits of alternative development strategies can be compared.

Re-use and courseware engineering

It is generally recognised that developing good multimedia courseware can consume large amounts of time and resources. Friedler and Shabo (1991) state that traditionally 'the development of courseware is considered to be an expensive process. There are varying estimates as to the effort required to develop an hour's worth of courseware: from 300 to 500 or even 1000 developer hours'. Commercial developers may even require 4000 developer hours of effort to create one learner hour of highly interactive multimedia courseware (Marshall *et al.*, 1994). With effort being expended at this rate there is a need for a more disciplined approach to the development of multimedia courseware analogous to software engineering (De Diana, 1993).

The adoption of a courseware engineering approach may in itself improve productivity. Similarly, the implementation of design techniques for re-use and transferability may reduce the total effort expended in development and maintenance during the lifetime of the courseware product. Unfortunately, there is no way to compare the effect of different design strategies unless a rigorous framework for measurement exists. At present any comparisons tends to be subjective because there is no standard measurement process (De Diana, 1993; Marshall *et al.*, 1994; De Diana and van Schaik, 1993). The starting point for research into the effect of re-usability and transferability is to define a number of measurements or metrics.

Multimedia courseware development lifecycle

The starting point for a metrics programme requires a clear definition of the development process on which to base measurements. Figure 1 shows a waterfall lifecycle model for multimedia courseware development, based on a number of existing instructional design and courseware engineering models (Tennyson, 1993). While de-emphasising the concurrent and iterative nature of multimedia courseware development, it forms the platform for base measurements.

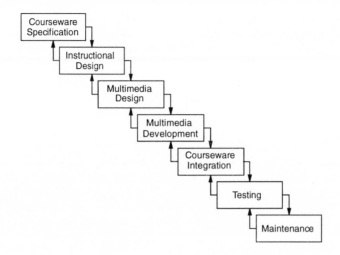

Figure 1 *The waterfall model of multimedia courseware development*

The following definitions are adapted from our earlier work on multimedia courseware (Marshall *et al.*, 1994).

For the purposes of development measurement the starting point is defined as the beginning of the instructional design phase while the end point is the completion of the testing phase. The maintenance phase is excluded from the initial development effort measurements, but it is essential for detailed records to be kept in this phase to track maintenance, reuse or cross-platform effort.

Elapsed time is the total time in days from the start of the instructional design phase to the end of the testing phase; **development time** is the number of hours taken to develop the multimedia courseware from the start of the instructional design phase to the end of the testing phase. During this period development time is measured in productive working hours used by the multimedia courseware project. Development time expended after the testing phase on maintenance or re-use is accumulated separately from the main development time.

Effort is measured in developer hours and describes the total amount of productive work expended developing the course:

$$\text{Effort} = \sum_{\text{Instructional design}}^{\text{Testing}} \text{Development time on phase} \times \text{Number of developers used}$$

Once the testing phase is finished, effort expended on maintenance or re-use is recorded separately.

Learner time is the amount of time spent by the learner using the courseware and has been called 'delivery time'. However, to prevent confusion with product delivery we propose to describe this measure as learner time. There is no agreed definition as to how it should be calculated and given self-pacing of instruction, the range of learner time for a group of learners can vary considerably. The mean learner time is measured using a representative group of 20 learners for whom the material was designed.

Productivity is measured in units of 'mean learner hours per developer hour' and normally results in a value less than one. The output measure is the number of hours of learner material delivered and the input is the development effort.

$$\text{Productivity} = \frac{\text{Learner time}}{\text{Effort}}$$

Effort to learner time ratios: The widely used 'development to delivery time ratio' is misleading and is better described as 'effort to learner time ratio' The following definition should be used.

$$\text{Effort to learner time ratio} = \frac{\text{Effort}}{\text{Learner time}}$$

Using this definition, it is measured in 'mean developer hours per learner hour'.

Measuring the effect

Having established a framework it is now possible to explore the effect of alternative design and development strategies on effort, productivity or other courseware metrics. There has been very little rigorous research into the effectiveness of designing courseware for re-use and transferability. Most research tends to be anecdotal in nature with little empirical evidence to support the claims. In this section, the effects on productivity of designing courseware for re-use during the development lifecycle will be explored.

Re-usable development tools and instructional templates

Avner (1988) described the effect of authoring tools and team size on courseware development productivity. In analysing the productivity of experienced courseware development teams it was noted that depending on the size of team there was an improvement in productivity of 30% to 43% between the first and second module. Table 1 shows the mean productivity against team size for the first and second module undertaken by the same team. The values are based on Avner's (1988) productivity rate figures inverted to match the consistent definition presented in this chapter.

Avner (1988) identified that most of the increase in productivity between first and second module could be attributed to 'the result of effort to identify or create tools to be used in subsequent modules'. Once the tools have been created they require only minimal maintenance effort or improvement. The result is to allow the team to concentrate on the development of courseware. Figure 2 shows the reduction in productivity of intra-team communications as the team size grows from one developer to six.

Table 1 *Productivity for first and second courseware modules*

| Team size (developers) | Teams in sample | Mean productivity (Mean learner hours per developer hour) | |
		Module 1	Module 2
1	10	0.020	0.026
2	17	0.011	0.016
3	13	0.008	0.010
4	13	0.007	0.010
5	4	0.007	0.009
6	4	0.007	0.010

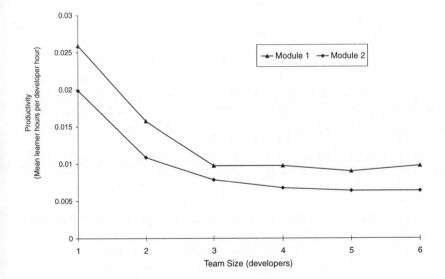

Figure 2 *Productivity against team size*

These two points support Sommerville's (1989) idea of a 'toolsmith' who creates tools to support software engineering teams. The dramatic effect of using the 'toolsmith' approach to develop courseware tools is described by Blalock (1994). American Airlines assembled a team who worked for nine months to create a unique set of development templates and shells to support future courseware production. These templates, development shells and models were then used to create 150 hours of interactive courseware. The key benefit claimed for this method was a 'dramatic improvement in the pace of courseware, proficiency reviews and proficiency evaluations development... Effective (well-designed) shells, templates and models will reduce development time and save money. Poorly designed shells, templates and models could, in fact, increase the overall development time and project cost' (Blalock, 1994). The use of shells and templates resulted in a productivity of 0.008 average learner hours per developer hour compared to 0.004 for previous traditionally developed projects.

Similar results are reported by Campbell (1988) who used a template-based design tool which was used to create over a thousand hours of instruction. The tool was designed to allow subject matter experts to pick one or more instructional templates from a predefined selection and enter appropriate content. Campbell (1994) reported making considerable savings in development effort in using the template system in comparison to traditional authoring systems. The creation of the templates by tool identifiers and developers along with tight management and training of the full team to use the tools can also reduce the intra-team communications overhead. By using templates design, format and methodology decisions were made leaving little for the team to communicate during the actual development.

Re-usable media and other libraries
Schooley (1988) identified in the CEAC cost estimation model that the availability of library assets can reduce the development time. In the case of CEAC, library assets were defined to include utility, application, graphics and character sets. The utility and application elements have already been considered in the previous section. The graphics and font libraries reflect the CBT basis of CEAC and can be extended to describe the availability of media libraries in multimedia courseware. Schooley (1988) estimated that the availability of media libraries could reduce the development effort by approximately 10%.

The availability of existing subject matter content has been viewed as potentially reducing the development effort required to prepare multimedia courseware. Kearsley (1985) in the CBT Analyst courseware estimation tool includes three questions that attempt to incorporate productivity gains associated with existing media or course materials. The existence of graphics libraries reduces the estimate of development time, while the development of new media or materials increases the development time. In the CBT Analyst estimation method these increases or decreases have a non-linear effect on the overall development time.

Post-development re-use
Very little research has been done on the effort required to implement changes for post-development re-use. That which does exist tends to be based on subjective opinion rather than on consistent measurement. Research into the development of multimedia courseware, as opposed to hypermedia-based systems, has been ongoing for some time. However, the only published evidence found by the authors into re-use post-development is provided by Department of the Air Force (1993) which provides informal estimates of the additional development time required to implement a change. Table 2 is based on the Department of the Air Force's Configuration Control Matrix.

Table 2 *Configuration control decision matrix*

| Type of change | Level of change | | |
	Minor example	Moderate example	Major example
Technical	Switch in the wrong position	Functioning of entire component must be changed due to an equipment modification	Introduce an entire new set of tasks
Instructional	Allow students two tries at a question instead of one	Change one test from multiple-choice to true/false	Introduce entire new strategy on how to test
Media	Change font	Add four full-motion video shots	Replace all graphics with video
Developer hours	< 40	40–160	> 160

These values in this table are based on expert opinion of the development time required to make changes to multimedia courseware and take no account of techniques to design re-useable courseware.

Effect of transferability

The need for transferability between computer and operating systems has become increasingly apparent over the last five years with commercial interest in producing authoring tools and systems which operate on a number of platforms. Authorware, Icon Author, CT and numerous other commercial products now allow the core code created on one platform to be transferred to another. Unfortunately, few of these systems deal effectively with the diversity of video, audio, graphics and animation formats used by computers. The result is that while the code may be transferred, the media seldom can. Unfortunately, we can find no research to indicate the effect on productivity of designing and developing multimedia courseware to be transferable across different hardware and operating systems platforms.

Design for re-use and transferability

One of the problems associated with the previous generations of technology-based learning courseware was that the development methods and techniques encouraged the encoding of most physical and instructional aspects of the courseware within the software. The result of this design technique is to limit re-use of instructional templates and tools during the development phase and recoding during the maintenance phase. This makes it difficult to re-use or transfer the courseware to another platform or to update it to meet new requirements. Figure 3 describes the various elements that are currently encoded by a typical authoring environment.

The subject matter knowledge, multimedia resources and instructional environment are normally designed into the final courseware product by the development team. The operational environment, such as the operating system and hardware, are normally predefined and major changes may require considerable recoding of the courseware. The presentational aspects of the courseware are also predefined by the authoring environment. Everything from the position of objects to the colour of the screen are normally encoded at the authoring stage.

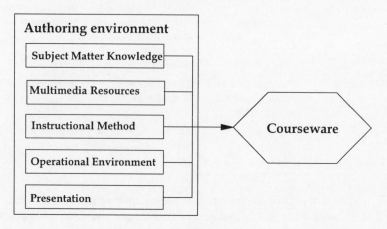

Figure 3 *Traditional courseware*

Merrill *et al.* (1990) indicated that to prepare re-usable courseware requires a change in instructional design and development techniques which decouples the media resources, knowledge base and instructional strategy. To support this work proto-type software tools have been developed to demonstrate some of the principles of re-use (Merrill, 1991; Merrill and ID2 Research Group, 1993; Merrill and ID2 Research Group, 1994; Merrill and Twitchel, 1994; Spector *et al.*, 1992). Unlike traditional courseware authoring techniques, these systems attempt to decouple knowledge (subject matter), resources (multimedia representations) and strategy (instructional). Figure 4 shows Merrill's architectural model for ID2 Expert development.

The separation of the knowledge, multimedia resources and parameters allows the transactional system to control the presentation of the courseware. While it would appear that decoupling allows multimedia courseware to be designed for post-development re-use and transferability, there is no published research into the effect on development effort or productivity.

Conclusion

The lack of an established framework of multimedia courseware metrics restricts our knowledge of the effect of design for re-usability and transferability on effort, development time and productivity. The calls for the establishment of a discipline of courseware engineering may result in a metrics framework to support further research into comparative evaluation of alternative design and development techniques. The metrics-based framework to assist comparative research into the development effort and productivity requirements for re-use and transferability described, forms part of an ongoing programme of research into the effect of different multimedia design and development strategies. It is hoped that the systematic analysis of the effect on productivity and effort of re-use and transferability techniques will enable developers to learn the lesson of previous attempts at technology-based training and create courseware that will last beyond the life of the original hardware and instructional design.

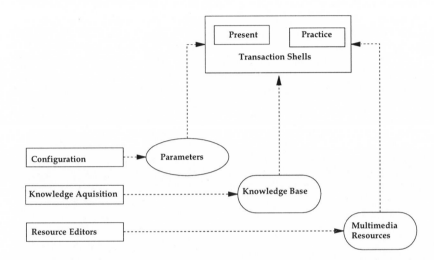

Figure 4 *Architecture of transaction-based instructional design system*

References

Avner, A (1988) 'Is there an ideal size for courseware production teams?' in *30th Association for the Development of Computer Based Instructional Systems*, ADCIS, Philadelphia, pp.143–7.

Baker, J (1994) 'One man and his dog', *Interact*, **1**, 3, 16–17.

Blalock, R H (1994) 'How models and templates = fast and creative development at American Airlines', in *16th Annual Conference and Exhibition on Interactive Systems for Training and Job Performance Improvement*, Washington Interactive Multimedia '94, Society for Applied Learning Technology, Washington, DC.

Campbell, J O (1988) 'Automated lesson generation for high volume computer-based instruction', in *Sixth Annual Conference on Interactive Instruction Delivery*, Society for Applied Learning Technology, Warrenton, VA.

Campbell, J O (1994) 'Template tools for computer-based training material', in *6th Summer Institute on Automating Instructional Design*, Utah State University, Logan, UT.

Cates, W M (1992) 'Fifteen principles for designing more effective instructional hypermedia/multimedia', *Educational Technology*, December, 5–11.

De Diana, I (1993) 'Editorial', *Education and Training Technology International*, **30**, 3, 190.

De Diana, I and van Schaik, P (1993) 'Courseware engineering outlined: An overview of some research issues', *Education and Training Technology International*, **30**, 3, 191–211.

Department of the Air Force (1993) 'Information for designers of instructional systems: interactive courseware (ICW) design, development, and management guide', *AF Handbook* 36–2235, Vol 5, Department of the Air Force, Headquarters, US Air Force, Washington DC.

Friedler, Y and Shabo, A (1991) 'An approach to cost-effective courseware development', *British Journal of Educational Technology*, **22**, 2, 129–38.

Kearsley, G (1985) 'The CBT advisor: An expert system program for making decisions about CBT', *Performance and Instruction*, **24**, 9, 15–17.

Marshall, I M, Samson, W B and Dugard, P I (1994) 'Multimedia courseware. Never mind the quality, how much will it cost to develop?', in *Proceeding of Association for Learning Technology 94*, University of Hull, pp.63–4.

McDonough, D, Strivens, J and Rada, R (1994) 'Current development and use of computer-based teaching at the University of Liverpool', *Computers in Education*, **22**, 4, 335–43.

Merrill, M D (1991) *An Introduction to Instructional Transaction Theory*, Research Report, Utah State University, Logan, UT.

Merrill, M D and ID2 Research Group (1993) *Automated Instructional Design and Development*, Research Report, Utah State University, Logan, UT.

Merrill, M D and ID2 Research Group (1994) *Instructional Design Theory for Automated Instructional Development*, Research Report, Utah State University, Logan, UT.

Merrill, M D and Twitchel, D G (1994) *Instructional Design Theory*, Educational Technology Publications, Englewood Cliffs, NJ.

Merrill, M D, Li, Z and Jones, M K (1990) 'Limitations of first generation instructional design', *Educational Technology*, **30**, 1, 7–11.

Schooley, R E (1988) 'Computer-based training (CBT) cost estimating algorithm for courseware (CEAC)', in *Interservice Industry Training Systems Conference*, pp.319–28.

Spector, J M, Gagne, R M, Muraida, DJ and Dimitroff, W A (1992) 'Intelligent framework for instructional design', *Educational Technology*, October, 21–7.

Sommerville, I (1989) *Software Engineering*, Addison Wesley, London.

Tennyson, R D (1993) 'Knowledge base for automated instructional systems development', in R D Tennyson (ed), *Automating Instructional Design, Development and Delivery*, Springer-Verlag, Berlin, pp.29–59.

Address for correspondence: **Ian Marshall** *et al.*, Software Quality Group, University of Abertay Dundee, Kydd Building, Bell Street, Dundee DD1 1HG.

31. Now You See Me: Video as a Tool for Teaching and Assessment

Professor Stephen Brown and **Iona Cruickshank**, *De Montfort University*

SUMMARY

This chapter describes an innovative two-fold strategy for the use of video technology to support the teaching and learning activities within De Montfort University. It shows how video can be used to provide a method of delivering lectures and demonstrations which would otherwise not be possible in a conventional lecture-room setting and how video recording of tutors' assessment comments, related to student work, can enhance the feedback process while reducing staff work loads. Findings show how the video-based learning resources can be used to improve flexibility of student access to information and skills, encourage learners to take increased responsibility for their own learning programmes, provide students with detailed comparative feedback on their own performance and free staff time for individual tuition and creative work.

Introduction

As part of its remit, the Lens Based Media Centre is responsible for the teaching of photography and video. Teaching is structured into modules, each module comprising 120 hours of student educational experience taught over a 15-week semester. Students are able to choose from a menu of modules which include photography and video.

Since the introduction of modularity there has been a dramatic increase in the number of students taking Lens Based Media modules, particularly photography. Students who enrol on the photography modules are of mixed photographic ability, some 63% having had little or no previous photographic experience.

The photography modules are practical in nature, based on a teaching and learning strategy that includes lectures, demonstrations, tutorials, practical project work and continuous assessment, at the end of which a student is required to produce a portfolio of work related to three or four project briefs. There is only one photographic module prerequisite, which is a level one module, 'Photography and Camera Vision'. Once that has been completed successfully, a student can choose to undertake any photographic module relevant to their year.

The challenge

During the academic year 1993/94 440 students undertook photographic modules. Of those, some 224 opted to take the prerequisite module 'Photography and Camera Vision', resulting in the module being repeated a total of 12 times.

Various ways of teaching large numbers of students were considered, such as lecturing to larger groups and then splitting them into smaller groupings for practical work. Repetition of the module was still required so that students could access 'Camera Vision' without timetable clashes.

Considerable academic and technical staff discussion related to student numbers occurred during the first semester. These highlighted particular areas of concern regarding the teaching of the prerequisite module, and the collection, collation and distribution of feedback at the end of each semester to all students on photographic modules. The main points raised were:

- The level of absenteeism per week resulted in the need to back-teach or tutor approximately 20 students per week, equivalent to a further module repetition.
- Giving the same lecture six times in a week on occasions had resulted in jaded delivery as the end of the week approached.
- The repetition of certain tasks was extremely time-consuming and tiring (particularly the demonstration of loading and unloading a film into a 35mm camera).
- The large number of visual images that required assessment created problems for the academic team in relation to achieving consistency in their marking over a number of days.
- The time spent on collecting, collating and distributing comments as feedback to students after assessments was staff-intensive, time-consuming and inefficient.
- Written verbalisation comments were not considered to be the most satisfactory method of giving feedback about visual imagery.
- Staff felt stressed and considered they would be unable to sustain the quality of teaching and learning.

The cause of these problems was not unique to Lens Based Media. Similar problems had previously been identified by the Teaching More Students Project (Gibbs, 1992) as being synonymous with a large increase in student numbers. It was acknowledged that to improve the situation, the Lens Based Media Centre's teaching and learning strategy required change. It seemed sensible to utilise the visual medium of video as a tool to interface between staff and students.

In the context of this case study, the use of video was considered to offer a method for improving the flexibility of student access to information and skills, as well as a means of freeing up staff time. A two-stage implementation process was used.

- The first stage involved the utilisation of video as a method of delivering assessment feedback to students.
- The second stage required greater preparation and was implemented several months later. This involved the recording on to video of lectures and repetitive tasks.

The implementation of the proposed strategy had to take account of issues expressed by academic staff such as the comparative educational effectiveness of delivering lectures and demonstrations traditionally or through the technological medium of video; and whether the utilisation of video offered a solution to the centre's teaching and learning problems.

Delivering student feedback

A challenge faced by Lens Based Media was 'How could a small number of staff give feedback to large numbers of students in a reasonable period of time?' Although critiques and ongoing verbal student feedback were an integral part of all photographic module content, the assessment at the end of the semester was the only time that all of a students' project work could be commented on together. Staff considered it advantageous for students to receive feedback associated with the breadth of their work as well as detailed information on a project-by-project basis.

The final end of semester assessment is held as a mini-exhibition at which each student is required to display their portfolio of project work. Up to 60 students per day, in designated module groups, are allocated display space. On average, some 210 students per semester are required to display a total of 2,280 photographic images. Each student is also required to produce a log book related to their concept generation, research findings and analysis of their photographs, on a project-by-project basis.

Previous methods of collecting and collating student feedback had been found to be too time-consuming and had required the typing of comments. These were:

- tutorials in one-to-one or small group situations;
- various methods of note taking, each of which required that the lecturer recorded the assessment panels' main comments either in long hand, into a tape recorder, or by dictation to someone who recorded in shorthand.

Using these methods had taken approximately one month to reach a stage where they could be distributed. By then the relevant students would either have commenced their second semester timetables, have started their summer vacation, or have graduated. It was considered that using the visual medium of video would enable the assessment panel to record their comments while addressing a student's photographic imagery.

In the field of operative dentistry education video has been used (Roberts *et al.*,1988) to enable students to receive feedback without affecting student–patient relationships. The findings show that video offered a rapid turnaround time between recording and delivery to students, as well as enabling the provision of a more objective record of a situation. From this evidence it was judged that video could be used to enhance a student's educational experience, while also offering a cost-effective method of solving the centre's previously identified problems.

Method

At the end of a group's assessment, the three members of the assessment team would take turns to talk to camera. The camera would be focused on an individual student's display of work while a tutor highlighted certain points or compositional factors and made constructive comments related to the team's final assessment of the work.

The camera was on a tripod and focused to include all of a student's work as full screen. One of the assessment team would operate the camera so that certain photographs could be shown full frame for clarification of detail. The team's comments were recorded via a clip microphone handed between the members of the team. It was decided that each would talk to one project. That way the students could see that they were assessed by a group, not just by one individual.

Results

We learned a great deal. We discovered that one of us was very natural talking to camera, while the other two struggled initially, particularly with the handover lines and with being able to build on the previous panel members' comments.

A positive aspect of this method of student feedback was the speed at which the feedback was available to students. The assessment would be completed on one day and the tape would be available for student viewing from 9am the following day. This proved very popular and enabled students to raise any problems with us quickly and ask for tutorial time. Data related to the pattern of student viewing and their interaction with the video showed that:

- 39% of students viewed the tape the day following their assessment;
- 20% viewed the tape several days later;
- 20% viewed the tape the following week;
- 20% viewed the tape several weeks later;
- 83% watched comments on other people's work as well as their own;
- 16% watched the comments on their work only;
- 50% watched the video on their own;
- 33% watched the video with a friend;
- 16% watched in a group.

Evaluation

Evaluation was undertaken in two stages.

Informal interviews were used to gather open-ended, subjective feedback from students. The main comments from students were as follows:

'Very good because we can see the work as you point to areas and talk about it.'
'Seeing other students' work and how you assessed their work in relation to mine meant I learned from the other comments.'
'It gives an average view of what was good and what wasn't across everybody's work.'
'It was like having a critique of the whole group's work.'
'The tape gives us an overview of our semester's work rather than just comments on one project.'
'It was good to have more than one tutor's comments, not just main module tutors, as we got another viewpoint.'
'I like how you related our written comments to the finished work.'

Constructive criticism mainly dealt with our camera and presentation skills:

- sometimes we pointed to work off camera;
- the sound level deteriorated if we turned our heads away from the microphone;
- extraneous noise was sometimes louder than our comments;
- occasionally our comments did not use expressions of encouragement and this was seen as hurtful.

Overall, the comments were such that it was decided to address our camera and presentation skills and continue with the use of video as a delivery tool.

The following semester a *structured questionnaire* was used as a method of data collection. The content of the questionnaire included the seven statements identified by students at the interview stage of the evaluation, and additional statements that staff considered essential to the evaluation process in that responses would clarify factors that were considered as possible negative aspects of this method of delivering feedback. The questionnaire was designed to collect data relevant to:

- the pattern of student viewing interaction with the video;
- a student's opinion of video as a method of delivering feedback;
- a student's preference in method of feedback delivery;
- additional comments students wished to make.

All 60 students who formed the target population were surveyed, 79% of whom had not previously experienced video as a method of delivering feedback. The results (Figure 1) show that the students strongly agreed with the majority of the statements that had been made at the initial interview stage. However, responses to two statements were not as positive. This alerted the team to a mismatch between the message the staff believed they were sending and what the students believed they were receiving. This was considered valuable feedback that would enable staff to address these points during future assessments.

One of our main concerns had been how students would feel about other students seeing and hearing their personal feedback comments, particularly if the comments were negative. Although some 15% of students did strongly express concern about this, 39% of respondents did not see this as a problem.

From the staff point of view the most significant data showed a positive response of 67% from students who had indicated that they preferred the use of video as a method of delivering feedback to other methods they had previously experienced.

Students' response to an invitation to make constructive suggestions for improving our method of student feedback could be categorised into three main areas. These were related to:

- requests for the inclusion of marks;
- comparisons between good and bad work prior to the start of each project, so that students can understand what tutors are looking for;
- the recording of the full discussions of the assessment panel.

The staff have undertaken to address the request for comparisons between so-called 'good work' and 'bad work'. Currently video is being used to record examples of work that meet the specified criteria for assessment across a full range of marks. The other two suggested inclusions are not logistically possible.

The results of the evaluation were such that the use of video as a delivery tool has continued. Currently operated across all of the photographic modules, it has become integral to the centres' assessment procedure.

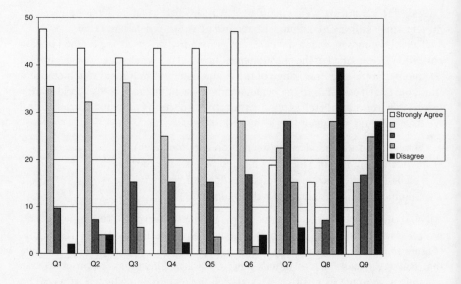

Figure 1 *Results of a five-point evaluation rating of nine statements, calculated in percentages*

Key to Figure 1

Q1. The video was very helpful because I can see the work as you point to areas and talk about it.

Q2. Seeing other students' work and how you assessed their work in relation to mine meant I learned from the other comments.

Q3. It gives a clear view of what was good and what wasn't across everybody's work.

Q4. It was like having a critique of the whole group's work.

Q5. The tape gave us an overview of our semester's work rather than just comments on one project.

Q6. It was good to have more than one tutor's comments (ie, not just main module tutor) as we got another viewpoint.

Q7. I like how you related our written comments to the finished work.

Q8. I feel uncomfortable with having my work commented on for all to see.

Q9. I was not clear why some of the criticism was being made by the tutor.

Conclusion

Video has enormous potential as a method for recording and distributing feedback to students, particularly in the areas of art and design education, or in educational situations which include practical project work. Positive aspects of this method include:

- the speed of turnaround for distribution to students – comments recorded one day can be ready for student viewing the following day;
- a saving in staff time – the length of time this activity now takes has shown a saving of 50% in staff time;
- it offers a preferable educational experience to students compared to other methods of delivery of feedback, in that it enables students to view their work and comments in relation to the panel's comments on the work of the rest of their group;
- it offers a more objective record of comments on visual imagery than is possible with a verbal description;
- it offers a record of past student work with academic comment which can be referenced by
  - academics to assist continuity in marking over a period of time
  - external examiners
  - students starting a module or considering enrolling on a module who are able to view previous work and gain an idea of the diversity of approaches and the standard expected in relation to the stipulated assessment criteria.

The successful use of video, together with the positive response from the students, gave the module team considerable confidence as they implemented the second phase of the strategy: the use of video to support and enhance the centre's delivery of teaching and learning.

Video recording of teaching and learning events

At De Montfort University video has been used as a teaching aid for a number of years, although its use has not been included within the teaching and learning strategy of the photographic modules. Students have previously been taught through traditional face-to-face delivery of lectures, seminars, tutorials and practical demonstrations. The remainder of a student's photographic educational experience was undertaken as self-directed study, which involved the student in research and practical project work, on location and in the centre's laboratories. Students were expected to be responsible for their own time management of these activities.

The success of television, film and video within education has been well documented. A considerable amount of the research carried out has investigated the educational effectiveness of instruction delivered through the medium of television compared to that delivered in a classroom situation. Commenting on evidence from such research, Schramm (1977) states 'there is no basis in the research for saying that students learn more or less from television than from classroom teaching', although what students learn and how effectively depends on how the programmes are designed (Bates, 1987). In this instance it was proposed to follow the advice offered by Bates that 'the most effective way to get the most out of television material, when interpretation and application are the main aims is through group discussion, guided by relevant questions for discussion'. To this end it was decided that the centre's strategy should include academic interaction with the student group prior to and on completion of a projection of a video lecture.

The decision taken by Lens Based Media staff, to deliver a complete module lecture programme to students through video, was unique within the university. One particular area of concern expressed by staff was related to the students' possible reaction to this method of delivery, given that all the other lectures they would attend in the university would be delivered in face-to-face situations. This concern was outweighed by the acknowledged benefits of video which would enable students:

- to work at their own pace;
- to access lectures if they had been absent;
- to take more responsibility for their own education.

Video recording of lectures also offered staff the potential to 'break down tyrannies' (O'Hagan, 1995) imposed by lecture schedules in higher education.

Not only was it believed that the use of video would enhance a student's educational experience, but that it also offered a cost-effective method of solving the centre's previously identified problems and enabled a saving of staff time that could be used to greater educational effect. It was seen as a strategy that would not necessarily involve the staff in too much additional work, as the lecture content already existed. The exception to this was the planned inclusion of a location shoot for an instructional demonstration based on the initial project. It was planned to use video to undertake an activity that time constraints and staffing had previously made impossible: to take the students on location through the medium of video. They would be able to follow a lecturer as he or she undertook the project and talked them through decision making. It was believed, from past experience of teaching similar student groups, that this would assist students who had little or no previous photographic experience.

Methodology

A production team was formed to plan and implement the programmes. Included were key photographic personnel, a video technician and a television expert, who took on the role of director. Initial decisions included the identification of the number and type of programmes that were considered essential to the proposed strategy. These included all five of the lectures, one practical demonstration and a repetitive task, which had been identified as the most staff-intensive. Constraints associated with time and staff availability resulted in certain of the demonstrations remaining as face-to-face interaction between staff and students.

During the initial pre-production meetings it was agreed that the aims of the production were:

- to record lectures, not make professional television productions;
- to make the production process cost-effective;

- to ensure that technical quality was of a standard that did not detract from the aesthetic detail of situations and imagery.

The recordings were undertaken in the video studio in order to achieve what was considered by the director and academics to be an acceptable standard.

Results
It was considered a beneficial learning experience by the production team, in that it had resulted in the need for staff to address:

- their teaching strategy;
- teaching performance;
- students' reactions to the learning experience.

Teaching strategy
Although it was normal for lecturers to review and update the content of their lectures, the fact that once recorded, it was not planned to update the video for a two-year period, resulted in a reassessment of the lecture content and the proposed learning outcomes. This led to refinement and restructuring and was seen by the academics as a positive method of focusing on their teaching strategy.

Teaching performance
Initial reaction of the staff prior to delivering to camera was one of anxiety based on the realisation that the end result would involve self-appraisal – an experience that was not relished by even the most confident of the staff. The self-appraisal came immediately after the initial recording, when the rushes were viewed, and decisions made in respect of reshoot. Comments, in the main, related to pace of delivery. On video, normal classroom delivery appeared slower, even hesitant in some cases. Pace became a key issue in the delivery of the remaining lectures, and has remained an issue for the staff in their continued face-to-face delivery to students.

The confrontation of the individual with their own teaching strategy was considered invaluable in that it enabled the teaching staff to check from the perceiver's viewpoint the organisation of content, and the clarity of the main points related to proposed teaching outcomes.

Student reaction
It had been expected that there might be some negative response to this method of delivering. This was unfounded, as was the concern that once the students realised they could sign the videos out to view in their own time, they would not attend the timetabled lectures. This was not the case – levels of student attendance remained similar to that of the previous year when teaching had been undertaken in a face-to-face situation. It had also been expected that the opportunity to view the tapes for further reference would be popular with the students. To facilitate this, an area was equipped with four video players each with a set of headphones. In fact the expected pattern of behaviour did not materialise until later in the semester.

The videos were found to be invaluable by staff dealing with students who would have otherwise been disadvantaged through absence from lectures. They were also used by several students who had not previously been able to undertake the prerequisite module at level 1, enabling them to catch up on the level of competence required for enrolling on level 2 photography modules.

At the time of writing, the second semester has commenced and the videos are being used as refresher aids by students who successfully completed the level 1 prerequisite up to 18 months ago. This use had not been anticipated.

It is interesting to note that level 2 students who have had the experience of being taught through video delivery expected to continue with this method and have started to request copies of videos of their current lectures for reference viewing. Staff have responded to this request by recording several level 2 lectures on video as back-up reference material.

Evaluation

Formative evaluation of the pilot project was undertaken through the collection of qualitative data. This enabled the module team to evaluate student perception of, and interaction with, video as a method of educational delivery, and student performance in relation to comparative learner outcomes.

Qualitative evaluation

On completion of the first semester all the students who formed the target population were surveyed through the use of a structured questionnaire, which included questions to identify the pattern of student interaction with the tapes. It was judged that such data would provide insights into the clarity of module content and instructor effectiveness, enabling appropriate changes to be made at a future date, if required. Open questions were also included offering students the opportunity to respond with opinions, constructive criticism or suggestions related to the teaching method or content of the module.

Results from all of the target population surveyed showed the following responses to the feedback questions:

- 93% of the students considered it helpful to be able to view the tapes in their own time;
- 68% of the students preferred to attend timetabled viewings rather than viewing entirely in their own time;
- 68% of the students did not wish the module to be taught by a different method;
- 56% of students replayed tapes for clarification purposes;
- 31% of students replayed tapes because they missed the timetabled projection;
- 84% of students took notes while watching a tape.

Some 54% of the students responded to the open questions. Of these around 15% made valid suggestions related to problems they had experienced while undertaking the lighting project. The main consensus was that a demonstration delivered through the medium of video was perceived by the students as an educational disadvantage compared to a face-to-face demonstration. This response was confirmed by the fact that 68% of the students reviewed the lighting demonstration tape, a greater percentage than for any of the other tapes. 'Camera technique' was the next highest, being viewed by 39% of students.

Learner outcomes

The effectiveness of learner outcomes was measured through a comparison of assessment scores of the target student population with those from the previous semester's students, taught through traditional face-to-face methods. The spread of marks was similar. The exception was in the failure rate of the target student population, which was less than that of the previous years. While it was recognised that this could have been through a difference in student competence rather than the use of video, overall the results suggest that the use of video enhanced the students' educational experience, and alleviated previously identified problems experienced by the staff.

On the basis of the results from this case study, the use of video technology to support teaching and learning appears to offer considerable benefits to higher educational in terms of:

- more effective communications between students and staff;
- more individualised student feedback and support;
- raised staff awareness of personal teaching effectiveness.

Its inclusion within a strategy related to providing for students within a decreasing unit of resource offers a method of educational delivery that can maintain quality standards while showing a saving on staff time. As it is acknowledged that further research testing, across a wider range of students, would be beneficial in confirmation of such statements, De Montfort University is continuing to address this issue through the development and implementation of a similar teaching and learning strategy within its textile technology degree programme. It is hoped that such results will show that the utilisation of video may offer a potential solution to some of the problems inherent in teaching and learning in the 1990s.

References

Bates, A W (1987) 'Learning from television', in M Thorpe and D Grugen (eds), *Open Learning for Adults*, Longman, Essex.

O'Hagan, C (1995) 'Custom videos for open learning', *Innovations in Education and Training International*, **32**, 2.

Gibbs, G (1992) *Assessing More Students*, No. 4, The Teaching More Students Project, The Polytechnics and Colleges Funding Council, London.

Roberts, D B, Kinzer, R L and KunihirA, S (1988) 'Clinical teaching by video-enhanced study club discussion sessions', *Journal of Dental Education*, **52**, 214–16.

Schramm, W (1977) *Big Media, Little Media*, Sage, London.

Stephen Brown is Professor of Media and Information Technology, De Montfort University, and formerly the Head of Distance Learning, British Telecommunications plc.

Address for correspondence: Department of Media and IT, De Montfort University, Gateway House, The Gateway, Leicester LE1 9BH, UK.

Iona Cruickshank is Head of Lens Based Media within the Department of Media and Information Technology at De Montfort University, and formerly worked as a professional photographer.

32. Encouraging Flexible Learning through Action Research: A Case Study of Student Perceptions

Karen Hinett, *University Central Lancashire, Preston*

SUMMARY

The use of records of achievement and 'personal development programmes' is increasing in higher education. This paper challenges assumptions made about the reflective process central to these developments through in-depth interviews with students involved in the 'Personal and academic development', which operates as a programme of action research at the University of Central Lancashire. It is informed by interviews with key respondents at institutions operating similar programmes. It begins with a brief outline of the university's 'personal development programme' followed by a discussion of the interim findings which examine the factors which affect the students' perception of learning and their reaction to a programme of 'flexible' learning.

Introduction

This chapter provides a brief outline of the institution and addresses four main points:

- the aims and intentions of the research;
- the case study of personal development and its location within the action research tradition;
- the outcomes of the research, namely, student perceptions of learning as articulated through interviews during 1994;
- conclusions and recommendations. All quotations from students used here are from interviews conducted in 1994 and as such this chapter represents interim findings.

The University of Central Lancashire at Preston is a 'new' university created as a result of the 1992 White Paper. It has a student population of approximately 16,000 of which 52% are women and 51% are over 22 years old. The university operates a modular, semesterised system which uses the Credit Accumulation and Transfer Scheme (CATS).

Aims and intentions of the research

Records of achievement and personal development programmes have been promoted through government initiatives such as the National Record of Achievement (NRA) and the Enterprise in Higher Education initiative (EHE). Such programmes are often linked to vocational training and the promotion of 'transferable skills'

(Ainley, 1994). Debate has taken place about the value of such innovations in higher education and distinctions have been made between a 'learning outcomes profile' which offers students accredited skills, and a 'personal or professional development portfolio' which aims to 'encourage a spirit of reflection and goal setting' (Assiter and Shaw, 1993).

Research at the University of Central Lancashire suggests that the bifurcation of skills and personal development is unnecessary. Instead, the acquisition of skills were located *within* a reflective process. The aim of the Personal and Academic Development Portfolio Unit (which will be referred to as the PDP from here on) is therefore to make the acquisition of skills meaningful by offering a context in which the student can understand his or her own learning and development. The research aims to question and assess the value of taking part in such a personal development programme.

The rationale for the PDP stemmed from existing research into student learning which suggests that:

> 'it would be beneficial to provide students with the concepts and theories emerging from the current research on student learning. Such a study skills course would draw attention to the importance of organisation and structure, to the contrasting styles and approaches, to the need to adopt versatile and appropriate strategies, and to the development of a personally satisfying style of studying which is idiosyncratic but effective.' (Ramsden and Entwistle, 1993)

The PDP aimed not only to offer students guidance in their learning but to facilitate independent learning and allow the students to become more responsible for their personal and academic progress. It aims to do this by employing a student-centred approach to learning.

There is much confusion and lack of conceptual clarity about personal development; phrases such as 'student-centred learning', 'autonomous learning' and 'independent learning' are used interchangeably. Boud (1988) argues that: 'The main characteristics of autonomy as an approach to learning is that students take some significant responsibility for their own learning over and above responding to instruction'. Gibbs (1981) says that the characteristics of student-centred learning are 'stressing students' independence and personal responsibility'.

The literature on student-centred learning argues for an approach that involves a shift in the traditional conceptions of learning and teaching. It requires the teacher to learn and very often for the students, as learners, to teach through presentations, groupwork and other forms of communication. The work of Hounsell (1984) and Boot and Reynolds (1983) reveals that lecturers are often more concerned with the transmission of material than on its reception. Student-centredness challenges the view that material can be packaged, delivered and then consumed by the students. More fundamentally, student-centred learning places emphasis on the learning and development of individual students rather than teaching per se.

The PDP aims to be student-centred through interactive class work and assessment which allows choice and negotiation. The programme aims to fulfil these intentions by using group exercises and discussion as the basis for learning. The programme combines elements of formal lecturing, group exercises which require discussion and feedback to the rest of the group, and experiential learning. Exercises vary depending on the topic being discussed but aim to encourage students to examine a subject or theory (such as Bloom's (1956) taxonomy of ways to gain knowledge) and to make judgements for themselves.

Placing the programme within the student-centred tradition is not without problems. To be truly student-centred the course would be flexible and allow content and assessment to be negotiated. This is a concern for any institution which operates a modular scheme as each module has to comply with the regulations of the structure. There are also pedagogic concerns: student-centred learning suggests an equal relationship between learner and teacher which is difficult to maintain when assessment is necessary for accreditation.

The PDP design was shaped by the work of Ramsden and Entwistle (1983) who suggest that the student's perception of the assessment is crucial to the approach they take to learning. Students are likely to adopt a reproductive, surface approach to their learning where the assessment is seen as threatening, where the syllabus is overloaded or where there are inappropriate assessment questions or techniques required. The assessment for the PDP thus aims to be relevant, challenging though not unrealistic, timely, and to encourage students to become more aware of their own learning. In addition the types of assessment are varied (see Figure 1). Students are assessed on their personal responses to learning through the completion of 'learning logs'. Learning logs guide the student through key stages identified by Boud (1985):

- Returning to the experience – recounting the events (describe the event).
- Attending to feelings – acknowledging feelings and removing obstruction to rational consideration (what did I learn?)
- Re-evaluating the experience – re-examining the experience in terms of new knowledge and applying it to future behaviour (action plan and review).

Course unit	Assessment guidelines	Student input
Presentation and communication	A ten-minute presentation	Students choose their own subject to present and can use any visual format, ie, video, slides
Information technology	A piece of word-processed work, or graphic design	Each assignment is negotiated with the student to suit their individual level of competence
Learning to learn	Four 'learning logs' and a written piece on their 'good and bad learning experiences'	Students are encouraged to reflect on their learning and to assess how new information relates to their previous knowledge. Each log is individual to the student and written in the first person

Figure 1 *PDP for one semester*

Action research and the personal and academic development programme

The PDP was devised as a pilot scheme that would enable students to acquire skills in key areas of presentation and information technology while encouraging them to be reflective learners. The course lasts for one semester (12 weeks) and operates twice yearly. The programme comprises three four week units:

- an introduction to information technology;
- presentation and communication skills;
- learning to learn.

The programme is available to all first-year students who can opt to take the course as an elective. The PDP is therefore additional to their main area of study and makes up one-sixth of their first-year work. Reservations were felt by the research team about implementing an add-on programme, as much of the literature suggests that to be successful such programmes should be embedded in the major course of study. However, the students were very mixed in their attitudes towards such a programme. This issue will be explored in more depth later.

The details of the PDP design were based on research at other higher education institutions and are intended to act as a pilot upon which an informed decision can be made about making such a programme available to all undergraduates. This prior research indicates that for an RoA scheme to be successful the aims of the innovation must be compatible with the culture of the institution (Trowler and Hinett, 1994). The PDP operates under the CATS scheme employed by the institution. The rationale is that students become socialised into the credit culture on entering the university and expect to be given credit for their work; it would therefore be against the culture of our institution to expect students to become involved in a new scheme without some incentive.

The PDP operates as action research in that the course design and delivery are open to change in the light of student opinion, current research, and the progress as noted by the programme leader. An original cohort of students were interviewed in 1994 about their expectations of higher education, their perceptions of learning and their reaction to the PDP programme. These students will be interviewed again in order to account for any change in perceptions as they mature as students and as they experience a range of other teaching and learning styles. In addition, a group of students participating in the course during 1995 will be interviewed to account for their perceptions of learning as they experience a revised programme. It is anticipated that the student discourse will illuminate the changes in the programme as perceived by the students and indicate the external influences which affect their personal development.

Before we proceed to an examination of student perceptions of learning it is important to acknowledge the various factors that affect the research. First, the programme operates within the boundaries of an action research case study and could be considered limited as it draws exclusively on the opinion of the students. While it ignores the other value frameworks of staff and peers it draws upon the relevant research and aims to provide outcomes which are generalisable to theory if not to context. Second, research has suggested that students naturally mature over time (Gibbs, 1992). The research aims to question this view and to provide an account of the factors that affect learning through student discourse.

Research outcomes
Of the 15 students interviewed, 13 were female and 2 male. Six of the female students were mature (older than 22), five returning to college after raising a family. Although this is an unequal gender distribution, it is representative of the students on the course. Many themes emerged; for simplicity these have been divided into four categories:

- the pedagogic factors affecting learning;
- independent factors affecting the student's personal development;
- student expectations of higher education and employment;
- the student attitude to the PDP.

Pedagogic factors affecting learning
The theme most frequently mentioned by students associated with the traditional model of learning was assessment. This includes:

- concern about the autonomy and control of assessment;
- linear learning and rote memorisation;
- an emphasis on grades.

Students revealed through the discourse a personal dichotomy: on the one hand, they learn better through interactive methods and find experiential learning more enjoyable; on the other, they do not trust or value their own judgement where self-assessment is concerned. Students suggest that they expected to be told what to do. 'you've been conditioned into it over the years through schooling to be taught at, you expect it'. It would appear that the majority of students expect what shall be called a 'teacher-centred' style of learning because that has been their experience prior to attending the university.

Many of the students describe being in prescriptive learning situations where they are told, 'you will do this' and mentioned the PDP where by comparison, 'there wasn't much talking at students so that's good'. This has obvious implications for the degree of interest and motivation the student shows, the difference between 'wanting to learn something and it being forced on you'. What the transcripts reveal is that the students often feel resigned to teaching styles and to passively follow the lectures: 'I'm not really into where you get a lecturer stood at the front telling you loads of information and not really giving you a chance to put your views across'. Part of this resignation to passivity is the students' preoccupation with note-taking: 'just writing down lots of facts, I don't learn very well like that'. The students claimed that they were unhappy with this style and resented being part of a 'prescriptive' system. However, their discourse suggested that they felt incapable of altering the system.

In addition, students articulated a concern, verging on the obsessive, with grades. The majority believed that the grades they received were a true measurement of their ability. One student described two different approaches she had applied to two different assignments and concluded that one style was more effective than another, 'because I got a four (CATS grade) for my marketing and a three for my business so I must have learnt something mustn't I?' The student has validated the quality of her work through the grade she received, although she still questions whether this is actually indicative of her learning. Issues of awareness are highlighted through the students' attitude to the award of grades:

> 'You do get into a mentality of "what am I going to get out of it" in terms of credits because you have to get your credits and if you want a decent grade you've got to get the grades within those credits. I suppose you become a bit selfish and you've just got to accept it.'

The student appreciates that this mentality is not perhaps the most conducive to learning but that it is necessary in order to progress. This uneasiness can be detected in the following quotation where the student defends, partly against her judgement, the traditional learning model as a way of getting through the system:

> 'There would be the occasional lecture that was slightly interactional but normally there are just streams of notes… We have one lecturer who writes down everything you need to know on an overhead and then while you're copying it down he'll tell you everything you need to know for the exam. At least I know with his notes I've got it all there.'

These opinions have important implications for curriculum design. The transcripts suggest a general discontent with the 'teacher-centred' model of learning being offered to the student. The opinion that formal lectures produce a 'captive' audience is ironically apt; students are not so much attentive as captive to assessment methods, which prey upon their insecurity and need to succeed. By comparison, the students expressed appreciation of the 'student-centred' model employed in the PDP:

> 'The way the lessons were structured and we worked in groups I found that I came up with things when I was talking to other people that I wouldn't have [thought of] if I'd just sat and written it down.'

None of the students expressed a negative response to the student-centred style of teaching and learning. Several students commented that they would have felt uneasy about all the activities had they not been given supplementary hand-outs because of their preoccupation with having notes from which to revise. When asked what they thought the PDP course had taught them, they were unanimous in their vote: improved self-confidence, confidence in giving presentations and using a computer.

Such positive comments should not suggest that the PDP was a resounding success. The students were wary about self-assessment and were cautious about the hidden agenda; why did they have to evaluate themselves – that was the teachers job? What was I looking for? As stated earlier, the students were asked to complete four learning logs, which are reflective pieces. The students are encouraged to re-evaluate learning experiences and to extract exactly how the experience led to 'new' learning. The logs were received with apprehension by the students who are locked into an assessment pattern which denies individual expression or negotiation.

'I didn't want to do it. If there was another option I would have opted to do something else, I'd have opted for a 5,000-word essay instead of doing the learning logs but I think I would have missed out on something and I wouldn't have got so much out of the course.'

The above extract reveals the difficult transition from one style of teaching to another. In a teacher-centred assessment model the student and lecturer are in a relationship based on power, the student as learner being subordinate to the lecturer as holder of knowledge. The student is thus reliant on the lecturer to provide him or her with the tools with which to complete assignments and sit examinations: she or he is also reliant on the lecturer for the grade she or he receives. In the student-centred model the student and lecturer are equal in their relationship, both as learners. The students are engaged in self-assessment and peer-assessment and are thus much more reliant on their own ability and are responsible for their own success. Some students were quite keen and claimed,

'It makes you stop and think about it. It helps you embed it in your brain a little bit more... you can only improve on what you're doing if you're conscious about it... you learn from what you're doing, you learn from your mistakes.'

The learning logs are an important part of the PDP in that they aim to challenge the students' conventional ideas of learning and assessment. Self-assessment is a necessary and important step in the transition from teacher-centred models of learning and encouraging individual progress and student-centredness.

Independent factors affecting personal development
Issues of personal development and how the student felt they had progressed or changed as a result of the PDP experience were explored in the interviews and several themes emerged:

- whether the student had any prior experience of reflective logs;
- the initiative and responsibility of the learner;
- the gender and age of the student.

Those students with prior experience of reflective logs were generally negative about them. Their main concern was that they were repetitive, the whole process being more of a chore than an educational enlightenment.

'On the BTEC we had to fill in similar things... for all your various competencies you have to write various things underneath... You end up writing the same thing... without giving much thought to what you were writing.'

All students with previous experience expressed similar sentiments. The logs were obviously given very low status and were undermined further by a lack of recognition by the college (all students with previous experience attended the same local further education college). Learning logs were generally accepted with the self-selected interviewees but as more students experience reflective work (which they consider to be a waste of time) in further education, the less likely they will be to engage in self-assessment at university and may opt for traditional 'safer' models.

The transcripts revealed a correlation between two factors: those students who took responsibility for their work, and age. In every case the students who acknowledged that they put effort into their studies were mature. There are several possible reasons for this. First and most obviously, the mature students have returned to college probably having had to work hard to gain entry qualifications before they arrived and are therefore very keen. Second, many of them did not complete their education or have a chance to go to university for various reasons and now feel that this is their time. Third, many have either worked in the home or held down paid employment and realise the benefits of being a student. However, it may also be the case that the diligent younger students may not admit to being diligent because of social pressure to conform to a stereotype of the young student who cares more for their social life than their studies (this sentiment of 'conformity' is backed up by Ainley, 1994).

Student expectations of higher education and employment
Only one student claimed that all she wanted from university was a degree. The other 14 ranged in their enthusiasm but all envisaged some kind of individual development. Some students emphasised the social aspect, leaving home, living on their own and experiencing life as an independent adult. The majority were keen to test themselves and accomplish something for themselves:

> 'I needed to do it for me, not just for the years ahead or career. I needed the time out to do something for me... I wanted to be educated and to have my mind opened and to learn new things. It's just as simple as that.'

The findings reveal that individual and career development cannot be separated. All the students were aware that presentation skills and information technology were important to employers and all but one thought they were important on a personal level too. Only one student was dogmatic in her view of education: 'it's all down to getting a job at the end, isn't it?' Other students were acutely aware of the importance of skills and some even suggested that the university deliberately incorporated these skills because they are useful in industry: 'I think employers look for people who can present themselves. If you can communicate in an effective manner I think that's going to get you more chance of a job really'. Clearly the students are aware of the need for interpersonal skills and the ability to communicate.

Student reaction to the PDP
Earlier it was stated that the PDP was designed as a credited elective. Research has suggested that such an add-on course 'divorces them [skills] from the cultural context' (Ainley, 1994). However, this add-on course was not considered to be ideal but as a compromise which would be congruent with the aims of the research and the idiosyncrasies of the university.

Despite such implementation problems, the students claimed that they enjoyed mixing with students from other disciplines. The students named variety of subject, different perspectives and general interest as the factors which aided this approach. 'It was more interesting to talk to people who were doing different things and what they had to say about the university'. As a group they seemed to relish the opportunity to meet students from other areas and many of the discussions on learning styles were informed by anecdotes from students who were taught in different ways (eg, lab work in the natural sciences and individual project work in computer science).

Conclusions and recommendations

This chapter is written with the assumption that the students of the 1990s are heterogeneous and demand a programme of study which will maximise their individual potential. The research suggests that students are discontented and frustrated by 'traditional' teaching styles and assessment methods which do not allow creativity or individuality. There is a discontinuity between what higher education offers and what the students want.

The research to date reveals that students are becoming much more selective in their choice of programme. They are aware of the pressure upon them to perform well not only educationally but at an interpersonal level. This has enormous implications for curriculum design and teaching styles. The gap between the 'traditional' single/combined honours degree and the more general education which includes proficiency in certain skills is widening as students become more aware of the need for interpersonal skills in the world outside higher education.

The students are quite clearly being sent mixed messages: on the one hand, they are encouraged to be computer literate and to discuss in class: on the other, they are forced to resort to traditional learning styles and a passive approach to learning in order to conform to the assessment criteria. The students, while they have not used the words 'student-centred', are moving towards a more liberal, student-centred approach. They recognise the importance of being responsible learners and are aware that certain interpersonal skills are necessary for their progress. They describe a frustration with formal lectures where they are denied the opportunity to participate. It should not surprise academics that students born in the late 1970s should find formal instruction through the use of outdated media 'boring' (Spender, 1994). It is evident from research so far that students shine when they can learn through media which has meaning for them and when they can control the way they respond to assessment criteria. The students may wish to present the content of their assignment through visuals rather than words, using computer graphics, camcorders and CD-ROM. This may mean allowing them to submit work on disc, through video, or via the Internet.

This chapter argues that a skills-based programme, which combines assessment which the students consider to be relevant to them with a student-centred approach, can help to improve students' confidence and equip them with the skills they consider necessary. Learning logs can help students to make sense of their learning as they develop and acquire new skills so that their learning is not in an 'intellectual vacuum' but grounded in the experience of each individual's programme of learning. The PDP is not offered as an ideal but one which helps to unite students in their ability to access information.

The following conclusions and suggestions are offered to practitioners and researchers who wish to implement a similar programme in their own institution.

- Student-centred learning requires a deconstruction of the traditional assessment model and requires a shift in emphasis from the staff to the student.
- Forces such as a modular scheme impinge upon the extent to which student-centredness can be facilitated. Student-centredness must therefore be defined in relation to the context of the institution.
- Assessment needs to be flexible to the extent that students can respond with individuality and through a variety of media.
- Used in conjunction with other subjects, learning logs can help to encourage reflectivity.
- Reflectivity often results in students becoming more self-aware, and can then begin to take responsibility for their own development.
- Understanding the students' perceptions about teaching and learning should be crucial to the facilitation of learning in a system of mass higher education.
- Finally, institutions attempting to implement personal development should foster a flexible and reflective pedagogy.

References

Ainley, P (1994) *Degrees of Difference: Higher Education in the 1990s*, Lawrence and Wishart, London.

Assiter, A and Shaw, E (1993) *Using Records of Achievement in Higher Education*, Kogan Page, London.

Bloom, J (1956) *Taxonomy of Educational Objectives. Book 1: Cognitive Domain*, Longman, Harlow.

Boot, R and Reynolds, M (1983) *Learning and Experience in Formal Education*, Manchester Monographs.

Boud, D (1985) *Reflection: Turning Experience into Learning*, Kogan Page, London.

Boud, D (1988) *Developing Student Learning and Autonomy*, 2nd edn, Kogan Page, London.

Gibbs, G (1981) *Teaching Students to Learn: A Student Centred Approach*, Open University Press, Buckingham.

Gibbs, G (1992) *Improving the Quality of Student Learning*, Technical and Education Studies, Bristol.

Hounsell, D (1984) 'Understanding teaching and teaching for understanding', in F Marton, D Hounsell and N Entwistle (eds), *The Experience of Learning*, Scottish Academic Press, Edinburgh.

Ramsden, P and Entwistle, N (1983) *Understanding Student Learning*, Croom Helm, Beckenham.

Spender, D (1994) Keynote speech at the 1994 International Experiential Learning Conference, Washington DC.

Trowler, P and Hinett, K (1994) 'Implementing the recording of achievement in higher education', *Capability*, Higher Education Council (HEC), Vol.1.

Karen Hinett is a research assistant at the University of Central Lancashire, Preston. She is currently involved in research in experiential learning and aims to complete her PhD on Student Learning in Higher Education in 1996.

Address for correspondence: Department of Public Policy, Harris Building, Preston PR1 2HE, e-mail: K.Hinett@uclan.ac.uk

33. 'I'd Like to do the Course but…'. Mentoring – Flexible Approaches to Staff Development: A Case Study from New Zealand

Doug Haynes, *Educational Development, Manukau Polytechnic, Auckland*

A mihi (greeting) from Aotearoa (New Zealand) to the conference:

> *Kia ora koutou katoa*
> *Rau rangatira ma*
> *Ko tenei taku mihi aroha*
> *Kia koutou e runga i tenei ra*
> *Mihi ki nga tangata o tenei whenua*
> *Mihi ki tenei whare e tu nei*
> *No reira*
> *Tena koutou*
> *Tena koutou*
> *Tena koutou katoa.*

SUMMARY

Mentoring is increasingly becoming a key tool for polytechnic staff developers in New Zealand. Lecturers in New Zealand polytechnics have pressures on their time which make attending traditionally delivered professional development courses and seminars increasingly difficult. This case study describes a range of flexible learning modules delivered at Manukau Polytechnic in Auckland, New Zealand. All of the modules have as their base the mentoring of individual staff engaged in independent learning. The modules are credited towards a Diploma in Adult and Tertiary Education. Participants in the modules work at their own pace but have regular meetings with the mentor or module leader. The views of mentors and module participants are explored on the role of the mentor and the nature of the independent learning projects. The advantages and disadvantages of this style of professional development are analysed.

Background

The last five years have seen far-reaching changes to the structure of tertiary education in New Zealand. Institutional autonomy, reduced government funding, quality requirements for accreditation, the introduction of a competency-based National Qualifications Framework, are but a few. One of the consequences is that tertiary institutions are having to do more with less. Many newly appointed polytechnic lecturers have not received any preservice training in adult learning and teaching. Each newly appointed lecturer is currently required to undertake 12 weeks of training in adult learning and teaching. This training has been delivered through modules running for a complete week or part-time over a term. Traditionally delivered staff development courses are proving increasingly difficult to fill: 'I'd like to do the course, but… ' is an increasingly common response from polytechnic lecturers when staff development sessions are mentioned.

The difficulties that are behind this response are common limitations of traditional course delivery. Cost is clearly a major factor. Heads of department are finding it difficult to fund replacements for lecturers attending staff development courses. Lecturers themselves find that the disruptions to their teaching and/or personal life from attending staff development sessions outweigh the benefits. The timing of traditional course delivery is difficult in a large institution with a diversity of timetables, terms and semesters. Traditional courses are sometimes perceived to be not relevant to the workplace needs of the participants. Lecturers are increasingly demanding professional development which directly solves problems they have in their work.

The Educational Development Section at Manukau Polytechnic teaches modules which lead to a Diploma in Adult and Tertiary Education. In the last two years, enrolment on some of the traditionally delivered modules has declined. In response, the section is giving greater emphasis to more flexible delivery. Two modules which are particularly popular are the Independent Learning Contract and the Teaching Development Contract. Both involve the lecturer negotiating professional development outcomes which will improve their own knowledge and their teaching. The lecturers work independently, meeting regularly with their mentor.

Action Research and Educational Management modules have been developed which are a mix of traditional delivery and a project done independently by individuals or groups. A module on Course Design and Development is now offered as a completely independent learning package. Two advanced Course Design and Assessment modules involve the participants identifying a project relevant to their curriculum work and negotiating appropriate assessment criteria with the module leader. It is anticipated that other modules currently delivered in a traditional mode will be converted to independent learning packages this academic year.

Seven module participants and three module leaders who had been involved with flexible learning and mentoring approaches in the modules described above were interviewed recently on video. This chapter in part draws upon the issues raised in these interviews.

The nature of mentoring

'Mentoring' is a term used in widely disparate ways in the educational literature. Healey and Welchert (1990, p.17) define mentoring as 'a dynamic, reciprocal relationship in a work environment between an advanced career incumbent (mentor) and a beginner (protégé) aimed at promoting the career development of both'. Several of the staff in Educational Development interviewed supported this view – that although the mentor may be perceived to have a higher level of professional acumen, they also gained knowledge and insights from the module participants they mentored. The notion of the mentor as one who helps learners reflect upon their experiences is a particularly valuable one in a staff development situation. In this context Ralph Tuck (1993, p.25) identifies three important functions of a mentor:

- an enabler of the self-assessment process;
- a 'mirror' to the learner's own ambitions and understandings;
- a provider of 'unconditional positive regard'.

Several of the responses of Educational Development staff and module participants supported and developed Tuck's definition of a mentor's function:

- a mentor is someone to bounce ideas off, someone who has a helicopter view;
- mentoring involves a sharing of experience;
- the mentor could be seen as a trusted friend and colleague;
- the mentor is a sounding board – someone who helps to solve problems.

The module participants interviewed shared many of the perceptions of the Educational Development lecturers on the nature of mentoring, but also raised some interesting additional insights. Some of these were:

- the mentor has to respect confidentiality;
- the personal relationship is important – trust is necessary;
- the mentor is someone who points you in the right direction;
- the chemistry between the mentor and the mentored needs to be right. There need to be options if the relationship does not facilitate learning;
- the mentor needs to be accessible and available when you want them;
- some found it difficult because they felt that they were not on the same wavelength as the module leader.

Several respondents raised the interesting idea that mentoring also involves peer mentoring. This was particularly so in the projects of the Action Research and Educational Management modules. Some responses included:

- 'We gained more from the help we got from each other than from the module leader because he was based on another campus.'
- 'One of the key things we gained from each other was encouragement.'
- 'Those of us who worked in pairs found the module much easier than those who worked individually with some meetings with the module leader.'

The nature of flexible learning

As with mentoring, the educational literature uses 'flexible learning' in a wide range of senses. In some definitions it is virtually synonymous with open learning; in others it has little to distinguish it from independent learning. The sense in which it is used here is based upon Scriven's (1991, p.299) notion of open learning: that it is characterised by the removal of barriers to participation which are inherent in the traditional system – such as the timing and location of delivery, the pace of study and the entry requirements; the giving of greater responsibility to learners to determine not only where they study, but also, for example, what they learn, how they learn and how they are assessed. It involves a positive commitment to the widening of access to education and to the promotion of learner autonomy.

The giving of greater responsibility to the learner inherent in flexible learning is not complete on any of the modules offered at Manukau Polytechnic. If one looks at placing the modules on the continuum shown below, many would be around the midway point, although the advanced assessment and course design and modules involve a great deal of student responsibility and self-direction. As Candy *et al.* (1994, p.129) make clear, most learning situations involve a balance of direction from the teacher and responsibility by the student, with a gradual relinquishing of control by the teacher.

Exercise of
control by
staff

Exercise of
responsibility
by students

There were interesting responses from the module participants and leaders on this issue. Clearly there is insecurity which accompanies greater responsibility.

- 'It was confusing to those who like structure.'
- 'Sometimes it seemed initially that the choices were just too broad.'
- 'I found negotiating the assessment criteria for my project particularly hard.'
- 'I realise now that I lacked the library and computing skills to do the topic justice.'
- 'I found it easier to meet with the module leader each week if only for a short time. Others did not come much at all.'

Some of the advantages of greater participant responsibility identified by the module leaders and participants include:

- 'It promotes deep rather than surface learning.'
- 'It enhances motivation.'
- 'Being able to choose a topic for study which was directly relevant to my work was a definite plus.'
- 'The flexibility in terms of the time when it had to be completed was a real advantage.'
- 'Participants were able to apply their learning to the workplace and reflect upon it.'
- 'Flexible learning enables people to take off. There were enormous leaps in learning.'
- 'At the time our firm was seeking ISO accreditation. I was able to do a project which produced a procedure required for accreditation.'

The future

The delivery of staff development modules at Manukau Polytechnic in the future may well be influenced by the growing accessibility of electronic media. As more polytechnic staff have access to electronic communications (PMail) on networked computers, it is anticipated that some of the module outcomes that are now delivered for assessment in hard copy form, will be sent electronically. Also the support and assistance of the mentor may in part be given by PMail. Interactive video may also influence the delivery of modules. However, it is important to bear in mind the reactions of module participants interviewed. Clearly they see personal face-to-face interaction as a vital aspect of the mentoring process and a balance of electronic communication and face-to-face interviews would seem to be desirable.

References

Candy, P *et al.* (1994) *Developing Lifelong Learners through Undergraduate Education*, Canberra, Australian Government Publishing Service.

Healey, C C and Welchert, A J (1990) 'Mentoring relations: a definition to advance research and practice', *Leadership*, December.

Scriven, B (1991) 'Distance education and open learning: Implications for professional development and retraining', *Distance Education*, **12**, 2.

Tuck, R (1993) 'The Nature of Mentoring', *The New Academic,* Autumn.

Address for correspondence: **Doug Haynes**, Curriculum Adviser, Educational Department, Manukau Polytechnic, Auckland, Box 61-066, Otara, Auckland, New Zealand.

34. Flexibility in Education for the Professions: The Case of the Property Profession

Dr Peter Hobbs BSc PhD ARICS and **Professor Alan Spedding PhD CEng MIStructE FRICS**, *University of the West of England, Bristol*

SUMMARY

This chapter provides an overview of the issue of flexibility for professional groups by concentrating on the property profession. It addresses three main issues: the growing pressures for flexibility in education for the professions; the dimensions of flexibility in such education; and the delivery of flexible property education.

It is argued that the growing pressure for flexibility in the workplace has implications for the very nature of the professions and that this, in turn, influences approaches to education for the professions. Within this context, this chapter explains the scope of a particular award to demonstrate an approach to accommodating flexibility within a structured framework which satisfies not only the students and educational establishments, but also the professional bodies and employers.

Introduction

The issue of 'flexibility' in the education of professionals is a huge topic, covering issues from the funding of higher education to the skill requirements of relevant professional bodies. This short chapter attempts, therefore, to provide an overview of the issue of flexibility for professional groups by concentrating on the property profession. This overview addresses the following three issues:

- the growing pressures for flexibility in education for the professions;
- the dimensions of flexibility in such education;
- the delivery of flexible property education based on an innovative approach developed at the University of the West of England.

The term 'flexibility in education' is used here to encapsulate education's responses to a range of views, in the property professions, on the ways in which vocationally oriented courses might be delivered to students. Employers are having to respond rapidly to the changing nature of work in the professions generally. Some of the professional institutions in the field have changed their attitude to the content and aims of courses in a response to the need for young professionals to be more adaptable and responsive to market and job changes. This may be particularly so in the light of the internationalisation of business. Also, expansion in higher education means that students are likely to be more diverse in their general educational background than previously, and they may also be mature employed students, wishing to study on a part-time or block-basis in order to enhance their qualifications.

Tensions between more traditional views of the nature of a profession and the day-to-day needs of employers have always had to be managed in the design of courses, although some suspect that these are becoming more acute. Our view, however, accords with that expressed some years ago by Lord Butler in his address to the Royal Institution of Chartered Surveyors when he said, 'The educationalist needs to have the most far-sighted vision, especially he who would school a modern profession for the tasks of a future where change will be rampant' (Lord Butler, 1968).

Flexibility in education for the professions

Growth and change in the professions

In order to understand the scope of flexible professional education, it is necessary to define the nature of professional activities and the approach to the education policy of key professional groups. This provides a basis for an overview of education policy in certain professions, identifying key professional requirements and outlining different approaches to professional education.

It is difficult to unambiguously define the 'professions', although for our purposes they can be defined as possessing the following characteristics:

'skill based on theoretical knowledge; an extensive period of education; the theme of public service and altruism; the existence of a code of conduct or ethics; insistence upon professional freedom to regulate itself; and the testing of the competence of members before admission to the profession.' (Bilton et al., 1987)

Much of the literature on the nature of professionalism in the property field records the change of emphasis from the traditional, confidential service rendered to an individual client to that of highly competent technocrat working within a code of professional conduct. James Nisbet, a well known chartered surveyor, summarised much of the problem in relation to the changing business environment when he said: 'In essence the growing requirement of the corporate client is for a competent technologist to supplement its manpower, and not a professional consultant' (Nisbet, 1977). These defining characteristics have important implications for the education of professions as well as the development of 'flexible' education. In particular, there are clear links between educational institutions and professional bodies in determining the proper scope of knowledge on which the profession is based. There are also implications for the way in which potential entrants to the profession are educated.

Whatever the definition, the professions have grown dramatically during the 20th century. It has been estimated that, by 1991, there were 2.7 million professionals in the UK (see Table 1). The growth in these professions has been particularly marked over the past 50 years with the advent of the welfare state leading to the emergence of the welfare professions (teachers, health professionals and social workers) and, from the 1970s, the rise of enterprise and management professionals.

Table 1 *The main professional groups*

Groups	'000s
Teaching professionals	1211
Engineers and technologists	507
Business and financial professionals	260
Health professionals	233
Miscellaneous professionals (eg, clergy, psychologists and social workers)	126
Natural scientists	122
Architects, town planners and surveyors	98
Legal professionals	75
Librarians and related professionals	27
Total	2659

Source: Watkins *et al.* (1992)

Superimposed on the growth of these different professional groups has been a shift in the nature of professional work. Over recent years, these changes have been associated with the move from 'Fordist' to 'post-Fordist' forms of production and activity. This shift involves a move away from high volume, bureaucratically managed systems, towards more flexible systems of production, administration and management. These new forms of work, variously termed 'post-Fordist' or 'flexible specialisation', are based on growing consumer sophistication and choice, a differentiation in services provided, the widespread adoption of information technology and changes in the organisation of service provision (Brown and Lauder, 1992).

These pressures associated with flexible specialisation are leading to flexible working patterns for the professions. These new flexible patterns:

'demand greater business involvement, higher levels of work, devolved decision making, high-level communication and negotiating skills and offer rewards based on measures of contribution.' (Watkins *et al.*, 1992)

In turn, these changes generate a range of pressures on the skill and training requirements of all professional groups. This is particularly the case for property professionals who, during the late 1990s and beyond, face the impact of information technology on professional practice, the trend towards greater specialisation, the changing organisational environment within which property professionals operate and competition from non-traditional sources such as accountants, solicitors and consultants. As stated by Shepherd (1993):

'A far more flexible work pattern will evolve whereby companies become smaller in staff terms and will probably consist of a basic management and specialist team at the core, with further skills bolted on as required to meet demand.... The long career ladders of the past will be the exception, and individuals will need to be more flexible and have the ability to operate on a wider functional basis, and it will be important to recognise and train for a broader range of skills.'

It is within the context of the growth and change in professional activity that approaches to professional education need to be examined. In particular, it is clear that professional activities have become more flexible in terms of their scope and the way in which they are delivered. A key issue is the implication of growing flexibility in professional practice on professional education.

Approaches to professional education

Over the past 50 years there have been marked changes in the approach towards the education of professionals. Two well-established models of professional education can be identified, along with the more recent development of a third model (Bines and Watson, 1992). The first of these models, the 'apprenticeship' or 'pre-technocratic' model, is where professional education takes place largely on the job, with some instruction through block and/or day release. Within this model, the curriculum concentrates on practical issues, with little emphasis on academic content.

The second model, the 'technocratic' model, has become the dominant approach for much professional education over the past 30 years (Bines and Watson, 1992). This model is characterised by three elements:

- development and transmission of a systematic knowledge base;
- interpretation and application of the knowledge base to practice;
- supervised practical experience in selected placements.

This technocratic approach to professional education was introduced in the 1960s and became the dominant form of professional education from the 1970s to the present day. The model has been responsible for educating a large number of students on vocational courses who were seeking to enter the emerging welfare and business professions associated with Fordist production. Indeed, the way in which the model has operated in practice has a number of Fordist principles. As stated by Stewart in 1990:

> 'in mass higher education, the bureaucratisation and mechanisation of education, an assembly line approach in which the product representing studentship is assembled by a number of specialists, many in narrow academic disciplines but some also in "support areas".... Mass higher education has acquired the characteristics and management approaches of large scale industry.' (Quoted in Farnes, 1993, p.14; see also Raggatt, 1993)

Despite the success in educating large numbers of students, this technocratic approach is not without its weaknesses. On the one hand, there are a range of conceptual and practical shortcomings such as the tendency to fragment learning into discrete and unrelated parcels, including a disjunction between theory and practice (Bines and Watson, 1992).

More fundamentally, however, there are growing weaknesses associated with the relevance of such an approach in the context of the pressures facing professional work outlined above. In particular, this change is associated with the different requirements generated by post-Fordism or flexible specialisation and the growing importance of information technology.

It is within this context that the third model of professional education, the 'post-technocratic' model, has started to emerge (Bines and Watson, 1992). The key feature of this third model is the emphasis on the acquisition of competencies. Importantly, however, these competencies are acquired through experience of practice and reflection on practice. Great emphasis is placed on individual student learning and progression.

Dimensions of flexibility in professional property education

The dimensions of flexibility can be explained in terms of the key components in award delivery, such as the content, delivery and length of courses. The main components of award delivery are set out in Table 2. For each of the components, the table reveals the major shifts in professional property education away from technocratic and rigidly determined structures to more flexible and student-centred approaches.

Table 2 *Emerging dimensions of flexibility in professional property education*

Component of course delivery	Technocratic: 'profession-led'	Post-technocratic: 'learner-centred'
Course content	• technical skills tightly specified • conceptual development	• technical skills loosely specified • conceptual development • personal/managerial skills

Method of delivery	• subject-centred: lectures/tutorials
	• examination-led assessment
		• student-centred: interactive
		• range of assessment:
		  – examinations
		  – coursework
		  – presentations and the like

Mode of attendance	• full-time dominant	• full-time dominant, but increasing range of alternatives, such as part-time, block release and distance learning
Length of course	• rigid	• rigid, but moving towards being extendable

This shift in the nature of property education parallels the move from the apprenticeship model to the technocratic model of education discussed in the preceding section. Prior to the mid-1960s, the usual route to qualification as a chartered surveyor was by professional examination (RICS, 1970), and formation of professional surveyors under the apprenticeship or pupillage model had generally been the model that was strongly favoured by the majority of senior partners of firms.

However, a change was signalled by a statement that 'pupillage does not fit contemporary conditions' and the principle of full-time academic study for the professional body's examinations, followed by two years' practical training, had begun to be accepted 'by implication' (Wells, 1960). It was suggested that the employer should undertake to give pupils 'adequate training'. This theme was developed into a policy that full-time education, including exemption from the examinations of the RICS, would become the main method of entry to the profession and this required adequate testing of postgraduate experience by a 'test of professional competence' (RICS, 1967).

As a result, between the mid-1960s and the mid-1980s, there was a massive change in the routes by which most chartered surveyors became qualified (RICS, 1978, 1989, 1994). A series of exempting degrees were established in polytechnics and universities accompanied by a minimum two-year postgraduate assessment of professional competence system (Cadman, 1980, 1987; Millington, 1984). In fact, by the early 1990s less than 5% of students were seeking to enter the profession through the examinations of the RICS (RICS, 1994).

The change in emphasis summarised in Table 2 suggests that flexibility and innovation might be characterised by the reduced significance of unseen examinations, greater credit for coursework and the right to unlimited resits where failure occurs. Some of these trends are apparent in all areas of higher education, while others are more specific to property education. In general terms, for instance, it is likely that: 'higher education will become less linear, with greater flexibility for students who will have a greater say in when, where and what they study, and the phasing of their study' (HEFCE, 1995).

The RICS has come to take a less prescriptive role in determining the nature of property education. On the one hand, the Institution has reduced the need for individuals to take their degree in one of the seven specific fields related directly to the division of the RICS in which they intended to qualify and practise. The result is that graduates from any RICS-accredited exempting course can now register to undertake their practical experience under the regulations of a division not specific to their degree. On the other hand, the Institution has moved away from regulating the number of graduates seeking to enter the profession, preferring to allow the level to be decided by employers (RICS, 1994).

Although becoming less prescriptive over undergraduate education, the RICS and certain other property-related bodies have sought to increase the level of 'structured learning' during students' postgraduate training and as part of their continuing professional development (CPD) activities throughout their professional careers (RICS, 1994, 1995).

The trend towards flexibility in property education is now widely established, certainly at an undergraduate level. Most undergraduate courses have become modular, have sought to broaden the range of student options and have attempted to become more student centred. There are, however, a number of serious concerns over these trends (Fraser *et al.*, 1994, 1995; Holdsworth, 1994). Perhaps the most fundamental of these concerns relates to the loosening of relationships between course content and eventual practice:

> 'The flexibility in course content now acceptable for accreditation is linked
> to the breakdown of the profession's divisional structure.... By relaxing core

syllabus requirements, the RICS seems to be hoping that curricula will broaden to underpin the expanding employment opportunities within the profession. In fact the outcome is liable to be a range of bland courses with introductions to everything and depth in nothing.' (Fraser *et al.*, 1995)

Such comments reflect a concern to maintain standards in the undergraduate stage of education of professions, and are illustrative of the conflict between the factual and procedural basis of a profession as seen by experienced educators and the rapid changes occurring in the market place. Within this context, professional bodies face an inherent dilemma. In the light of the pressures on working patterns, professional bodies need to encourage the adoption of more student-centred and flexible approaches. In order to respond effectively to change in the workplace, professionals need to develop an ability to respond to changing circumstances.

This increasing focus on student-centred approaches to learning challenges one of the defining characteristics of 'professionalism', namely that professions should possess 'skills based on theoretical knowledge' (Bilton *et al.*, 1987). The more pronounced the shift away from the development of a body of knowledge towards developing the cognitive and synthesising skills of the learner, the harder it will be to justify the case for the existence of the relevant professional body. This dilemma facing the professional bodies is part of a broader issue associated with the deregulation of restrictive professional practices in response to growing consumer pressure and government attempts to encourage competition (MAC, 1985; Watkins *et al.*, 1992).

These changes, and this central dilemma, might be seen as threatening the very nature of professional education. Alternatively, it is possible to develop a more positive and constructive approach to professional education based on a recognition of the need for greater flexibility. It was within such a context that the Real Estate team at the University of the West of England (UWE) saw such developments as signalling the increased need for coordination of undergraduate study and employment-related postgraduate education and training.

The delivery of flexible property education

The scope for flexibility

The need for change in education for the professions and vocational fields generally has been a matter of concern which has grown over the last 15 years. The 'Education for Capability' initiative of the RSA, which was started in 1980 and reformed in 1988, gave expression to these concerns. The intention of the initiative was to encourage the correction of the imbalance between 'education' and 'training'. Their manifesto (HEC, 1988) stresses the view that:

'Individuals, industry and society will all benefit from a well balanced education concerned not only with excellence in the acquisition of knowledge and skills of analysis but also with excellence in using and communicating knowledge, doing, making, designing, collaborating, organising and creating'.

What is called 'The Capability Approach' also suggests that people enhance their capability when they are *responsible and accountable* for their own personal, educational, vocational and professional development.

For some years the Surveying team at UWE had operated a thick sandwich BSc (Hons) Quantity Surveying degree which had incorporated some of the principles of interaction between students' academic work and practice in placement (see also Stapleton and Netting, 1986). In particular, the choice of topic for Honours dissertation normally arose from this interaction. In the real estate field it had not been thought to be as beneficial to students due to the different nature of the work which a third-year undergraduate might be expected to undertake. However, the Real Estate team decided to investigate the next logical step, which was to consider the potential relationship between study undertaken for the BSc (Hons) in real estate and the extra study and practical experience needed for the minimum two-year postgraduate professional assessment stage of the formation of the professionally qualified surveyor.

Inevitably, graduates would be employed in a wide range of professional firms of different sizes in different geographical locations, and their work experience would vary according to the workload of the firm and levels of responsibility taken by the graduate. The team therefore recognised that flexibility needed to be built into any proposed postgraduate award route. Flexibility was required in the method of delivery of course material, in alternative course content within the real estate theme, in the modes of attendance, and also in the overall length of the course.

Reflection on our own experiences with young professionals, consideration of the capability approach, and a series of discussions with our professional liaison employers group led us to seek to develop a postgraduate Diploma and Masters degree in the real estate field which would allow a more student-centred learning approach. Our aim was to make the total formation of the surveyor into a relatively seamless process from undergraduate academic work through a blend of practical experience and related higher study to professionally qualified status.

The Real Estate team at UWE have had close links with the Incorporated Society of Valuers and Auctioneers (ISVA) for over 20 years and have provided a unique undergraduate award which affords our graduates complete exemption from the Society's examinations, leaving graduates to take only the professional assessment of the Society. The Society has shown itself to be receptive in the past to innovation in collaborative work with UWE, and so we approached their education committee with our proposals for a postgraduate award linked to their procedures.

Dimensions of flexibility in the PG Dip/MSc Real Estate

The concept of the award
The overall aim of the award is to enhance the skills of student practitioners to enable them to better understand and exploit changes in demand for professional property services. The award seeks to relate the practical experience of the student to best professional practice and developing theory in the field. It also provides an opportunity for students to further their education by developing specialisms in specific areas of professional practice.

This central aim is achieved largely by integrating components of academic study with the work undertaken for the professional assessment of the ISVA. This training period is itself flexible in terms of the length of time over which it might be completed and in terms of areas of professional experience covered. Essentially, the period of professional assessment requires the submission of written evidence of specific areas of work undertaken in practice, including a journal giving details of professional experience gained and an extensive site-oriented assignment.

The award builds upon these practice-based submissions in order to incorporate associated elements of learning and intellectual development which are then assessed and given credit towards the award of the postgraduate Diploma. Over two-thirds of the credits required for the PG Diploma are based upon components of the ISVA professional assessment (see the award structure in Table 3). The concept behind this structure is that the ISVA looks for evidence of satisfactory professional experience *per se*, but academic staff look for evidence of intellectual development related to the qualities expected of the property professional.

The team defined graduate development in terms such as evidence of the integration of academic and practical knowledge, development of specialist property knowledge and skills, a broadening of the understanding of the context of professional problems and responsibilities, and the communication of the results of analytical and self-critical reflection.

Table 3 *Structure of the PG Diploma/MSc Real Estate*

Postgraduate Diploma

The award of the Postgraduate Diploma requires the successful completion of three distinct types of module (ISVA Related, UWE Core and Award Module Options), as follows:

SVA Related Modules – total of four and a half modules, all of which are compulsory.

Module title	Credits	Relevant ISVA Component
First Stage Experiential Learning	1 module	Stage 1 Journal
Real Estate Practice	half module	Stage 2 Case Study
Second Stage Experiential Learning	1 module	Stage 2 Journal
Practical Assignment	2 modules	Pre-Qualification Assignment

UWE Core Module – total of a half module, which is compulsory.

Professional Practice Management	half module	not relevant

Award Module Options – total of one module, selected by student from Postgraduate modular programme.

MSc Stage

In addition to credits gained for the PG Diploma Real Estate: +

Dissertation	3 modules	not relevant
Award module options selected by student	1 module	not relevant

---

Students therefore, in addition to justifying the professional content of their work to the ISVA, have to satisfy tutors through associated assignment work that the other objectives of each module have been achieved. In addition, students choose modules from a selection of modules available on the Built Environment postgraduate modular programme and can, due to the ISVA timescale for professional assessment, complete the PG Diploma within a two to four year period. The MSc stage takes at least another year and involves the choice of an extra module plus submission of a dissertation.

Dimensions of flexibility

The award has been devised so as to maximise the scope for flexibility within a coherent structure. Flexibility exists on a number of dimensions, including course content, length of the award, method of delivery and mode of attendance. In terms of the course content, there are several aspects of flexibility. First, a large component of the course is based on the professional assessment. Within this assessment, students choose to develop their experience in a variety of different areas from, for instance, auctioneering to mortgage valuations to international property finance. There is, therefore, considerable flexibility to accommodate the professional and personal preferences of the student. A second aspect of this flexibility is the scope for student choice in developing specialisms through the range of module options, and the dissertation.

In addition to the scope for student choice, there is the emphasis placed on developing the skills of students at being able to identify and respond to a wide range of challenges in the workplace. These skills are developed through the experiential-related modules and the core module, professional practice management. Within the experiential-related modules, students agree a work-based plan which requires them to produce evidence of their achievements in respect of their professionally based work experience. The emphasis is on demonstrating an ability to reflect on their workplace experience in the context of developing theory and best practice.

The two key areas in which development is monitored are *self-development*, which involves initiative, analytical and critical ability, persistence, creativity and innovation; and *task-oriented or managerial development*, involving skills of planning, negotiation, communication, interpersonal relations and leadership. Such an approach is used to develop the cognitive, synthesising and practical abilities of the students. In essence, we encourage the students to identify and find the relevant information or understanding, and then apply that information or understanding to issues facing themselves as individuals, the organisation for which they work, or the profession as a whole. As such, we seek to develop the skills of students to respond in a flexible, unprejudiced manner, to problems in the workplace.

The award makes use of flexibility in a range of additional areas such as the length of the award, the method of delivery and the mode of attendance. The emphasis on the accumulation of relevant, module-based credits rather than the completion of 'years' or 'stages' of the award, means there is considerable scope for variety in student progression through the award. In order to accommodate the requirement for geographical flexibility, the award is offered on a distance learning basis. Each of the distance learning based modules require attendance at the UWE at two half-day or full-day workshops.

Conclusions

Obviously, the success or otherwise of a programme depends on the way in which it is implemented. For instance, the distance learning material needs to be well-designed so that the students actively engage in the material while away from the academic institution (Race, 1994). In addition, the assessment criteria need to be clearly specified and a framework for regular contact between students, and between staff and students, needs to be established. The emphasis in this chapter has been on setting out the framework and philosophy of the award, rather than the, nevertheless, critically important procedures for ensuring its successful implementation.

We have had two years of experience of operating this award, and we have received positive feedback from the student evaluation process.

The implementation of flexible learning has shown that a carefully designed scheme can be beneficial to students and rewarding to staff who are kept in close contact with the professional tasks that students are undertaking. In fact, savings in class contact time in operating the distance learning elements allow staff to concentrate on the qualitative objectives of the experiential modules. The emphasis has therefore shifted from a factual knowledge base to the acquisition of many of those transferable skills which the largest professional firms need in the competitive property field.

The opportunity for students to choose when they undertake the academic modules (within the overall course length) appeals to them, but requires a robust system to record student progress. It also requires the administrative process to cope with charging fees on a modular basis, and not by stage or year, and to give clearer advance notice of availability of modules and timetabling arrangements for block release or occasional part-time attendance. The need for clarity in the academic organisation has also to be matched by an atmosphere of cooperation and collaboration between staff and students. We believe that our experience so far has shown that flexibility in provision of education for the professions is possible and rewarding, and also offers a pattern for other courses in the future.

References

Bilton, T et al. (1987) Introductory Sociology, 2nd edn, Macmillan, Basingstoke, p.381.
Bines, H and Watson, D (1992) Developing Professional Education, SRHE/OUP, Buckingham.
Brown, P and Lauder, H (eds) (1992) Education for Economic Survival: From Fordism to Post-Fordism? Routledge, London.
Cadman, D (1980) 'Professional education', Estates Gazette, 2 February, 253, 253–4.
Cadman, D (1987) 'Professional education: a personal view', Estates Gazette, 7 February, 281, 521.
Farnes, N (1993) 'Modes of production: Fordism and distance education', Open Learning, 8, 1, 10–20.

Fraser, W, Crosby, N, MacGregor, B and Venmore-Rowland, P (1994) 'Education of GP Surveyors: Confusion worse confounded', *Estates Gazette*, 15 January, 9403, 113–15.

Fraser, W, Crosby, N and MacGregor, B (1995) 'Issues of quantity and quality', *Estates Gazette*, 18 February, 9507, 116–18.

HEC (1988) *The Capability Manifesto*, HEC, Leeds.

HEFCE (1995) *Review of Higher Education: Submission by the Higher Education Funding Council for England*, HEFCE, Bristol.

Holdsworth, P (1994) 'Education: Revision exercise', *Property Week*, 23 June, 33–43.

Lord Butler of Saffron Walden (1968) 'The professional man in society', *The Chartered Surveyor*, June.

MAC (1985) *Competition and the Chartered Surveyor: Changing client demand for the chartered surveyor*, RICS, London.

Millington, A (1984) 'Development of estate management degrees', *Estates Gazette*, 11 February, 269, 480–82.

Nisbet, J (1977) 'The changing nature of professional practice', *The Chartered Surveyor*, April.

Race, P (1994) *Open Learning Handbook*, 2nd edn, Kogan Page, London.

RICS (1967) *Report of Educational Policy Committee* (The Eve Report), Royal Institution of Chartered Surveyors, London.

RICS (1970) *Surveyors and Their Future*, Report to the RICS, Royal Institution of Chartered Surveyors, London.

RICS (1978) *Review of Educational Policy*, Report to the RICS, Royal Institution of Chartered Surveyors, London.

RICS (1989) *Future Education and Training Policies*, Report to the RICS, Royal Institution of Chartered Surveyors, London.

RICS (1994) *Education Policy: A strategy for action*, Report to the RICS, Royal Institution of Chartered Surveyors, London.

RICS (1995) *The Assessment of Professional Competence: A review and proposals for reform*, Report to the RICS, Royal Institution of Chartered Surveyors, London.

Raggatt, P (1993) 'Post-Fordism and distance education: A flexible strategy for change', *Open Learning*, **8**, 1, 21–31.

Reed, M (1989) *The Sociology of Management*, Harvester Wheatsheaf, Hemel Hempstead.

Rumble, G (1995) 'Labour market theories and distance education 1: Industrialisation and distance education', *Open Learning*, **10**, 1, 10–20.

Shepherd, P (1993) 'An industry perspective on qualification reform', in CISC *Report of Proceedings of CISC National Conference*, 15 July, London, pp.29–38.

Stapleton, T and Netting, R (1986) 'Not all theory?' *Estates Gazette*, 8 March, 277, 932–3.

Watkins, J, Drury, L and Preddy, D (1992) *From Evolution to Revolution: The pressures on professional life in the 1990s*, University of Bristol and Clerical Medical Investment Group, Bristol.

Wells, H (1960) 'The education of the chartered surveyor', *The Chartered Surveyor*, November, 217–19.

Addresses for correspondence: **Peter Hobbs**, Boots Properties, Hargreaves House, Wollaton Street, Nottingham NG1 5FJ; and **Alan Spedding**, Faculty of the Built Environment, University of the West of England, Coldharbour Lane, Bristol BS16 1QY.